WHAT DID YOU SAY?

A GUIDE TO THE COMMUNICATION SKILLS

Third Edition

ARTHUR KOCH
STANLEY B. FELBER

Milwaukee Area Technical College

PRENTICE-HALL, INC., Englewood Cliffs, New Jersey 07632

Library of Congress Cataloging-in-Publication Data

Koch, Arthur, [date]
   What did you say?

   Rev. ed. of: What did you say? / Stanley B. Felber,
Arthur Koch. 2nd ed. c1978.
   Includes index.
   1. Communication.   I. Felber, Stanley B., [date].
II. Title.
P90.K58 1985   001.54   84-6865
ISBN   0-13-951989-0

Editorial/production supervision and
   interior design: Lisa A. Domínguez
Cover design: Lundgren Graphics, Ltd.
Manufacturing buyer: Harry P. Baisley

Printed in the United States of America

10 9 8 7 6 5 4 3 2 1

0-13-951989-0   01

Prentice-Hall International, Inc., *London*
Prentice-Hall of Australia Pty. Limited, *Sydney*
Editora Prentice-Hall do Brasil, Ltda., *Rio de Janeiro*
Prentice-Hall Canada Inc., *Toronto*
Prentice-Hall of India Private Limited, *New Delhi*
Prentice-Hall of Japan, Inc., *Tokyo*
Prentice-Hall of Southeast Asia Pte. Ltd., *Singapore*
Whitehall Books Limited, *Wellington, New Zealand*

In memory
of our fathers,
Carl and Jack

CONTENTS

PREFACE

This Third Edition of *What Did You Say?* features considerable revision
and updating, a new format, and three new chapters. While the book
continues to combine the communication skills in an integrated framework whenever possible, it emphasizes writing to a greater extent than
did the previous two editions. In response to suggestions from many of
our colleagues, we have included three new chapters: "Writing and Rewriting," "The Opinion Essay," and "A Handbook." Readers familiar with
previous editions of *What Did You Say?* will notice that some sentences
have been changed from singular to plural constructions or otherwise rewritten in order to avoid sexist language.

Although these changes have given *What Did You Say?* a new look,
the primary purpose of our book remains the same, to provide occupa-
tionally minded students with the language skills of writing, speaking,
reading, and listening that will enable them to function with efficiency
and perception in society.

We begin each chapter with a list of learning objectives in the belief
that students learn better when they know exactly what is expected of
them.

The text is divided into four parts: *Preparation, Writing, Speaking,*
and a *Handbook.* Part I, Chapters One through Six, introduces the expressive and receptive skills, emphasizing their interrelationships. This

section focuses primarily on planning and gathering materials for purposeful communication. Chapter 2, "Reading and Listening," has been expanded considerably with new sections on the précis, listening, and notetaking.

The chapters entitled "Persuasion," "Logical Proof," and "Psychological Proof," from our earlier editions have been combined and condensed in our new Chapter 5, "Persuasion."

Part II, Chapters 7 through 11, begins with a new chapter, "Writing and Rewriting," which stresses revision as the key to success in writing and practice as the means of achieving it.

The next three chapters form a writing unit which begins with the sentence, moves to the paragraph and ends with a second new chapter, "The Opinion Essay." "The Business Letter," which has an expanded and updated section on the résumé, concludes part II.

Part III, Chapters 12 through 14, presents the skills of public speaking and group discussion. Material from the "Attention" and "Audience Analysis" chapters of our earlier editions have been integrated into the speech chapters.

Part IV, "A Handbook," provides the student with a brief review of basic English structure and a quick reference for checking basic English usage.

With the Third Edition of *What Did You Say?* our debt to our colleagues at the Milwaukee Area Technical College has increased. We are grateful to John Lewinski for updating and expanding his chapter on the business letter; to Gary Longrie for his contributions of poetry and précis writing; and to C. T. Bluemel and the members of the Departments of English and Speech for their many constructive suggestions.

We are also indebted to Jewell M. Burney, Rosemary A. Kenny, and Mary A. McQuaid for evaluating the revised manuscript and making us more aware of student needs outside of MATC, to Lisa Domínguez and Phil Miller of Prentice-Hall for their invaluable help in producing this book, and to our wives Betty and Estelle for their understanding and support.

PROLOGUE

The role of the broadcaster, the communicator, the advertising copy writer, the public relations man, the public speaker, the guy who writes the business letter, the guy who writes the love letter, the guy who writes the letter home—is to get ideas and information across simply, in an easy to understand and attractive way. Elizabeth Barrett Browning, in one of her Sonnets from the Portuguese, "How Do I Love Thee," said more in a very few lines about love than many of us could say in our broken prose if we filled up as many pages as are in a Sears Roebuck catalog.

What it all boils down to is this: Anybody who has anything to say in words or in pictures to be transmitted from one mind to another—regardless of all the modern electronic paraphernalia and hard work you go through to reach that reader, viewer or listener—has to ask himself the question "What did you say?" before he begins to transmit. The only way we can be sure that our ideas achieve their objective is to be clear about what we want to say and who we are trying to reach. That means understanding the guy on the other end. . . .

William A. Nail, "What Did You Say?"*Vital Speeches,* 38, no. 23 (September 15, 1971), 726.

WHAT DID YOU SAY?

CHAPTER 1

An Overview

After studying this chapter, you should be able to:
1. Answer the question, "Why study communication?"
2. Explain the philosophy of communication that governs this text.
3. Define and briefly describe the expressive communication skills.
4. Define and briefly describe the receptive communication skills.
5. Define a communicative act, indicating its essential components.
6. Explain how communication breakdowns occur.
7. Analyze communication situations, identifying essential components or indicating where breakdowns occur.

WHY STUDY COMMUNICATION?

If you are like most high school graduates, the prospect of additional study in language skills far from excites you. You have formally studied our complex, at times illogical language since elementary school, and you have engaged in the process of communication all your lives. Now college. And more reading, writing, and speaking!

Communication skills teachers often pride themselves on the importance of their discipline. "We are the largest department on campus and rightly so. All students, regardless of future educational and vocational objectives, need to learn to communicate more effectively. A good command of language skills can lead to a challenging, creative future. Inadequate mastery of the techniques of communication can only lessen the possibilities available to you."

In recent years, Communication skills teachers have found a powerful ally in industry. Employees are frequently sent to college at company expense in an effort to improve their communication skills. The following excerpt from an industrial publication addressed to technical students is typical of industry's concern with language skills:

To understand and be understood. A good education provides the tools for understanding. The first and most important of these tools is language for communication. It may surprise you that we've begun by putting the need to study English first rather than stressing science or mathematics. After all, our business is primarily concerned with science and the useful application of technological developments. Nevertheless, we are convinced that no matter what your career, a command of the English language is the most important skill you can acquire. Learning rules of grammar and acquiring the abilities to write effectively and to read accurately are vital. This background provides the skill to express yourself in speaking and writing and to extract maximum meaning from the spoken and written words of others.

This process is called communications. In today's world, and even more so in tomorrow's, the person who cannot communicate clearly labors under a tremendous handicap.

The young engineer, for example, might have his most brilliant idea rejected if he is unable to explain its significance to others. In addition, he will be unable to keep up with advances in his own field if he cannot get the facts from the flood of technical information available to him.

Think of any career you like: teacher, naval engineer, actor, salesman, auditor, lawyer, physician, news reporter. Is there one in which you won't have to communicate effectively with others in order to perform successfully?

A time to prepare. The best foundation for whatever career you eventually choose is a broad-based education that increases your understanding and appreciation of everything in life.

It is essential that you start "building in" this kind of background now, for there is no way that you can predict the exact requirements of life or what your interests will be in the future. In short, now is the time to prepare for an education rather than a job.

Obviously, most successful careers today call for special training—often long and intensive. Does this mean that you must commit yourself now to a specific plan of action? Not necessarily. How can you plan for a career that may not even exist today?

The answer is stay flexible. Don't cut yourself off from the future. Keep to the march of knowledge in general. Top careers will more and more demand people with specialized skills in combination with diversified backgrounds.

If there is one rule you can apply that will keep the door open to almost any future career, it is this: when you have a choice of courses, pick those which will help broaden your background—mathematics, language, physical sciences, literature, the social studies.

There's always the chance you'll want to switch your field of study in midstream. Why not? That's one and only one of the advantages of starting with a sound basic education and staying flexible.

Reprinted with the permission of General Electric Company.

You probably agree that the arguments of education and industry have validity, but somehow a continuance of the day-to-day struggle with "nouns and verbs and stupid things like that," as one student put it, leaves you a bit cold. Perhaps you feel that English cannot be as stimulating as a course in your area of specialization, but we don't want you to think of your communication study as just another English course.

The pages that follow will involve you in the practical aspects of written and oral communication. You will discover that in the performance of one of life's most important functions—communicating effectively with your fellow human beings—language can be one of the most exciting and demanding of studies.

A PHILOSOPHY OF COMMUNICATION

Traditionally, language study has been fragmented and compartmentalized, involving separate courses in grammar, composition, and literature. Reading and listening have recently emerged as highly specialized fields within the study of language. Most high schools and colleges offer reading workshops, reading and study skills programs, and courses in speed reading. The last named has become a lucrative enterprise for private educational concerns that capitalize on our inability to assimilate ever-increasing amounts of printed material with speed and comprehension. According to the *Harvard Business Review*, "The busy executive spends 80% of his time . . . listening to people . . . and still doesn't hear half of what is said." *Nation's Business* reports that most of us "really absorb only a scant 30%" of what we hear. Our increasing awareness of the importance of effective listening has resulted in some highly specialized listening courses. The subject matter of this book—language and communication—has been subdivided into numerous highly specialized fields which are usually studied separately. For practical and philosophical reasons, we propose to treat the study of language as a single subject.

Our treatment of communication is primarily intended for you, the college student. Because most of your course work is directly related to your chosen field of specialization, the amount of time set aside for general education courses in your curriculum is necessarily limited. It is usually impractical to schedule separate courses in speech, composition, literature, grammar, reading, and listening. Although the study of literature is beyond the scope of this book, we include a discussion of all of the remaining communication skills. Despite their distinctive aspects, these skills have much in common. We propose to indicate both their similarities and their differences throughout our study. Furthermore, we believe our integrated approach to the study of communication to be philosophically sound.

THE SKILLS OF COMMUNICATION

Expressive Skills

Speaking and writing are generally referred to as expressive skills; they provide the means whereby we express ourselves to others. Both skills are usually discussed under the same heading, because effective speaking and writing involve many similar problems, such as selecting an appropriate subject, communicating purposefully, relating material to a single, dominant idea, and organizing logically.

Obviously, there are also important differences. Writing is a relatively private affair between you and your reader, allowing ample time for revision and correction. When you are speaking publicly, however, all eyes are focused on you. A mistake cannot be readily erased. Speaking and writing employ different means to achieve emphasis and variety, but the primary purpose of both skills is the same: to get the message to your audience in an interesting way.

Receptive Skills

When we listen or read, we receive information through the spoken word or printed page. However, frequently we *hear*, but do not really *listen*. An entry in the *American College Dictionary* clarifies the distinction between these two terms:

Hear, Listen apply to the perception of sound. To hear is to have such perception by means of the auditory sense: *to hear distant bells*. To listen is to give attention in order to hear and understand the meaning of a sound or sounds: *to listen to what is being said, to listen for a well-known footstep.*

Similarly, sometimes we read words without understanding their meaning. Have you ever spent an hour or so reading an assigned chapter without having more than a vague notion of its contents? Perhaps you were distracted by interruptions or your own thoughts. Concentration is essential to both listening and reading, the basic difference being that if you cannot concentrate on what you are reading, you can always return to it at another time. You cannot, however, expect your instructor to repeat the lecture after class because your thoughts drifted during the presentation. Both skills involve breaking down a communication into main ideas and supporting details. Listening to your instructor's lecture is more demanding than listening to a friend relate a personal experience; reading Spenser's *The Faerie Queene* requires more concentration than reading a popular novel. However, all effective reading and listening share a common purpose: to receive messages clearly.

THE COMMUNICATIVE ACT

Communication results when a response occurs to a stimulus. For example:

Stimulus	Response
1. Strong winds and heavy rain	Baby cries
2. Strong winds and heavy rain	Man closes window

Our stimuli for the above examples, strong winds and heavy rain, produce varied responses from different people. The baby is frightened by the stimuli, and his response is an automatic one based on fear. In the second example, the man's response is motivated by other considerations, perhaps his desire to block out outside noise, or to protect his family and his belongings. Because he must decide among alternatives, the man's response involves reasoning. Thus, we see that a response to a stimulus may or may not be automatic.

Let us consider another stimulus-response situation:

Stimulus	Response
3. Dog barks	Baby cries
4. Dog barks	Man feeds dog

The baby's response to the stimulus is again an automatic one based on fear. The man's response is a nonautomatic one—feeding—to the same stimulus. Thus far we have seen how stimuli can produce automatic and nonautomatic responses.

The stimulus in a communicative act includes a sender and a message. Study the following analyses of stimuli previously referred to:

Stimulus	= Sender + Message
1. Strong winds and heavy rain	Depending upon your philosophical and theological convictions, you may conclude that "nature" or a supreme being is the *sender;* the *message,* strong winds and heavy rain, is then transmitted to a receiver.
2. Barking dog	The dog is the *sender;* his bark is the *message.*

Before you can respond to a stimulus (sender and message), you must first receive the message. Therefore, the response in an act of communication implies a receiver. Initially we defined communication as a response to a stimulus, but our modified definition now includes a sender, a message, a receiver, and a response.

	Sender	Message	Receiver	Response
1.	"Nature"	Strong winds and heavy rain	Baby	Crying
2.	"Nature"	Strong winds and heavy rain	Man	Closing window
3.	Dog	Bark	Baby	Crying
4.	Dog	Bark	Man	Feeding dog

Finally, a message may be sent through a variety of *media.* For example, the sender might (1) shout to a person standing nearby that a building is on fire, (2) make a telephone call and transmit the same information, or (3), if a mobile "on-the spot" television camera crew happened to be on the scene, broadcast the message to thousands of viewers instantly. While the actual words of the message might remain the same in each case, "A building is on fire. . . ," you can see that impact will differ, depending upon the *medium* chosen.

The *medium* represents the final modification of our definition of communication, which can now be summarized as follows:

1. The sender perceives something in the environment.
2. The sender *encodes* the message—that is, he puts the message into code.
3. The sender transmits the message through a particular medium.
4. The message is received . . .
5. and *decoded.*

6. The message is understood by the receiver in the same way it was meant by the sender.

7. The receiver responds (provides feedback) to the sender.

A communication "loop" has been formed. Communication is now complete. In everyday situations, communicative acts are not isolated. Instead, they flow one into the other and become part of a process. Understanding the steps involved in a single communicative act will provide you with a better understanding of that process. The following chart illustrates these steps.

How Communication Works

When a breakdown in communication occurs, one or more of the basic requirements have not been fulfilled. If you tell a friend you will meet him outside a building after your class, and he waits patiently in front while you wait near the side entrance, the message you sent to him was either incomplete or misunderstood. If your instructor must ask you to repeat your answer to her question in an audible voice, you, as a sender, have failed to establish meaningful contact. If you jump the gun at a traffic light because you were thinking of tomorrow night's date instead of concentrating on the signal, a traffic citation may be your reward. If you fail to hear your instructor announce a quiz for the next class meeting because you were talking to a classmate, you cannot respond with study to a message you never received. If we are to function effectively, communication breakdowns must be kept to a minimum.

EXERCISES

I. Analyze the following cartoons as examples of communication, indicating the sender, message, receiver, and response. Where breakdowns in communication occur, indicate why.

Cartoon by Sanders © Used with permission of The Milwaukee Journal.

The Family Circus, by Bil Keane. Reprinted courtesy of the Register and Tribune Syndicate, Inc.

'Where am I? What's been going on here?'

Cartoon by Sanders © used with permission of The Milwaukee Journal.

From Parade Publication, Inc. Cartoon by Boltinoff. Reprinted by permission.

II. From your own experience, cite two examples of breakdowns, one involving speech, one involving writing.

1. Identify the causes of the breakdowns.

2. State what could have been done to improve the communication.

III. The following photographs are intended to stimulate a written or oral response. Choose one or more that you can relate to from your own experience. Then write a response to the picture, to be used either as a topic sentence for a paragraph, or as the main idea statement of a longer paper or speech, as your instructor directs.

With permission of the photographer, David Bernacchi.

Losing can be . . .
I wonder if . . .
Why did I . . .
I'll never be able to . . .

With permission of the photographer, Greg Gay

Loneliness can be . . .
When no one cares . . .
Being old is . . .
A pet can be . . .

Used with permission of the photographer, Arnold Gore.

Being pregnant is . . .
Childbirth involves . . .
Mothers are . . .
Love is . . .
Being a parent means . . .

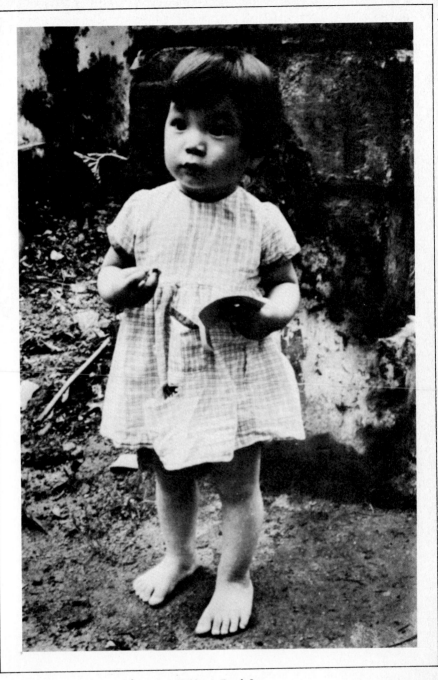

Love is . . .

Caring means . . .

Helping can be . . .

Responsibility involves . . .

Reprinted with permission of the Milwaukee Journal.

Pollution could . . .
Unless we control our . . .
Without enough energy, we . . .
Our nation needs . . .

CHAPTER 2

Reading
and
Listening

After studying this chapter, you should be able to:
1. Identify "key" parts of a chapter before reading it in its entirety.
2. Formulate the kinds of questions that will increase your understanding of the material being read.
3. Retain the information you have learned for a longer time.
4. Identify similarities between reading and listening skills.
5. Write an effective précis.
6. Discuss the procedure to follow in preparing to listen.
7. Recognize and limit external and internal barriers to listening.
8. Take notes more effectively.

This chapter was written in part by **Mary Jane Irwin**.

WHAT DID THE AUTHOR SAY?

How do you study your daily assignments? Does your instructor assign a particular number of pages to be read? Does the instructor give you questions to be answered? Does the instructor ask for an outline or summary of the material?

When only a designated number of pages are assigned, most students begin at the beginning and read straight through the lesson. Most students know "how to read" the words. When they have finished reading every word of the lesson, they may say to themselves, "I have completed my assignment, which should give me a good grade in this class." Wrong! Just reading the words in an assignment will never guarantee understanding what the author said. *And* you must not only understand what the author said, but you must also be able to remember and apply it.

Sometimes highly intelligent students have trouble in school. They may read well, but they do not realize that reading is only a part of studying. On the other hand, less intelligent students frequently earn good

*"Don't worry about passing reading.
Take a remedial course when you get to college."*

grades because they have learned how to study. Just reading an assignment will not guarantee a good grade on a quiz or in the course.

In order to *study* a lesson, you must first consider what your purpose
is in reading it. The purpose in reading assigned material in a textbook
is usually to master it. In order to *study* the written words of any assignment, you must (1) prepare to read, (2) read to answer questions, (3) reflect on what you have read.

Preparing to Read

The first step in preparing to study a lesson is to determine the specific purpose for which the material is being studied. Is it necessary to
master the material by understanding the main ideas and show the relationship of the details to the main ideas? Or is it just necessary to hit the
high spots? Mastery is not always required.

When you have determined how much you are going to have to
"know" about the lesson, it is necessary to know what the author is writing
"about." A student's first reaction is, "How do I know what she is writing
about until I have read it?" Of course, you won't know what she *says* until
you have read it, but you can find out the subject of the lesson by reading
the title carefully and *thinking* about what it says. (Some students don't
bother with the title at all because they are anxious to "get into the chapter" and get the studying finished as quickly as possible.) When you have
determined the subject, ask yourself what you already know about this
subject. No one ever read anything with any degree of understanding
knowing absolutely *nothing* about the subject.

For example, if the title of a lesson were "Atomic Energy," your first
impulse might be to say, "I don't know anything about this subject." This
is because you think it is necessary to know the scientific aspects of the
splitting of the atom. Detailed scientific knowledge is not necessary in order to prepare to read about atomic energy, but you must set your mind
in motion in the proper direction so that you can build on your present
knowledge. Your present knowledge may be limited to the fact that energy from the atom is extremely powerful—so powerful that it can power
submarines and electric power plants as well as cause devastating destruction. Now your mind is ready to receive further information about atomic
energy.

After you have understood the subject of the lesson and have recalled what you already know about the subject, read the first and last
paragraphs, putting into your own words what the author has said. Most
writers tell you at the beginning what they are planning to write about,
and at the end they sum up what they have said. *Do not read the entire lesson yet.* It is all right to skip from the first to the last paragraph in a text-

book assignment because your textbook is not like a novel that has a plot, and the textbook material will never build up to a climax or contain a surprise ending. Your textbook author is trying to help you understand subject matter.

Next read the main and subordinate headings, which will allow you to understand exactly what aspects of this subject the author has emphasized. One of the most difficult tasks for students is to determine what is important in a lesson. These preparatory steps to reading an assignment will tell you exactly what the author thinks is important.

If there are maps, charts, graphs, or pictures in the lesson, be sure to read the captions and try to understand the reason the author included them.

Using this preparatory process, it should take you no more than five minutes to find out what 30 pages are "about" in a textbook assignment.

Let's review *how* you find out what a textbook lesson is "about" *before you read it.* Study the:

1. Title
2. First and last paragraphs
3. Main heading and subheadings
4. Pictures, charts, maps, and graphs

Below is an example of how you would go about *preparing* to study a 30-page chapter in a psychology textbook. *Before* you read the chapter in its entirety, you would read only these parts. Follow along carefully, and you will see how much information you can get just by reading certain parts that reveal what the author has decided is important.

Title   MEASUREMENT AND INDIVIDUAL DIFFERENCES

First   "In whatever way we look at individuals we find differ-
paragraph   ences: in size, health, strength, ability, and emotional stability. Each differs in one way or another from everyone else. This is no recent discovery—for some time you have been aware that there are others who possess more intellectual ability than you have, and some who possess less. Even the ancients recognized such differences and took account of them in training their youth. Why the psychological emphasis today in this area?"

Headings   *Measuring Units*
Mental Age/Chronological Age
Intelligence

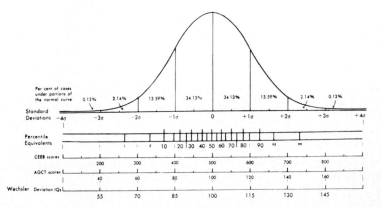

Chart   **Distribution of IQ's (From Madigan, *Psychology*, 5th Ed.)**

Heading   *Innate and Acquired Differences*

Chart   **The individual is a product of heredity and environment (From Madigan, *Psychology*, 5th Ed.)**

Headings   *Causes of Individual Differences*
DEVELOPMENTAL FACTORS
RACIAL FACTORS
FAMILY FACTORS
SEX FACTORS
AGE FACTORS
Temperamental Differences
ENVIRONMENTAL INFLUENCES
HUMAN DRIVES OR MOTIVES
ATTITUDES AND EMOTIONS

Physiological Differences
SENSE ORGANS
GLANDULAR CONDITIONS
PHYSICAL CAPACITY
STRENGTH
SENSITIVITY TO PAIN
REACTION TO FOOD AND DRUGS
Recognition of Individual Differences

**Last
paragraph**   "The causes of individual differences are designated as heredity and environment. Heredity sets the limit to the pattern of potential growth, but environment maximizes or minimizes this development."

Textbook extracts from *Psychology, Principles and Applications,* 5th ed., by Marion East Madigan. St. Louis: C.V. Mosby Company, 1970.

Now that you have "hit the high spots" in this chapter by reading only certain parts of it, you have discovered what the author is talking "about." If this were an actual assignment in your textbook and you had called to mind what you already know about heredity and environment, you would have a good idea about the author's main ideas. Then when you actually read the chapter, it would be easier for you to sift and sort the details that support these main ideas.

The Importance of Questioning and Curiosity   If you have been *thinking* as you read these particular parts of the assignment, your curiosity would probably help you formulate questions that the author will be likely to answer. There are different kinds of questions you might formulate. Some would be "surface" questions in which all you do is turn a heading into a question. Others might be called "in-depth" questions, which enable you to delve further into why the author has included something in order to make a point.

Using the above material from an actual textbook, you might formulate some surface questions as follows:

Heading   *Innate and Acquired Differences*
Surface question   What are innate and acquired differences?

Heading   *Measuring Units*
Surface question   What are measuring units?

Heading   *Mental Age/Chronological Age*
Surface questions   What is mental age?
                         What is chronological age?

Heading	*Causes of Individual Differences*
Surface question	What are the causes of individual differences?

Since reading is a *thinking* process, it is not enough to resort to surface questions alone. You must think more deeply and come up with some in-depth questions. These are questions that show a relationship between a heading and the title of the chapter, or perhaps they will show the relationship between a subheading and its heading. Here are some examples:

Title	MEASUREMENT AND INDIVIDUAL DIFFERENCES

Heading	*Measuring Units*
Surface question	What are measuring units?
In-depth question	How are these measuring units used to determine individual differences?

Heading	*Causes of Individual Differences*
Subheading	DEVELOPMENTAL FACTORS
Surface question	What are developmental factors?
In-depth questions	How do these developmental factors cause individual differences?
	What are the individual differences caused by these developmental factors?

All in-depth questions must be formulated within the area of the title. As you formulate these questions, you are beginning to think. You may even guess what answers the author is likely to give to these questions. When you have speculated on the answers, you will be delighted as you read the chapter to find out that the author's ideas agree with yours. If you find that your answers do not agree with the author's, your curiosity will be aroused and you may develop further questions. In either case you will be reading *actively,* and you will become involved in what is written just the same as you become involved in watching a good television program. You always enjoy a movie when you anticipate what is to come next. Asking questions *before* you read can make a dull and uninteresting subject come alive.

It is absolutely necessary for anyone to know *before reading* what questions the author is likely to answer. Everyone realizes it is absolutely necessary for you to know what you lost before you begin to look for it; otherwise, how would you know when you had found it? And yet, students begin reading an assignment without the slightest idea of what they are looking for; thus, they are very unlikely to find it.

Although it has taken a long time to explain *how to prepare to read* an assignment, to actually apply this to a textbook assignment takes very little time. Just knowing how to prepare to read is not enough. You must be able to apply these techniques on your own lessons, and this takes practice.

EXERCISE

Fill in the blanks at the end of these instructions *as* you accomplish each task. The blanks and tasks have corresponding numbers. Use a lesson which has been assigned for another class and one *which you have not read*. (Any textbook will be all right. Perhaps psychology or sociology may be easier for your first practice lesson, but the technique works equally well with a math or science lesson.)

1. Write the name of the *course* in which this lesson has been assigned.
2. Write the complete title of the textbook lesson.
3. What do you already know about this subject? Write some specific facts. Do not tell when or where you studied this subject, but give some specific facts you learned about it.
4. Read the first paragraph. *Restate* the main idea *in your own words*.
5. Read the last paragraph. *Restate* the main idea *in your own words*.
6. List the main heading and subheadings. (If you are reading an essay or a textbook without headings, read *only* the first sentence of every third or fourth paragraph and write *in your own words* what the author said in each of these sentences.)
7. Were there any pictures, charts, maps, graphs in the lesson? If so, study them and write the main idea expressed in the heading under each one.
8. For each of the headings in this assignment, write (1) a surface question and (2) an in-depth question.

(When you have become adept at using this technique for preparing to read, you will not have to write out all of this information. Writing it is time-consuming, but it is necessary until you perfect the technique.)

Fill in the blanks:

1. Name of the course for which you are reading this assignment.

_____

2. Give the title of the lesson to be studied.

_____

3. What do you already know about this subject?

_____

_____

_____

_____

4. RESTATE the main idea in the first paragraph. USE YOUR OWN WORDS.

_____

_____

_____

_____

5. RESTATE the main idea in the last paragraph. USE YOUR OWN WORDS.

_____

_____

_____

_____

6. LIST the main heading and subheadings.

_____

_____

_____

_____

_____

_____

7. LIST pictures, maps, graphs, charts, etc.
KIND of pictorial aid   Write the caption under each of these aids

_____   _____

_____   _____

_____   _____

_____   _____

8. Formulate a SURFACE QUESTION for each heading and subheading. Write it under A. Formulate an IN-DEPTH QUESTION for each heading and subheading. Write it under B.

A. (surface) _____

B. (in-depth) _____

A. _____

B. _____

A. _____

B. _____

A. _____

B. _____

A. _____

B. _____

Reading to Answer Questions

The questions you have raised about your assignment and your review of what you already know about the subject should increase your interest and curiosity. When you have become interested in and curious about what you are going to read, it is much easier to find out what the author "says."

You already know how to read words, or you would not have reached this point in the textbook. You already know what important questions the author is likely to answer. Now the problem is to find out how the author answers these questions.

How to Read Sentences   In order to understand what a sentence "says," it is necessary to understand sentence structure. More detailed information regarding sentence structure is found in chapter 8 of this book.

In reading to answer questions, you must know that each sentence tells about someone or something, and it tells what is said or done about that someone or something. If you were to read directions, your purpose for reading them would be to find out what you were supposed to do. Here is a good example of how you could do the wrong thing if you were not able to read sentences properly. Here are the directions: "A synonym or an antonym for the word in Column I can be found in Column II." Some students find this to mean that the sentence is talking about the "word in Column I." This is *not* what the sentence means. It is talking about the "synonym or antonym in Column II." The next sentence in the directions states, "The word should be written on your paper. Indicate whether this word is a synonym or antonym." This time "word" refers to the synonym or antonym in Column II, the very thing the author was talking about in the first sentence. When the student writes the "word" from Column I rather than the choice from Column II, the answer will be wrong because the student has not read the sentences properly.

HOW TO READ PARAGRAPHS

Paragraphs do not make much sense if you cannot read a sentence.

For many years before a student reaches college, instructors have been asking him to pick out the most important idea in a paragraph or to underline the topic sentence. Seldom is the student told *how* to do this.

When the author writes the paragraph, she has one main idea to convey to the reader. It will be about one particular subject. By reading rapidly you can identify the subject by noticing that each sentence of the paragraph will refer to that one thing or idea. Each sentence will say something different, but each sentence will be about the same subject. When you have discovered what this thing or idea is that the author is writing about, you must decide what is so important about it that she found it necessary to devote an entire paragraph to it. Many ideas may be expressed in a paragraph, but the author will write only one main idea, with all of the other ideas supporting this main idea. Sometimes an author will give examples or an explanation of a point she is trying to make. These are given to help you understand the main idea and are relatively unimportant if you understand the author's idea itself. Some students are able to remember the examples or explanations, but they can't remember what the point was the author was making. The author uses many methods to make a main idea clear to you. You must understand what material is supportive to the main idea and this requires *thinking*. Reading is a *thinking process*.

In a way, reading a paragraph is similar to reading an entire lesson. First, you find out what the author is talking "about," and then you find what she "says" by recognizing the difference between her main idea and the supportive details.

Authors develop the main idea of a paragraph by using a variety of methods:

1. Use of a definition to give the main idea
2. Use of examples and illustrations to explain main ideas
3. Use of comparison and contrast to show similarities and differences
4. Use of explanations or descriptions to expand a main idea and clarify the meaning of the paragraph
5. Use of a combination of some of the above

EXERCISE

In each of the following paragraphs, the author has used one of the above methods to develop a main idea. Indicate by using the proper number which method has been used for each of them.

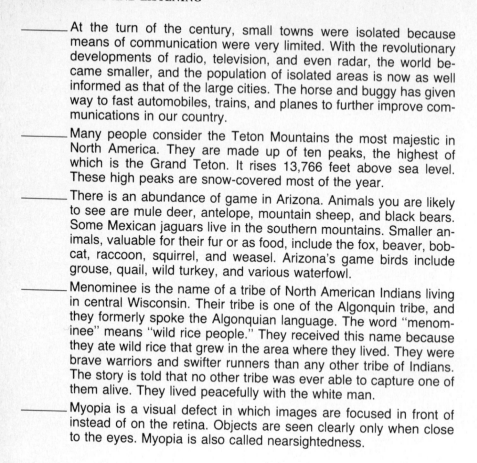

_____ At the turn of the century, small towns were isolated because means of communication were very limited. With the revolutionary developments of radio, television, and even radar, the world became smaller, and the population of isolated areas is now as well informed as that of the large cities. The horse and buggy has given way to fast automobiles, trains, and planes to further improve communications in our country.

_____ Many people consider the Teton Mountains the most majestic in North America. They are made up of ten peaks, the highest of which is the Grand Teton. It rises 13,766 feet above sea level. These high peaks are snow-covered most of the year.

_____ There is an abundance of game in Arizona. Animals you are likely to see are mule deer, antelope, mountain sheep, and black bears. Some Mexican jaguars live in the southern mountains. Smaller animals, valuable for their fur or as food, include the fox, beaver, bobcat, raccoon, squirrel, and weasel. Arizona's game birds include grouse, quail, wild turkey, and various waterfowl.

_____ Menominee is the name of a tribe of North American Indians living in central Wisconsin. Their tribe is one of the Algonquin tribe, and they formerly spoke the Algonquian language. The word "menominee" means "wild rice people." They received this name because they ate wild rice that grew in the area where they lived. They were brave warriors and swifter runners than any other tribe of Indians. The story is told that no other tribe was ever able to capture one of them alive. They lived peacefully with the white man.

_____ Myopia is a visual defect in which images are focused in front of instead of on the retina. Objects are seen clearly only when close to the eyes. Myopia is also called nearsightedness.

The following paragraph, from Dr. Madigan's *Psychology, Principles and Practices,* may help you to understand how to read a paragraph.

MEANINGFULNESS (This is a subheading)

Significant material is more slowly forgotten than nonsense syllables. Nonsense material barely learned is almost forgotten in four months, but poetry barely learned has been known to be retained for twenty years. Material in which the elements are related as parts of a whole is more readily learned than nonsense material. This is due to interrelationships which in turn depend on past experience. The reader would probably have no background to utilize in committing to memory a sentence written in Greek.

As a student reads this paragraph quickly, he can see that the underlined words in each sentence are making comparisons of material that may be either meaningful or meaningless. Anything that relates to one's experience or shows relationships between parts of a whole must be meaningful. The subheading has already told the student that the paragraph has to do with "meaningfulness."

The heading under which this subheading comes is entitled "Retention and Forgetting." Now it is easy to see that the writer is trying to convey to the reader that meaningful material is more readily remembered than nonsense material.

If the student were to use the question technique, he would find:

Heading   RETENTION AND FORGETTING

Subheading   *Meaningfulness*

Question   What does meaningfulness have to do with remembering or forgetting?

If you go back and read the paragraph, it is easy to come up with the same answer this time: Meaningful material is more readily remembered than nonsense material. This, of course, is the idea the author is trying to emphasize.

Any of these techniques will help you come up with the main idea of a paragraph. As you sift and sort when you read, you will select those points the author considers important, and you will find the answers to your questions.

Each time you find an answer to a question you should stop, look away from your textbook, think about it, and recite the answer in your own words. This means that you will *learn as you read*. As you think about these new ideas, you will relate them to what you already know about the subject. In this way you place these ideas in your mind in an organized fashion, keeping in mind the relationship of the supporting details to the main ideas. Organization always aids memory of material. No one's mind soaks up knowledge the way a sponge soaks up water; rather it is more like a sieve through which ideas and words are likely to leak. It takes much *thinking* to *learn from reading*.

If at first you are unable to find answers to your questions, do not become discouraged. It takes much practice to be able to turn headings into surface and in-depth questions. If you have done a good job of speculating on what you are looking for, you are quite likely to find it. And when you find the answer to a question, you will know that the idea is an important one. If, however, you did not develop the proper questions, you will be sufficiently interested at this point to be impressed with the information that you do find. Formulating good questions comes with practice.

It is not necessary for you to study the entire chapter all at once. You can take only a few pages at a time if you wish. The amount of material you learn at one time may depend upon how profound or detailed the lesson turns out to be. It may also depend upon what your purpose is for studying it. Must you master it? Or do you need only the main ideas?

Thinking About What You Have Learned

It is not enough to prepare to read by finding out what the lesson is about, formulating questions, and then learn while reading. True, at this point you have *learned,* but now it is necessary for you to *remember* what you have learned. Most forgetting takes place soon after something has been learned; therefore, a review soon after something has been learned is necessary as well as at frequent intervals thereafter. As you review, you will find there are some things you must go back and *relearn.* This doesn't mean that you have a poor memory, because it happens to everyone. However, if you can recite what you have learned perfectly some time after you have learned it, it means that you have *overlearned*—something that is necessary in obtaining good grades in college.

How should you review? First, if you have written in your notebook the questions you have formulated and have found the answers to them, you may record these answers below the questions. This will give you good notes for review. Of course, you will not have written the answers in your notebook until you have turned away from the textbook and recited them in your own words. To review these notes, cover the answer, read the question, and recite the answer aloud. It is easy to uncover the answer and check to see whether or not you were correct.

There are other ways to *think* about what you have learned. When the entire lesson has been studied and you have given some thought to the answers to your questions, you might find someone who would be willing to listen to what you have just learned. The listener will not learn much, but you will have fixed many ideas and concepts more securely in your mind as you told him what you learned from the assignment. If you can't find anyone who is willing to listen to you, you can always go into a room, close the door and repeat to yourself aloud what you have learned. In either case you will have *tested* yourself to see exactly what you have learned. Don't forget that *learning* takes place *while* you read. Everyone is capable of *forgetting;* thus, *review* is necessary for *relearning* and *remembering.*

EXERCISE

1. Choose a reading assignment made for another class in which you are enrolled.
2. Prepare to read the lesson by reading the title, first and last paragraphs, headings, and subheadings, and look at the charts, maps, and graphs.
3. Recall what you knew about the subject before you looked at the chapter.
4. Turn the headings and subheadings into surface and in-depth questions.
5. Write these questions on a sheet of paper, leaving room for answers.
6. Read several pages until you have found the answers to eight or nine questions.
7. Write the answers to these questions in the space left on your paper for this purpose. Use your own words.
8. Continue reading several pages and writing answers to the questions until the entire lesson has been completed.
9. Review: Cover your answers, read the questions, and recite answers to test your learning. Check immediately to see if you were correct. If you were not correct, this is the time to relearn.
10. Reviewing should be done soon after the lesson has been studied and periodically until the final examination. Daily preparation of this kind will rule out the necessity for cramming before examinations.

THE PRÉCIS

The précis (pronounced pray-see) is a particularly useful assignment. The term, which comes from the French, means "to cut off or prune." When you write a précis of a selection, you are writing a concise summary of its essential parts in your own words. A well-written précis is *your* copy, in miniature, of the original. Therefore the précis of a story will be the same story written in a much condensed form, usually about one-fourth of the original.

Perhaps the greatest benefit of précis writing is that it promotes careful and thoughtful reading. In order to write an effective précis, one must be able to recognize an author's main and supporting ideas and separate them from the less essential supporting detail. This requires the ability to read in depth in order to find exactly what the author wants to communicate.

Other advantages to précis writing are listed below:

1. It develops the skills of observation and analysis which are essential to writing.

2. It eliminates the planning and preparation stage of writing, allowing more time for practice.

3. It deals with those qualities necessary for effective writing: unity, coherence, voice, conciseness, completeness, and correctness.

Keep in mind when writing your précis that you must include those details essential to the purpose and meaning of the selection. Furthermore, although you are writing in your own voice, you must be faithful to the organization of the original. Finally, although a précis is a summary of someone else's writing, it is also a sample of your own so you will want to make it as effective as possible. Here are some specific suggestions for writing a successful précis:

1. *Unity*—Study the selection carefully to determine what the essential details are. Include those which clarify or support the controlling idea thereby providing *unity* to the selection.

2. *Coherence*—Do not rearrange the writer's ideas in your précis. Follow his order of arrangement exactly. Since a précis should be as *coherent* as the selection you are summarizing, provide smooth transitions between sentences and paragraphs.

3. *Voice*—Use your own *voice* when writing a précis. The clearest indication that you have an understanding of something is to be able to say it in your own words.

4. *Conciseness*—Remember, the précis is a condensed version of the original. Be simple, direct, and succinct.

5. *Completeness*—Although the précis is a miniature version of a composition, it must be *complete*. After you have finished the first draft of your précis, read it over carefully to be sure you haven't omitted anything of importance.

6. *Correctness*—Before you turn in your précis to be evaluated, proofread it carefully to eliminate errors in grammar, punctuation, and spelling. Check for those kinds of errors you have made in the past. If you are in doubt as to what is *correct*, consult a dictionary or the handbook at the back of this text.

Examples of Précis Writing

Listed below are concrete examples of précis writing. They include passages that are narrative, expository, descriptive and poetic.

The Narrative Précis

In a narrative it is the essential details and events which must be saved, rather than the central thought. Therefore, the précis of a story is usually much shorter than that of an exposition or description.

JAMES THURBER
University Days

I passed all the other courses that I took at my University, but I could never pass botany. This was because all botany students had to spend several hours a week in a laboratory looking through a microscope at plant cells, and I could never see through a microscope. I never once saw a cell through a microscope. This used to enrage my instructor. He would wander around the laboratory pleased with the progress all the students were making in drawing the involved and, so I am told, interesting structure of flower cells, until he came to me. I would just be standing there. "I can't see anything," I would say. He would begin patiently enough, explaining how anybody can see through a microscope, but he would always end up in a fury, claiming that I could *too* see through a microscope but just pretended that I couldn't. "It takes away from the beauty of flowers anyway," I used to tell him. "We are not concerned with beauty in this course," he would say. "We are concerned solely with what I may call the *mechanics* of flowers." Well," I'd say, "I can't see anything." "Try it just once again," he'd say, and I would put my eye to the microscope and see nothing at all, except now and again, a nebulous milky substance— a phenomenon of maladjustment. You were supposed to see a vivid restless clockwork of sharply defined plant cells. "I see what looks like a lot of milk," I would tell him. This, he claimed, was the result of my not having adjusted the microscope properly; so he would readjust it for me, or rather, for himself. And I would look again and see milk.

I finally took a deferred pass, as they called it, and waited a year and tried again. (You had to pass one of the biological sciences or you couldn't graduate.) The professor had come back from vacation brown as a berry, bright-eyed, and eager to explain cell-structure again to his classes. "Well," he said to me, cheerily, when we met in the first laboratory hour of the semester, "we're going to see cells this time, aren't we?" "Yes, sir," I said. Students to right of me and to left of me and in front of me were seeing cells, what's more they were quietly drawing pictures of them in their notebooks. Of course, I didn't see anything.

"We'll try it," the professor said to me grimly, "with every adjustment of the microscope known to man. As God is my witness, I'll arrange this glass so that you see cells through it or I'll give up teaching. In twenty-two years of botany, I — —." He cut off abruptly for he was beginning to quiver all over, like Lionel Barrymore, and he genuinely wished to hold onto his temper: his scenes with me had taken a great deal out of him.

So we tried it with every adjustment of the microscope known to man. With only one of them did I see anything but blackness or the familiar lacteal opacity, and that time I saw, to my pleasure and amazement, a variegated constellation of flecks, specks, and dots. These I hastily drew. The instructor, noting my activity, came back from an adjoining desk, a smile on his lips and his eyebrows high in hope. He looked at my cell drawing. "What's that?" he demanded with a hint of squeal in his voice. "That's what I saw," I said. "You didn't, you didn't, you *didn't*!" he screamed, losing control of his temper instantly, and he bent over and squinted into the microscope. His head snapped up. "That's your eye!" he shouted. "You've fixed the lens so that it reflects! You've drawn your eye!"

—630 words

Précis of "University Days"

I passed the courses I took at my university, except for botany. The problem showed itself in the laboratory where all botany students spent hours looking at plant cells through a microscope. I was never able to focus in on a plant cell. My instructor was patient with me at the beginning, but soon his patience gave way to rage. Even when he adjusted the microscope, all I could see was milk.

Since the course was required for graduation, I finally took a deferred pass and tried the course the following year. My instructor was again enthusiastic, but I was still unable to see anything.

Determined, my instructor leaned on his twenty-two years of teaching botany, and "with every adjustment known to man" tried again. With one of these adjustments I did see something which I drew. He returned to see what I had drawn. "What's that?" he squealed. "That's what I saw," I said. He lost control, looked into the microscope and then at me. He shouted, "You've fixed the lens so it reflects! You've drawn your eye!"

—179 words

The Descriptive Précis

The effectiveness of description usually depends upon how specific the details are. Therefore, to make what is already specific even more concise is a challenging and worthwhile activity.

Las Vegas

It's a 24-hour figment of some surreal imagination, a jerry-built collection of neon rising out of the red desert sand.

Covered with sagebrush and tumbleweed, and decorated with several billion dollars' worth of glass, plastic, steel and concrete—Las Vegas transcends the normal definitions of reality.

It is a town of high heels and sneakers, designer jeans and Levi's, gold neck chains and pale-green polyester leisure suits.

It's a town where absolute strangers can meet at a bubbling fountain of free champagne, exchange life histories while filling their glasses, and depart, each knowing that neither will have to prove the truth of anything said to the other.

They treat $100 bills like matchsticks here, but you can still make a public telephone call for a dime. Thirty-year-old blackjack dealers here have 50-year-old eyes. And 70-year-old hands.

You can get a bacon, egg, toast and hashbrown breakfast at dinnertime for 99 cents, or a New York strip steak breakfast for $2.95. And you can catch a glimpse of Sinatra at Caesar's Palace, after a 2-hour wait, for $40—cocktails at $3.50 each, extra.

This is a city of 6-foot showgirls not counting the feathers, of lavish and elaborate musical stage productions, of real celebrities doing real things like waiting for elevators.

It is a town of 24-hour wedding chapels where there is no waiting period, and no blood test is required; where a marriage license may be obtained any time between

8 a.m. Friday and midnight Sunday, and between 8 a.m. and midnight any other day; where almost 58,000 people were married last year, and where 9,000 were divorced.

It's a city where a blissful couple, heedless of the 40-degree midnight temperature, can be found in their bathing suits sipping cocktails and dangling their legs in the heated waters of the hotel's outdoor swimming pool.

Las Vegas averages only about 4 inches of rain each year, but a 5-minute cloudburst in the mountains can trigger a flash flood that might close roads as well as schools.

It is a city of 42,000 slot machines and 45 major casinos that last year grossed $1.75 billion; where 42%, or almost 70,000 of its 164,000 residents hold casino or allied jobs.

It's a town of 50,000 motel and hotel rooms with a convention center large enough to require electric-cart security patrols, a town with an international airport, 12 taxi companies, 10 bus firms, 3 limousine services, 14 golf courses, 3 shopping malls, 9 hospitals, 11 nursing homes, 110 primary and secondary schools, 9 public libraries, and the 10,000-student University of Nevada at Las Vegas.

It's Las Vegas Blvd.—The Strip—and Fremont St. downtown; it's umpteen-zillion lightbulbs that never stop blinking and an equal number of bells, buzzers and chimes that never stop ringing, buzzing or chiming.

It is residential areas leaning toward beige adobe and red tile, and Tudor-style row houses, a community where it is against the law to build a home without air conditioning.

It is, also, a bunch of ordinary citizens who work normal, 8-hour days, who raise children and educate them, who watch television and worry about inflation and jobs and crime and who, most deeply, resent the implication that everyone who lives and works in town is either a gambler, an entertainer, a tourist or a hustler.

But Las Vegas is what it is—glitter and glamor, mostly, a "complete" resort city in the minds and eyes of the convention industry people, a 24-hour city to most visitors where anything and everything is available around the clock, 365 days a year.

—610 words

Donald A. Bluhm, *The Milwaukee Journal*, March 20, 1983. Reprinted by permission.

Précis of *Las Vegas*

It's a 24-hour desert mirage set in sagebrush and capped with billions worth of glass and steel—Las Vegas needs to be looked at through a special prism.

Here, people wearing the latest trendy clothes meet to share their stories with flair, knowing that anything they say is a part of the moment, and then gone.

High-rolling spenders fast-flow large amounts of money, while real bargains can still be found. Age is deceptive here, and you can see big name people doing ordinary things outside the glamor of showtime.

Marriage and divorce happen with ease and spin around the clock, like neighboring roulette wheels.

In spite of occasional heavy rains, good weather smiles down on a complex of hotels, motels and entertainment businesses which make up the largest portion of the city's economy.

Underneath it all, the natives live and work and worry much the same as in less flashy cities, and reject the image that they are all somehow connected to the gambling and entertainment industry with its neon personality.

Yet looking at the reality, Las Vegas is a Mecca to the convention industry, and to visitors the city where you get anything you want at any time.

—203 words

The Expository Précis

Exposition is communication which explains a concept, idea, belief, or process. The ability to effectively summarize exposition is a must for any student. Below are two expository paragraphs together with a précis of each:

Plumbing work is divided into two categories: rough-in work and finish work. Rough-in work involves the installation of water supply lines, drain pipes, and other items that will be enclosed in the floors and walls when the building is completed. Finish work involves installing all plumbing fixtures such as sinks, lavatories, and water closets and making all the necessary pipe connections to put them in operating condition. It may also involve completing piping that will be exposed in basement areas.

—80 words

Stanley Badzinsk, Jr., House Construction: A Guide to Buying, Building and Evaluating (Englewood Cliffs, N.J.: Prentice-Hall, 1976), p. 124.

Précis

Plumbing involves rough-in and finish work. Rough-in work is installation of systems later enclosed in floors and walls. Finish work is installation of fixtures, connections, and exposed basement piping.

—29 words

Genetic information is transmitted from parents of offspring through a complex series of processes. Twenty-three pairs of chromosomes in the human germ cells divide into 2 gametes by meiosis, giving to each of these mature germ cells (female ovum and male spermatazoon) one-half of the genetic material necessary for producing a new individual. The specific hereditary information is carried on the chromosomes by thousands of genes, but the expression of gene characteristic is not a preprogrammed, unchangeable process. According to the Jacob–Monod hypothesis, there are 3 different types of genes. Only one type is directly responsible for growth. The other two regulate genetic activity as a result of information from the rest of the reproductive cell. These synthesizing genes do not automatically perform the processes contained in their genetic code; their function is to be sensitive to environmental conditions within the cell. Thus, gene expression is affected by the prevailing cellular environment of the fetus and the uterine environment, which are active in determining the structure and organization of each fetal system. Variation in the human results from common factors, such as crossover of genes in a variety of combinations, mutations, unusual sexual configurations, and other abnormalities in genetic process. Many chromosomal defects can now be diagnosed.

—210 words

Ruth Beckmann Murray, and Judith Proctor Zenter, *Nursing Assessment and Health Promotion Through the Life Span,* 2nd ed. (Englewood Cliffs, N.J.: Prentice-Hall, 1979), p. 8.

Précis

Genetic data transmits through a complex series of processes. Chromosome pairs divide into 2 gametes by meiosis. Ovum and spermatazoon receive half of the genetic material for a new individual. Specific data carried by three types of genes are expressed based on dominant cellular environment, and variation in the human results from common factors. Many chromosomal defects can be identified.

—60 words

The Poetic Précis

Writing a précis of a poem is often quite difficult. Inverted sentences, poetic language, and figures of speech can obscure the main ideas the poet is trying to communicate. However, for some students, summarizing poetry can be a thought-provoking, worthwhile assignment.

National Brotherhood Week

Oh, the white folks hate the black folks
And the black folks hate the white folks—
To hate all but the right folks
Is an old established rule.

But during National Brotherhood Week,
National Brotherhood Week,
Lena Horne and Sheriff Clark are dancing cheek to cheek.
It's fun to eulogize the people you despise.
As long as you don't let them in your school.

Oh, the poor folks hate the rich folks
And the rich folks hate the poor folks—
All of my folks hate all of your folks,
It's American as apple pie.

But during National Brotherhood Week,
National Brotherhood Week,
New Yorkers love the Puerto Ricans 'cause it's very chic.

Step up and take the hand of someone you can't stand;
You can tolerate him if you try.

Oh, the Protestants hate the Catholics
And the Catholics hate the Protestants
And the Hindus hate the Muslims
And everybody hates the Jews.

But during National Brotherhood Week
National Brotherhood Week,
It's National Smile at Oneanotherhood Week.
Be nice to people who are inferior to you;
It's only for a week, so have no fear—
Be grateful that it doesn't last all year!

—173 words

Précis of National Brotherhood Week

1. That one race hate another is an old established right. But during National Brotherhood Week they mix with some delight, even praise each other but keep each other in their place. Rich hate poor and poor hate rich; it's American to hate. But during National Brotherhood Week it's in to tolerate. And one religion hates another and all do hate the Jews. But during National Brotherhood Week like someone you choose.

    —69 words

2. Black and white, poor and rich, Protestant and Catholic—hate each other well. But during National Brotherhood Week everything is swell. So take that step cheek to cheek; it's only for a week.

    —33 words

3. Everybody hates somebody; it's the American Way. But during National Brotherhood Week everybody likes somebody until the seventh day.

    —19 words

WHAT DID THE LECTURER SAY?

Words are heard with one's ears, but it is necessary to listen to ideas with the mind in order to understand what has been said.

Although many students will say they learn more in a lecture class than they do from studying their textbooks, listening to a lecture can be a difficult task. Listening is an active process requiring full attention and concentration. Students may "miss" a large part of a professor's lecture because they have never learned to *listen*.

Preparing to Listen

The same techniques are involved in listening well that are involved in reading well. You must prepare to listen. The question is: How can you do this when you can't look at the lecturer's headings and subheadings beforehand to find out what the lecture is to be "about"?

You must prepare to listen by knowing something about the subject beforehand so that you can think ahead of and along with the speaker and thus listen actively rather than passively. In addition, if you know something about the subject beforehand, you will have something with which you can associate the new material and thus be better able to understand and remember it.

First of all, the instructor usually gives some kind of title to his lecture. In this case it is necessary for you to *think* about the subject and recall what you already know about this subject. It is not enough to say to yourself, "I learned all about that in high school." You must try to remember *what* you learned about the subject in high school. This will help you to become involved and interested in what the speaker has to say. *Thinking* is an extremely important process in good listening, just as it is in reading.

When you know beforehand the subject of the professor's lecture, it is easy for you to enter the lecture room with information about the subject. If you have no information stored away in your brain, you should go to the library *before* the lecture and obtain information that will help you to understand what the speaker has to say. When you are well enough acquainted with the professor's mode of operation, you can anticipate whether or not the lecture will be on the same material you studied from the textbook. You can always study the lesson beforehand for this kind of lecture class and be informed about the subject before you enter the classroom.

Good students are usually questioning ones. When they have some information on a subject, it is easy for them to raise further questions that the speaker is likely to answer. It is difficult enough to concentrate on a familiar subject, but much more difficult if the subject is an entirely new one. Everyone will agree that students are likely to be more interested in subjects with which they are familiar—and when you are interested, your listening task is much less difficult.

LISTENING TO LEARN

You learn by listening every day in all kinds of situations. On the other hand, you can "turn off" your listening if what you hear is something in which you are not interested or something you do not agree with or understand. That is why it is necessary to listen when you have some knowledge about the subject.

Assuming that you have prepared yourself for the listening experience, one of the most important things you must do is to identify the main ideas of what the lecturer is saying. The first clue will be in the title or the subject of his lecture. Then it takes concentration and clear thinking to sift and sort out main ideas from the details, explanations, and examples.

The good speaker will plan a lecture around several main ideas. As you listen, you must recognize each new idea as well as the technique the speaker is using to make a particular point. Is the speaker supporting each new idea with explanations or examples? More than likely the speaker will come back frequently to the main ideas, and you must be aware of this repetition.

If the instructor has prepared the lecture well, he or she will begin by introducing the subject, possibly take a stand on the subject, and even give a purpose for choosing this particular subject. Listening to the introduction is like reading the first paragraph of an assigned textbook lesson. Then the instructor will give a point-by-point presentation of the steps in this discussion of the subject. In order to follow the speaker's reasoning as this information is presented, you must listen carefully for words that will show the direction of his or her thinking. Is the speaker using such words as "furthermore" or "consequently" to show that the ideas are moving forward, or is "on the other hand" or "however" being used to show that they are being reversed? There are many of these transitional words the speaker will use to help to direct your thinking. Everyone would agree that when a driver returns to his parked car and finds a policeman writing out an overtime parking ticket, the driver quickly reverses his thinking when the policeman says, "I was going to give you a ticket, *but* now that you are here, I'll tear it up." The small word "but" made the driver reverse his thinking.

The conclusion of the lecture, of course, pulls all of the speaker's ideas together, and these words are similar to those in the final paragraph of a reading assignment. However, when you listen to a lecture, you cannot hear the summary or conclusion until the end of the lecture, whereas in reading you can read the final paragraph before you study the lesson.

When a professor begins a lecture with, "Today we shall talk about the five good reasons why . . . ," you must "pick out" and remember these five reasons. You must think about them and translate them into your own words and relate them to what you already know about the subject. In other words, you must become so actively involved in the lecture that you will be *learning* as you are *listening*.

When a speaker suggests that an idea is important, you should trust that and make special mental note of what is being said. When an example is given or an anecdote told to clarify a point, you must listen carefully to the example; however, the example or anecdote is not important in itself. What is important is the idea or concept the speaker is trying to explain. Unfortunately, some students remember the funny story but are unable to remember what point the speaker was trying to make. Here again, it is a good idea for the student to think of this point in his or her own words and to relate it to what has already been learned. Remember, the professor is not likely to include the anecdote or example on the examination.

Why do students take tape recorders to class? Probably the only reason is to be able to replay the lecture. What a waste of time! You can learn *as* you are listening the first time just as well as when you replay a tape. When you tape a lecture, all you are doing is postponing your learning and wasting your time in class. You are admitting to yourself that you have not yet learned how to listen. The one advantage of a tape is that it can be replayed again and again if the lecture was on a particularly difficult subject. However, few students replay the tapes, and because they have the information on tape they seem to feel they have it in their heads.

Notetaking, on the other hand, can effectively aid listening and retention. Anne Bradley points out the value of taking notes while listening. She writes:

1. What has been discovered about learning can be applied to a very real, immediate and practical college success skill—notetaking. When you take notes, your ears take in the information and your hands and brain transform the words and ideas into a visual form that can be re-read and reviewed. You've taken a weak auditory input (15%) and changed it into a stronger form (visual—85%) that has permanence.

2. The second reason to take notes during lectures is related to the first. Notetaking during lectures will help you to *concentrate in the classroom.* If you simply sat there passively listening, the information would literally be going "in one ear and out the other." Taking notes is an effective way of making a deep impression on your brain, of "filing" information in your brain's memory banks to be retrieved later when reviewing.

3. A third reason to take notes is to help you *prepare for tests.* In fact, "studying for a test" consists mostly of reviewing and memorizing information from lecture notes. So it's certainly important that these notes be complete, readable, accurate, and well-organized.

4. Another way good notes will help you prepare for tests is that they often are a source of valuable clues to what information the instructor thinks is most important, and therefore what he or she will most likely *include on exams.* This is only common sense. If you were an instructor, would you spend most of your time discussing topics that were unimportant and therefore not likely to be on a test?

5. Finally, notes are important because often they consist of *information that is not found elsewhere.* Instructors generally choose one or several textbooks that contain basic and detailed information about the subject matter. Then they spend lecture time explaining the basic concepts introduced in the text, or they may use text concepts as a base and add their own personal and professional expertise. Taking notes is a way for students to produce their own textbooks, to make the lecture material their own.

Anne Bradley, *Take Note of College Study Skills* (Glenview, IL: Scott, Foresman, 1983), p. 114.

It is easy for you to "turn off" what you are hearing if it is not what you want to hear. Often a lecturer presents ideas that are diametrically opposed to yours. In such situations it is even more important for you to listen in order to be informed on all sides of a controversial question. As you listen, you must try to understand the lecturer's point of view in order to remember how he or she feels about the topic, because these ideas will be reflected in the way any examination that is given on the material will be scored. If the class discusses the issue at a later date, it is necessary for you to understand the ideas you are going to have to refute if you wish to give your side of the argument.

It is necessary for you to understand every point the professor makes in a lecture. You must understand the organizational pattern of what is said so that you can distinguish between the main ideas and the supporting details. However, it is not enough to understand the organizational pattern and every point that is made. You must also learn to evaluate the information in the light of what you already know about the subject.

Remember, a professor is able to present fewer ideas in an hour than a good reader can get from reading a book for the same length of time. Learn to listen actively to what is said, and learn *while* you listen.

To be a good listener you must:

1. Prepare to listen by knowing something about the subject.
2. Identify main ideas.
3. Understand relationships of supporting details to the main ideas.
4. Think along with the speaker, anticipating what will be said next.
5. Translate the speaker's ideas into your own words.
6. Take effective notes when it is important to retain and review the information.
7. Evaluate what has been said.

EXERCISE

1. **Prepare to listen to the lecture in one of your other classes by recalling what you already know about the subject.**
2. **Raise questions in your mind that you think the speaker might answer in the lecture.**
3. **Translate the speaker's main ideas into your own words and jot them down in your notebook. Then include the important details that support the main ideas. (Most students should *think more* and *write less* while listening to a lecture.)**

4. As you listen, think along with the speaker and anticipate what will be said next.

5. Write a summary of what has been said as soon as possible after the lecture is finished.

BARRIERS TO LISTENING

Distractions

Two types of distractions, external and internal, can interfere with concentration and make it difficult to listen. External distractions refer to noises both inside and outside of the room. Paper rattling, coughing, whispering, and street noise are just a few of the things that make it difficult to pay attention. To limit external distractions when attending a speech or lecture, arrive early enough to find a comfortable seat close enough to the speaker to be able to see and hear easily. Avoid sitting close to an entrance or exit.

Internal distractions occur when a listener is so caught up in problems of his or her own that attention is diverted from listening. Ask yourself how many times you were supposed to be listening but found yourself thinking of an upcoming test, a broken romance, or a loved one in the hospital. When you are bothered by internal distractions, you must redouble your efforts to concentrate.

Emotional Reactions

Certain words can cause emotional responses that interfere with listening. Labels like "commie," "pig," and "honky" can trigger responses that interfere with our ability to concentrate. When we hear a speaker use one of these words our response is often immediate and negative. Try to avoid emotional reactions by determining to hear everything a speaker has to say before you judge him or her.

Defensiveness

Try to keep an open mind when listening. The practice of mentally debating with the speaker is a significant barrier to listening. If you get caught up in a rebuttal of the speaker's ideas, you will probably miss the rest of what he or she has to say. Use the same approach for avoiding the barrier of defensiveness as you would for avoiding emotional reactions: Listen to everything a speaker has to say before disagreeing.

Fatigue

If you know an important speech or lecture is coming up, make sure you are well rested. Active listening requires energy. If you are tired, you will find it difficult to concentrate on what the speaker is saying, particularly if the subject being discussed is complex or uninteresting.

Daydreaming

While a lecturer can speak at the rate of 100–125 words per minute, the listener can think at a rate eight to ten times faster. This often results in a tendency to let the mind drift into a period of daydreaming. The daydreaming might be momentary or extended. Extended daydreaming often results in losing the speaker's continuity of ideas. To avoid daydreaming, spend your time distinguishing between fact and opinion, drawing inferences, determining the main and supporting ideas, and taking notes.

Listening Only for Facts

A speaker supports his or her ideas with facts in the form of examples, explanation, testimony, statistics, and comparison. These supporting materials are sometimes more interesting than the ideas they support. Sometimes a listener can get so caught up in an interesting anecdote or an alarming statistic that the point the speaker is trying to make is missed. Avoid this pitfall by outlining the speaker's major ideas in your head or by taking notes.

Faking Attention

Most of us have been guilty at one time or another of faking attention. We might have done so to avoid being accused of not wanting to learn or of being discourteous. The danger of faking attention is that it can be a difficult habit to break. Being aware of how you will benefit from listening will make it less likely that you will fake attention.

Ineffective Note Taking

While effective notetaking is a valuable aid to listening, without an organized system, a student might be better off not taking them. A common mistake in taking notes is trying to take down too much of what a speaker says thereby concentrating on writing rather than listening. The way to avoid this problem, of course, is to develop an effective system for taking notes.

Reasons for Taking Notes

1. They indicate what the lecturer feels is important.
2. They help you remember information.
3. They provide information not found outside the lecture.

4. They aid in studying for exams.

5. They can give you a clear picture of the important ideas in the lecture.

Tips for Notetaking

1. Put down only important ideas.

   Try to capture the speaker's main points. Watch for emphasis of voice or facial expression by the speaker which will indicate key ideas. Listen for signals like, "Let's examine some of the reasons that . . ." or "Probably no other factor contributed more . . ." Phrases like these tip you off to the fact that important ideas are forthcoming.

2. Be brief.

   A common mistake in notetaking is the attempt to write down too much. Don't get so involved in writing that you miss the speaker's main ideas. It would be wise to develop a type of notetaker's shorthand. Use symbols, numbers, abbreviations, etc. The less time you spend writing the more you will have to concentrate on what the speaker is saying.

3. Use your own words.

   The best indication that you understand something is to be able to write it down in your own words. This practice will make it easier for you to both reconstruct what your instructor said on the subject and to remember it more easily.

4. Don't worry about spelling.

   The notes you are taking are for your own use. If you are not sure how a word is spelled write it phonetically. You can check spelling later when you review.

5. Don't erase.

   Don't waste your time by erasing. Just draw a line through your mistake and continue. If you are a stickler for neatness, you can rewrite or type your notes later.

6. Keep up.

   When you realize that your notetaking is falling behind, skip a few lines and begin again. Later, when you review, you can fill in the missing information. If you find that you cannot remember what was missing, ask a classmate or your instructor.

7. Write legibly.

   Make sure your notes are easy to read. If your notetaking is so hurried that you can't write legibly, you are probably writing down too much.

8. Copy all definitions, diagrams and drawings.

   The fact that a speaker goes to the trouble of putting a definition, diagram or the like on the board, means he or she feels they are important.

9. Date your notes.

Get into the habit of dating each set of lecture notes. This practice will insure your being able to check your notes with your classmates or the instructor.

10. Expand your notes.

It is a good idea to expand your notes as soon after the lecture as possible. Since most of your forgetting will take place during the first 24 hours, you should expand and clarify notes within that period.

CHAPTER 3

Purposeful Communication

After studying this chapter, you should be able to:

1. Classify the primary purpose of a communicative act under one of the following headings: to inform, to entertain, to convince, to actuate, or to reinforce.
2. List and briefly explain five considerations for selecting a subject.
3. Determine, after examining a list of subjects, which ones are sufficiently restricted for a composition or speech of a specified length.
4. Formulate a statement of specific intent for a subject you have selected and adequately restricted.
5. Explain how a statement of intent differs from a main idea statement.
6. Revise unsatisfactory main idea statements.
7. Plan and execute a written and/or oral communication for which you have determined the primary purpose, selected and restricted an appropriate topic, and formulated a specific intent statement and/or main idea.

CLASSIFYING THE PURPOSE

The purpose of this course is not to teach you how to communicate, but rather to help you communicate more effectively. This distinction is not merely one of semantics, since we have all engaged in the process of communication with varying degrees of success from the day we were born.

When we were hungry, we cried, and our message was answered. When we experienced pain or discomfort we made our feelings known long before we learned to talk, and our parents responded. We sent and received messages of sorrow, despair, frustration, joy, and ecstasy. As we learned our native language, our messages and responses became more sophisticated, and consequently our communication grew more complex. As we matured, we learned how to manipulate symbols, starting with pictures, progressing to letters, and finally to words, word groups, and sentences. Because the process of communication parallels the life cycle, we have experienced and will continue to experience hundreds of thousands of communicative acts. Our purpose, therefore, is not to learn new skills, but to refine and polish those we already possess.

Have you ever listened to a speaker ramble on without a sense of direction? Have you ever, merely to get the job over with, written a paper about a subject of no particular interest to you? When we try to communicate about a subject without sufficient organization, without relating each point to a controlling dominant idea, our speech or paper will lack a *sense of purpose.*

The effective speaker or writer has a purpose in mind during the planning stages of the communication. The overall purposes of a communicative act may be divided into the following categories:

1. *To inform,* to add to the knowledge of the reader or listener. News stories, weather reports, wedding invitations, stock market closings, traffic reports, baseball scores, and simple descriptions are examples of informative communication.

2. *To entertain,* to provide pleasant diversion, to amuse, to hold a passive audience's attention. All forms of comedy, television, games and quiz shows, music, sports events, and escape literature have entertainment as their primary purpose. Humor, while frequently employed, is not necessarily a prerequisite of entertainment.

3. *To persuade,* to convince, to reinforce, or to actuate. Because persuasion is more complex than information or entertainment, we shall deal with the three types of persuasion separately.

   a. *To convince,* to change a reader or listener's mind, or to commit an undecided person to our point of view on a particular subject. A politician addressing an audience previously committed to another candidate or as yet uncommitted to any candidate must first convince them that he or she is the best person for the job. For example, Republicans have seldom received strong labor support in recent national elections. While a Republican may realistically write off the support of the organized labor movement, he or she will, nevertheless, attempt to *convince* working people to support his or her candidacy. In urban areas, Republican candidates must *convince* growing numbers of traditionally Democratic voters to support them if they are to win elections, while the converse is frequently the situation in rural areas. The politician must analyze the constituency in order to decide who must be convinced and how best that task can be accomplished.

b. *To reinforce,* to strengthen and invigorate those previously committed to the point of view of the communicator. Note the basic distinction between persuasion to convince and persuasion to reinforce. In the former, the sender attempts to change his receiver's point of view; in the latter, the sender and receiver are already in agreement.

c. *To actuate,* to put into action. In our previous example, the politician's task was to convince constituents to vote for him or her. Having accomplished this purpose as well as possible with available resources, convincing large blocks of voters—blacks, Jews, business people, white collar workers, blue collar workers, professionals—the purpose then shifts to one of *actuation.* If voters committed to his or her candidacy do not actually get to the polls in sufficient numbers, that candidate will not be elected. Many a politician has lost an election because prospective voters never exercised their ballots. A change in the weather may keep the farmer on the farm and lose the election for the candidate. In 1948 pollsters and political analysts agreed that Thomas E. Dewey would easily defeat Harry Truman for the Presidency, yet the ballots returned President Truman to office in the major political upset of our century. The postelection analysis was that Dewey supporters suffered from complacency, staying away from the polls in the conviction that their candidate could not lose. The Republicans failed to actuate sufficient qualified voters committed to the Dewey candidacy. Jimmy Carter's unprecedented, meteoric rise in popularity in the months preceding the 1976 Democratic Party convention is a more recent example of a politician's ability to convince, then actuate his constituency.

Why would a communicator attempt to persuade a receiver with whom he or she is already in agreement? Consider a coach who talks to a team before an important game. The team does not need to be convinced of the importance of winning. But the coach does want to prepare them psychologically and emotionally for the big game. The late coach Vince Lombardi was a master of persuasion to reinforce.

In another example of reinforcement, it has become customary for both major political parties to designate a keynote speaker to address their national conventions. The speaker's fellow party members are generally committed to the same candidates and political philosophy, so his or her primary purpose is to emphasize party unity and deemphasize minor differences, thus enabling the party to emerge from the convention on a positive, unified note.

The football coach and political keynoter in our two previous examples are both addressing members of their respective teams. Because they seek to strengthen those previously committed to their points of view, their primary purpose is to reinforce.

EXERCISES

What is the primary purpose in each of the following situations—(a) to inform, (b) to entertain, (c), to convince, (d) to actuate, or (e) to reinforce? Be prepared to explain and defend your answer in class discussion.

1. A defense lawyer's pleading for the acquittal of a client during the final summation to the jury
2. A eulogy at a funeral
3. A short speech entitled, "How to bounce a meatball."
4. A speech entitled, "What we owe senior citizens."
5. A course in beginner's bridge
6. An instruction booklet for your own camera
7. An episode of your favorite situation comedy show
8. A door-to-door salesperson who would like to demonstrate the company's latest vacuum cleaner for you
9. A solicitation for a contribution to charity
10. A debate

SELECTING AND RESTRICTING A SUBJECT

Once you understand clearly the purpose of a speaking or writing assignment, you are ready to think about a specific choice of subject. Your decision should be based on a number of considerations:

1. Is my subject in keeping with the general purpose of the assignment?
2. Is my subject interesting to me?
3. Is my subject one about which I am sufficiently knowledgeable?
4. Will my subject be of interest to my audience or reader?
5. Is my subject sufficiently restricted?

Let us consider each of these questions in some detail.

1. *Is my subject in keeping with the general purpose of the assignment?*

Assume that you are asked to prepare a composition or speech whose primary purpose is to inform. If you select as your tentative subject, "Why I Believe Air Bags Should Be Required in All New Cars," your communication will be primarily persuasive, not informative. However, air bags could be a proper subject for an informative or even an entertaining communication. If you concentrate on *how* the air bag works, your communication will be in keeping with the informational purpose of the assignment. When the writer of a television skit has the air bag misfire at a drive-in movie, his primary purpose is to entertain.

2. *Is my subject interesting to me?*

Students rightfully complain when they are assigned such chestnuts as "How I Spent My Summer Vacation." When you have the opportunity of selecting your own subject, choose one in which you are genuinely interested. Your communication will thus be easier to prepare, because interest leads to enthusiasm.

3. *Is my subject one about which I am sufficiently knowledgeable?*

Interest and knowledge are not necessarily synonymous. You may be interested in finding out about a given subject, but if your interest is relatively recent, you may not have had sufficient time to acquire enough information to prepare a well-developed communication. When selecting a subject for an impromptu, adequate knowledge is especially important; the wrong choice will invariably result in superficial communication.

Even when you have the time to plan and prepare at a more leisurely pace, it is usually a good idea to select a subject with which you are already familiar. An introductory course in communication skills is not primarily a course in research. Your instructor is interested in purposeful, well-organized, and well-developed communication. Selecting subjects close to your own experiences will help you to achieve positive results.

4. *Will my subject be of interest to my audience or reader?*

At this point our emphasis shifts from the communicator and his message to the receiver and his response. Let us assume that your assign-

ment is to prepare a demonstration speech for classroom presentation. You tentatively decide to explain how to score a bowling match and to accompany your explanation with an enlarged score sheet. This subject is in keeping with the purpose of the assignment, and you are interested in and knowledgeable about it. Is it, however, a subject which will engender the response you desire from your audience? For those who bowl regularly, your explanation would be repetitious, while those who do not bowl may have no reason for learning how.

Perhaps your part-time job involves skills that are particularly interesting and valuable to you, but ask yourself whether a speech about them would be of interest and value to your audience. You must adapt your communication to your audience. Of course, it is impossible to interest different individuals with varying backgrounds in everything you say or write about. The point is simply to consider your receiver and prepare your communications accordingly.

5. *Is my subject sufficiently restricted?*

The secret of a well-developed communication is to begin with a subject which is sufficiently restricted and then to develop that restricted subject in detail.

A former student recently told us about his experience in an undergraduate course in modern poetry. His assignment was to select an appropriate subject, restrict it, submit it to his instructor for approval, and then write a term paper. Remembering what he had learned about the importance of beginning with a properly restricted subject, he decided to write about a single poem, T. S. Eliot's *The Waste Land*. He further restricted his discussion to the symbolism in the poem and submitted to his instructor the following tentative subject: "An Interpretation of the Symbolism in T. S. Eliot's *The Waste Land*."

After the student received his instructor's approval and began his research, he decided to write a line-by-line, symbol-by-symbol interpretation of the lengthy, four-part poem. However, he found that his discussion of Part One alone occupied about twenty pages of manuscript. Continuing with his original plan would have resulted in a manuscript of approximately 80 pages, well beyond the scope of the assignment. Should he change his subject to one less ambitious and involved? But what about all the time and effort already expended on research? He resolved the problem satisfactorily by changing his title to "An Interpretation of the Symbolism in Part One of T. S. Eliot's *The Waste Land*."

When we are involved in research, we cannot always know beforehand whether a tentative subject is sufficiently restricted. The problem of adequate restriction is not as difficult when we prepare a communication based on our own experiences, because the subject is thoroughly familiar to us before we begin.

Sometimes a subject which appears to be sufficiently restricted at first glance really isn't. A recent trip may provide you with a good subject for a speech or composition, but any trip, even a short one, is a combination of many experiences. Listing some of these should help you to further restrict your tentative subject.

My Trip to Washington, D.C.

I.   The Plane Ride to Washington
II. Visiting John Kennedy's Grave at Arlington
III. A Visit with Senator Nelson
IV. The Lincoln Memorial at Night
V.   Our Nation's Capitol
VI. The Smithsonian Institution—A Magnificent Complex

If you attempt to deal with all of these experiences, your communication will read like a shopping list. A "first we did this, then that" approach, with a sentence or two devoted to each experience, would result in an uninteresting and superficial communication. Let us continue to analyze our tentative choice of subject, a trip to Washington, D.C.

Restricted Subject	Analysis
I. The Plane Ride to Washington	The flight attendant spilled some coffee on my suit when the plane hit an air pocket. Perhaps I should describe this experience in detail?
II. Visiting John Kennedy's Grave at Arlington	I was deeply moved. Could I recreate in words the feelings I experienced as I watched the eternal flame?
III. A Visit with Senator Nelson	Meeting the Senator gave me the opportunity to chat with him about his proposal to recycle glass, metal, and paper products. I could share these thoughts with the class.
IV. The Lincoln Memorial at Night	The photographs I took would help me to recall the specific details of this scene and to recreate them for the class.
V. Our Nation's Capitol	Much too broad. Perhaps I could restrict this subject to my visit to the Senate Gallery.

VI. The   Smithsonian   Institution—A   Again, much too broad. There are nine
     Magnificent Complex   different Smithsonian buildings, each
                                            containing a multitude of exhibits.

EXERCISES

Determine which of the following subjects are sufficiently restricted for a three-minute speech or a 400-word composition. Further restrict those subjects that are too broad to be developed adequately.

1. Photography
2. My Most Unusual New Year's Eve Celebration
3. How to Bathe a Poodle
4. Grocery Shopping on a Shoestring
5. The Drug Problem
6. The Aftermath of Watergate
7. Is There Really Love at First Sight?
8. How to Study
9. My Visit to a Bohemian Night Club
10. The Equal Rights Amendment
11. Is Religiion Relevant?
12. Is There a Pollution Solution?
13. Hitchhiking to Mexico
14. Political Protest
15. Recycle Your Scrap!
16. Stamp Out VD!
18. The Women's Movement
18. How to Build a Good Hi-Fi Speaker for $15.00
19. The Gas Guzzler—And What to Do About it
20. Registration—A Twentieth-Century Horror

STATING THE INTENT

Once the purpose of an assignment is clear to you and your subject is carefully selected and sufficiently restricted, you are ready to formulate a statement of specific intent. We have classified purposeful communication under three main headings: to inform, to entertain, or to persuade.

Our next task is to relate this purpose to the specific content of our communication. Note the following examples:

1. **To Inform**
   a. to explain how to take pictures with a Polaroid camera
   b. to describe the view from my bedroom window
   c. to define "love"
   d. to summarize the Mayor's five-point approach for eliminating substandard housing from our town
   e. to relate the difficulties I encountered when registering for classes
2. **To Entertain**
   a. to poke fun at television comedies
   b. to prepare a program of folk music for our talent show
   c. to tell my favorite mother-in-law story to a recently married friend
3. **To Persuade**
   a. to convince you to support my candidacy for the presidency of the student body
   b. to explain why the President's wage and price freeze is unfair to labor
   c. to convince members of the Council to support a new sports arena for our town

All of these statements of specific intent are infinitive phrases beginning with the infinitive form of the verb: to explain, to describe, to define, and so on. When the intent of your communication is to develop a main idea, and this is generally true of persuasion, stating that main idea in a complete sentence will help you plan your communication.

Statement of Specific Intent: to convince you to support my candidacy for the presidency of the student body

Main Idea: My election to the presidency of the student body will insure organized student resistance to a raise in tuition.

Statement of Specific Intent: to explain why the President's wage and price freeze is unfair to labor

Main Idea: The President's wage and price freeze is unfair to labor because profits, insurance rates, and dividends are not included.

Statement of Specific Intent:	to convince members of the Council to support a new sports arena for our town
Main Idea:	Building a new sports arena will attract professional hockey to our town.

The main idea statement should fulfill four specific characteristics:

1. It should state a point of view, not a fact.
2. It should be restricted to that which can adequately be developed in a subsequent communication.
3. It should deal either with a single idea or two closely related ideas.
4. It should contain specific language.

Main Idea: The unemployment rate in our community is 6.2 percent.

Analysis: Since this is a statement of fact, not a point of view, it requires no further development.

Revision: The unemployment rate in our community will continue to increase unless new jobs are created more rapidly.

Main Idea: There are many reasons why the Yankees will again be American League Champions.

Analysis: "Many reasons" is too broad. It is better to restrict your main idea to one or two specific reasons and develop them in detail.

Revision: The Yankees will again be American League Champions because their pitching depth and long-ball hitting are superior to those of the other contenders.

Main Idea: Raising tropical fish and collecting stamps are interesting hobbies.

Analysis: This main idea statement contains two flaws:
1. Raising tropical fish and collecting stamps are two entirely unrelated activities.
2. The word "interesting" is vague.

Revision: Stamp collecting is a painless way to learn world geography.

EXERCISES

Analyze the following main idea statements. Revise any that are not satisfactory.

1. The Milwaukee Bucks are the most interesting team in professional basketball.
2. My sewing machine enables me to keep up with the latest fashions and still stay within my budget.
3. Employer commitments to affirmative action have successfully combated the adverse effects of discrimination against minorities and women.
4. Speeders lose their licenses in New Jersey.
5. The Women's Movement has irreparably harmed American family life.
6. Stock car racing is an exciting sport.
7. Jogging is a great way to stay physically fit, and physical fitness is necessary for a full life.
8. Gays are people, too.
9. Prostitution should be legalized.
10. Our welfare system is obsolete.

Assignment

Plan and execute a composition, a speech, or both (as your instructor indicates), according to the following procedure:

1. Indicate the primary purpose of your communication:
   a. to inform,
   b. to entertain,
   c. to convince,
   d. to actuate,
   e. to reinforce.
2. Does your subject fulfill the following criteria:
   a. Is it in keeping with the primary purpose indicated above?
   b. Is it interesting to you?
   c. Is it one about which you have sufficient knowledge?
   d. Will it be of interest to your audience or reader?
   e. Is it sufficiently restricted?
3. Formulate a statement of specific intent and deliver a main idea statement, if needed.
4. Write your composition and/or deliver your speech.

CHAPTER 4

The Forms
of Discourse

OBJECTIVES

After studying this chapter, you should be able to:
1. Define narration and explain how it may be employed in informative, entertaining, and persuasive situations.
2. Define exposition and explain how it may be employed in informative, entertaining, and persuasive situations.
3. Define an abstract word, following the three-step procedure indicated in this chapter.
4. Distinguish between denotative and connotative language.
5. Explain two techniques for achieving effective description.
6. Explain how description may be employed in informative, entertaining, and persuasive situations.

Once the purpose of your communication has been clearly established, you are ready to begin developing your subject. Which form of discourse will be best to help you accomplish your purpose? Should you tell a story? Explain a process? Describe a person, place, or event? One of these forms of discourse should suffice for brief communications, while longer communications may require combinations of the different forms.

NARRATION

Can you imagine one of your ancestors attempting to relate a personal experience to a friend? Perhaps he was stung by a bee as he walked through the forest seeking food or shelter. Later, when the pain subsided, he recreated this experience for his companion by imitating the buzzing of the bee, gesturing to depict its flight, and uttering a sound that articulated the pain he suffered when he was stung. A baby's early attempts to communicate follow a similar pattern. The baby frequently imitates the sound associated with a particular animal or object, and this sound becomes a word in his limited vocabulary. The cat is a "meow," the dog a "bow-wow," and the train a "choo-choo." An exclamation of joy— "Ah!"—or pain—"Ow!"—accompanied by an occasional gesture help him to tell his story. Narration or storytelling is our oldest form of communicating experiences.

Classifying Narration According to Purpose

We have stressed purposeful communication as one of the primary objectives of the planning stage. A narrative may be employed in a communication whose purpose is to inform, to entertain, or to persuade.

If you simply relate to a friend the events that occupied your day, the purpose of your narrative is to inform. You might, however, attempt to communicate a humorous experience. Perhaps when you opened the front door to get your morning newspaper one cold, January morning, the wind blew the door shut, leaving you stranded outside in your T-shirt and jockey shorts. You ultimately saw the humor of the situation, although it may not have been evident to you when the door first blew shut. In relating this experience you would want to provide your friend with an understanding of the events themselves, but your primary purpose would be to entertain.

Frequently an experience is incidental to its message. Anecdotes, fables, parables, and some personal experiences are examples of narration whose primary purpose is to persuade. Consider the following example of persuasive narration:

I am forty-four years old now and have a wife and two small children. By 1963 I had reached a comfortable salary level with an insurance firm and the future seemed bright for us all. In May of that year I developed a slight difficulty in swallowing. Our family physician said that if it persisted for another week he would arrange an appointment for me with a throat specialist. It did persist. The specialist diagnosed it simply as "a case of nerves," a diagnosis he was to reaffirm in October of 1963. Finally, in January of 1964, convinced that it was more than a case of nerves, I entered a hospital, where I learned that I had cancer of the throat.

The writer goes on to describe in detail the horrors he experienced in the cancer ward of a well-known hospital. He employs a narrative technique to accomplish the primarily persuasive purpose of his article. This purpose is clearly indicated in the two concluding paragraphs:

If anyone tells me it hasn't been proven that smoking causes cancer, I won't argue with him. The chances are his mind is made up anyway.

If, on the other hand, what I've written here can save even one man, woman or child from the horrors I've known, I'll be content.

From "They've Never Been to Seven-East," Copyright 1967 by the Christian Herald Association, Inc. Used with permission of the writer, Hugh J. Mooney, and the *Christian Herald*.

EXPOSITION

Do you want to build a shortwave receiver? Bake a cake? Design your own dune buggy? Add some electrical outlets to your home? Operate a sewing machine? Tile your basement floor? Make a fortune in the stock market? Ferment your own wine? Tune your car's engine? Just go to your library or local book store, borrow or buy the appropriate do-it-yourself book, and follow the "simplified, illustrated instructions."

We define exposition as communication which explains a concept, idea, belief, or process. In the examples above we act as receivers of expository prose. The writer is the sender; his book, pamphlet, or instruction sheet contains the message to which we respond. Some manufacturers take pains to enclose a clear set of instructions with their product. They have learned that clear expository communication is in their own best interest. Other manufacturers, however, have yet to learn this lesson. On Christmas Day, for example, thousands of fathers sit on living room floors attempting to assemble their children's newly acquired toys. After an hour or so of frustrating trial and error, Dad may utter some angry words, return the parts to their original container, and decide to replace the item with something easier to assemble. The child is disappointed, the parents frustrated, and the manufacturer has lost a sale because of unclear exposition. One manufacturer, obviously blessed with a sense of humor, began his instruction sheet as follows: Step one—mix yourself a good, stiff drink.

The accompanying assembly instruction for a utility bin cabinet are typical of expository material which accompanies products that must be assembled by the consumer. Notice how the various steps in the assembly process are clearly and concisely described. Key words are underlined, and repeated references are made to the accompanying drawings.

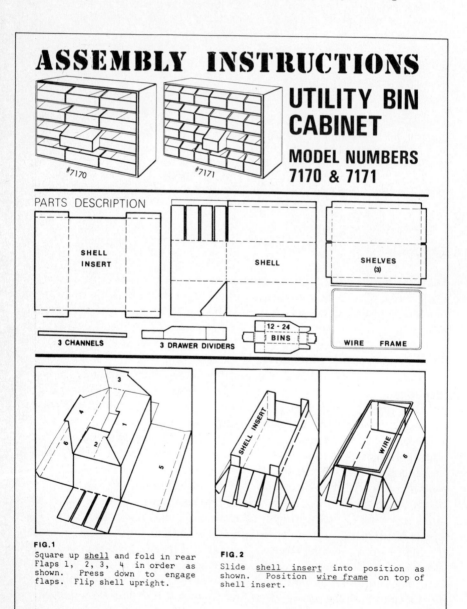

ASSEMBLY INSTRUCTIONS

UTILITY BIN CABINET

MODEL NUMBERS 7170 & 7171

#7170 #7171

PARTS DESCRIPTION

SHELL INSERT

SHELL

SHELVES (3)

3 CHANNELS   3 DRAWER DIVIDERS   12 - 24 BINS   WIRE FRAME

FIG.1
Square up shell and fold in rear Flaps 1, 2, 3, 4 in order as shown. Press down to engage flaps. Flip shell upright.

FIG.2
Slide shell insert into position as shown. Position wire frame on top of shell insert.

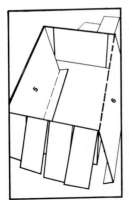

FIG. 3
Fold flaps 5 & 6 up and over wire and tuck down inside shell.

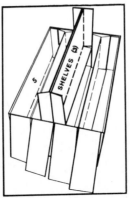

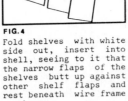

FIG. 4
Fold shelves with white side out, insert into shell, seeing to it that the narrow flaps of the shelves butt up against other shelf flaps and rest beneath wire frame as shown.

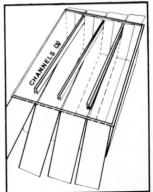

FIG. 5
Firmly press shelf channels over shelf.

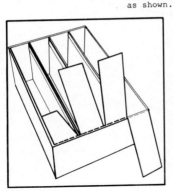

FIG. 6
Fold in remaining flaps and tuck securely against inner wall.

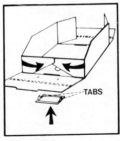

FIG. I BINS
Insert card holder tabs into the slots provided. Fold tabs over. Fold sides up, fold attached end flaps (front & back) over as shown.

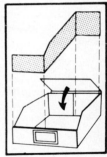

FIG. 2
Fold end panels up and over at double crease. Engage tab in slots on bottom Repeat operation opposite end. Add drawer divider as shown above.

Fidelity Products Company *A Division of Fidelity File Box, Inc*
705 PENNSYLVANIA AVENUE SOUTH, MINNEAPOLIS, MINN. 55426 • TELEPHONE (612) 544-6644

EXERCISES

I. Describe to the class an experience you had in attempting to assemble a product for which the instructions were not clear.

II. Bring an instruction sheet (similar to the example) to class, and comment on its effectiveness as exposition.

III. In a paragraph, explain as clearly and concisely as you can an everyday process with which you are thoroughly familiar. Assume the reader has never performed this process himself.

Suggestions

1. How to lace your shoes
2. How to make a cream cheese and jelly sandwich
3. How to brush your teeth
4. How to fry an egg

Classifying Exposition According to Purpose

Exposition is sometimes referred to as utilitarian prose because its effectiveness is measured by its usefulness and clarity. By definition, pure exposition is informational; however, it may also be employed in persuasive and entertaining communication.

Tom decides to convince his friend Bill to meet him at the stadium for a big football weekend. Sensing Bill's reluctance, Tom decides on a positive, enthusiastic approach:

Tom: I've got a couple of great seats for the State game. After the game Joe's throwing a big beer bash, and we're invited. Meet me at the Stadium Saturday at two, and we'll have a gas of a weekend.

Bill: Thanks for asking, Tom. But you know my sense of direction; I'd never find the place. Besides, I've got some studying to do for Monday's history exam.

Tom: Nothing to it, Bill. Take I-93 to the Iroquois Road Exit, about fifty miles north. When you exit, drive due East for four miles, and you'll run right into the stadium. We'll all be leaving Sunday, right after breakfast, so you'll get home in plenty of time to study.

Bill's tentative refusal is based on two reasons: He doubts his ability to find the stadium, and he needs time to study for Monday's examination. While Tom's primary purpose is persuasive (to convince), he utilizes exposition to answer Bill's first argument. Second, by arranging for an early Sunday departure so that Bill has ample time to study, Tom's chances of convincing Bill to join him have been enhanced.

Surely you have seen performers who employ varying degrees of audience participation in their acts. The singer who asks the audience to join him or her in the refrain or the MC explaining the rules of a TV game to contestants is involved with exposition. Explanations should be clear and brief when the purpose of a communication is primarily persuasive or entertaining. Exposition is merely a means to an end.

Definition: A Special Type of Exposition Involving Denotative and Connotative Meaning

Look around you. Regardless of where you may be at the moment, you see numerous objects whose names are familiar to you. The names we assign to objects like *door, window, book, desk, floor, ceiling, grass, tree,* and *shrub* are concrete words, relatively easy to define specifically. The literal definition of a word is its *denotative* meaning. If we tentatively define a desk as a piece of furniture, our definition is too general, because there are many pieces of furniture that are not desks. The *American Heritage Dictionary* definition—"a piece of furniture typically having a flat top for writing and accessory drawers or compartments"—is more specific, and consequently more satisfactory. Notice that this definition is still sufficiently flexible to include unusual desks. The dictionary's use of the word "typically" indicates that some desks may be atypical, thereby deviating from the usual pattern.

The words indicated all refer to objects, which are easy for us to visualize. Sometimes, however, words refer to concepts, ideas, or emotions, and mean different things to different people; consequently, they are more difficult to define satisfactorily. Words like *communism, hate, love, sorrow,* and *idealism* are abstract words referring to no specific objects. They are *connotative* in that different people have favorable or unfavorable attitudes about them, depending upon individual associations and experiences. The dedicated Communist's definition of his political ideology would be very different from that of a Wall Street banker. Defining an abstract word is a more demanding task than defining a concrete word, because the communicator must go beyond the literal meaning.

If you are asked to define an abstract word, a good starting point would be a reliable, up-to-date dictionary. The more information you discover about your word, the more complete your definition. Therefore, you might wish to consult an unabridged dictionary.

You should also pay particular attention to synonyms for the word you select. (Synonyms are words that have meanings similar to other words in the language.) However, since no two words have exactly the same meaning, distinguishing differences among similar abstract words will help you to make your definition clear and complete, and aid you in selecting precisely the right word for each situation. How, for example, does communism differ from socialism? How does hate differ from loathing, animosity, or dislike? How does love differ from affection, fondness, or infatuation? If your general language dictionary does not contain lists of synonyms, consult a specialized dictionary of synonyms and antonyms, or a thesaurus.

Our main concern thus far has been with the literal or denotative meaning of a given word. Once you have established a working definition with the help of a good dictionary, you continue the process of definition through reference to your own attitudes, values, and experiences. Your definition of "love" is probably different from your neighbor's. One of your primary objectives in defining an abstract word is to make your connotative meaning clear to your reader or listener. You might view love between the sexes as primarily a physical attraction, while another might see it as a meeting of the minds on such issues as raising children, and sharing similar moral and religious convictions. Someone else might think of love as synonymous with companionship. Each of you has an obligation to supply specific examples that will enable the receiver to understand your connotative definition.

The process of definition of abstract words can be summarized as follows:

1. Consult a good dictionary, preferably unabridged, to establish a complete denotative definition.

2. Distinguish the denotative meaning of your word from that of similar abstract words with the help of a good dictionary, a specialized dictionary of synonyms and antonyms, or both.

3. Supply your own connotative definition, supporting your judgments with specific examples.

EXERCISES

Define an abstract word in an extemporaneous speech or short composition, as your instructor directs. Follow the three-step process summarized above.

Sample Words

1. love
2. sorrow
3. idealism
4. faith
5. success

6. despair

7. solitude

8. individualism

9. tenacity

10. hope

Indicate whether the italic terms in the following sentences are denotative or connotative. If the term is connotative, determine whether the connotation is favorable or unfavorable.

1. I think John is *thrifty;* Mary thinks he is a *tightwad.*

2. Jim always addresses the *policeman* on the beat as *"officer"* but calls him a *pig* behind his back.

3. Sally, the *hairdresser* at Antoine's, refers to herself as a *beautician* or *cosmetologist.*

4. My *boss* is a *slave driver* if there ever was one.

5. Sam Farber is a *real American,* but all the *do-gooders* will vote for his *egghead* opponent.

6. I waited more than two hours for the *doctor* to see me; boy, those *pill pushers* don't care how long a *patient* is inconvenienced.

7. Fred thinks he is *honest* and *straightforward,* but he is really rather *simple.*

8. Two members of the history faculty *collaborated* on a book about Nazi *collaboration* during World War II.

9. For a *lawyer* who has been out of school for only a year, he certainly has been a busy *ambulance chaser.*

10. How's a *brother* going to make it if *Whitey* runs the establishment?

DESCRIPTION

Simple descriptions of people, places, and events are part of our everyday communication. A friend requests a description of your date's roommate before agreeing to a blind date. A classmate stops you at registration to ask whether you know the teacher of the history section she plans to enroll in. You make a mental note to write home to the folks, describing your new college campus. You tentatively select your senior high school trip as the subject of your next composition.

Your response to each of the above messages is primarily descriptive. Description, like exposition, is basically informational. Our primary purpose with both forms of discourse is to add to the knowledge of our audience. Expository communication, at its best, is generally simple, clear, direct, and detached. Description is more personal, more subjective. Its effectiveness depends upon how specific our details are.

Sensory Appeals

One method for achieving specific detail in description is to employ effective combinations of sensory appeals (the five senses being sight, hearing, taste, touch, and smell). Although it isn't necessary to employ all five in a single description, appeals to different senses will enable you to communicate a more complete description. Which combination is most effective will depend, of course, on your choice of subject.

Let us assume that your assignment is to describe a place on campus. The overall purpose of the assignment is to inform, but the specific choice of subject is left to you. After considering your English classroom, the library, the testing center, and the automotive shop as possibilities, you tentatively decide on the student center, a place with which you are thoroughly familiar. Checking your tentative choice against the criteria detailed in Chapter 2, you conclude that your subject is in keeping with the general purpose of the assignment (to inform), is interesting to both you and your prospective audience, and is one that you are sufficiently knowledgeable about. But can it be further restricted?

Perhaps the most obvious way of restricting your subject is to describe only one part of the student center, such as the snack bar. It might also be helpful to further restrict your subject to a place in time. The snack bar during the hectic rush of lunch hour is very different from its relatively deserted atmosphere of late afternoon. Eventually you decide on "The Snack Bar at Noon" as the revised subject of your descriptive communication.

Regardless of how familiar you think you are with the snack bar, it would be a mistake to attempt to prepare your communication from memory. Go there again, notebook in hand, to find specific details that will eventually be incorporated into your finished work. Recording these details as separate sensory appeals will provide you with the raw materials needed for successful description.

Sight:	long lines of students patiently awaiting their hamburgers and fries, long-haired, jeans-clad students rapidly munching their food at crowded tables, the blue and white tiled floor covered with litter carelessly dropped by students oblivious of the perils of pollution, one unhurried couple, holding hands, having eyes only for each other in the ever-changing crowd.
Hearing:	endless clanging of plastic trays making contact with the steel food rails, the din of happy, care-

free voices, the raucous sound of rock music blaring over the intercom, the voice of the order-taker barking out the jargon of his trade—"BLT down"—to the busy short order man.

Taste and Smell: spicy chili, frothy malts and shakes, freshly baked cakes and pies, the aroma of freshly brewed coffee, the smell of stale tobacco throughout the eating area.

Touch: bodies brushing against one another as students enter and leave the crowded area, the constant blast of warm air from the powerful, wall-mounted heater, the intermittent blast of cold air as entering students bring the winter chill with them.

The Snack Bar at Noon

The relative calm of coffee break time at the snack bar changes to chaos as the noon hour approaches. At exactly 11:50 A.M. the bell tolls; fifth hour class has ended, and hundreds of students converge on the northwest side of the student center, where the snack bar is housed.

Bodies brush against one another as students hurriedly enter the crowded area, bringing a bit of winter's chill with them. The freshly scrubbed blue and white tile floor is soon covered with litter carelessly dropped by those oblivious to the perils of pollution. Jeans-clad students noisily await their hamburgers and fries. The constant clanging of plastic trays making contact with the steel food railings competes with the raucous sound of rock music blaring over the intercom. Smells of spicy chili, freshly baked cakes and pies, and richly brewed coffee fill the air.

The voice of the order-taker barks out the jargon of his trade—"BLT down," "One burger, with"—to the busy short order man. The customers dig down into their pockets for change, pay for their selections, and scramble for the few vacant butcher block tables.

Students rapidly munch their food amidst the din of happy, carefree voices. One unhurried couple holds hands, having eyes only for each other in the ever-changing crowd.

Gradually the food line begins to subside. Students empty their trays into the huge, gray rubbish containers, then bundle themselves for departure. When the bell signals the end of the lunch hour, bodies converge on the exits, some leaving their debris behind on the tables. Soon the maintenance crew will tackle the seemingly endless job of preparing for the next stampede.

You may have noticed that not all of the sensory appeals in the notes were incorporated into the composition, and a few appeals that were in the composition are not found in the notes. Since effective communication involves repeated modification and revision, it is not necessary for you to follow your record of sensory appeals to the letter. Remember, you have merely made a random listing of initial impressions; additions, deletions, and modifications are expected and desirable.

The composition that you have just read represents one student's attempt to write an informative description. How successful is it? Is it sufficiently specific? Is it well organized? Purposeful? Interesting? Perhaps you can make suggestions for improvement.

Specific Language

A closely related technique for making details vivid is to use specific language. Try walking into your local market and asking the clerk for three pounds of fruit. He knows the meaning of the word "fruit" as well as you do, but he cannot fill your order without more specific information. What *kind* of fruit do you want? "Three pounds of apples, please," is better, but still not specific enough. As the clerk visualizes his stock of Delicious, Winesap, and Macintosh apples, he might become impatient with your lack of specificity. A critical reader or listener becomes equally disenchanted with vague description.

EXERCISES

Write a descriptive sentence about each of the following, employing appropriate sensory appeals and specific details. A sample sentence is provided for the first phrase.

1. A pair of shoes—My two-tone, black and rust sueded ties with wing-tip styling are perfect back-to-school shoes.
2. Something good to eat
3. A rock singer or group
4. Your room
5. A teacher
6. A musical instrument
7. A soft drink
8. A game-winning touchdown
9. A treasured possession
10. An article of clothing

Classifying Description
According to Purpose

The primary purpose of most simple descriptions of people, places, and events is to inform. But sometimes the information is subordinate to another purpose: to entertain or to persuade. Notice how the effective use of sensory detail and specific language enables the reader to experience vicariously the scene described in the following example of entertaining, descriptive poetry:

The Once-Over

The tanned blonde
        in the green print sack
in the center of the subway car
        standing
        though there are seats
        has had it from

1 teen-age hood
1 lesbian
1 envious housewife
4 men over fifty
(& myself), in short
the contents of this half of the car

Our notations are:
long legs, long waist, high breasts (no bra), long
neck, the model slump
        the handbag drape and how the skirt
cuts in under a very handsome
        set of cheeks
'stirring dull roots with spring rain' sayeth the preacher

        Only a stolid young man
        with a blue business suit and the New York
        Times
        does not know he is being assaulted

So.
She has us and we her
all the way to downtown Brooklyn
Over the tunnel and through the bridge
        to Dekalb Avenue we go

all very chummy

She stares at the number over the door
and gives no sign
        yet the sign is on her

Paul Blackburn From *The New American Poetry*, edited by Donald M. Allen © Grove Press, New York, 1960.

Has your mouth ever watered over an advertising brochure's description of a new summer outfit, a stereo receiver, or a vacation in some far-off exotic place? In advertising description, the information given is subordinate to the persuasive purpose of selling the product or service.

After studying the following example of persuasive description, answer the questions provided:

Fly away to Nassau's most fabulous world of complete resort activities . . . Nassau Beach Hotel. Just steps from your room are 660 yards of sunny, soft sandy beach washed by waters as clear, blue and warm as the breeze-swept Bahamian sky. Start your day with a suntan à la chaise, punctuated by periodic plunges into our ocean or sparkling pool. Explore the underwater world off-shore with snorkel, mask and fins. Skim the waves on water skis or sail a salty catamaran. Charter a sporty cruiser for deep-sea fishing. Go scuba diving around a coral reef. Dry off with a spot of volleyball, a shot of shuffleboard, a set of tennis. Cool off with a Tropical Temptation from our beachside bar. Then, head off on a jaunty golf cart for an afternoon round of 18 challenging championship holes at the Nassau Country Club right next door. If you prefer spectator sports, don't miss the crab or goat races down by the beach . . . with the added excitement of parimutuel betting! Go sightseeing in Old Nassau town by scooter, bike, . . . or hire a clip-clop carriage to squire you around (your horse may be wearing a straw hat). See the Old World pomp of Rawson Square. Climb the Queen's Staircase for a panoramic view of Nassau. Visit the native Straw Market. Buy free-port booty along bustling Bay Street. But don't linger too long downtown . . . Nassau's most exciting nightlife begins right here at the Nassau Beach Hotel. Stop in at the Out Island Bar or the romantic Rum Keg for an exotic cocktail (and try the hot conch fritters appetizers). Then there's the gleaming candlelight atmosphere and gourmet dining on native and continental cuisine in the elegant Lamplighter Room. Spend a lively hour or two in the colorful Rum Keg dancing to native rhythms, disco, steel band or Calypso. And come to the glittering sophistication of the Colony Room for the greatest nightclub shows. Wrap up your evening with a walk through our tropical garden under the stars and watch the moon turn the waves to silver along our beautiful beach. You'll understand the magic that makes one resort the most successful vacation spot on the Island . . . Nassau Beach Hotel.

With permission of Needham & Grohmann, Inc., and the Nassau Beach Hotel.

EXERCISES

ANALYSIS OF NASSAU BEACH HOTEL DESCRIPTION

1. Formulate a statement of specific intent for the foregoing advertising copy.

2. Which of the five sensory appeals (sight, hearing, taste, touch, smell) are represented? Give examples.

3. Which of the five sensory appeals predominates? Why?

4. Which sensory appeals are particularly effective? Are any of them trite, or otherwise ineffective?

5. Briefly comment on the effectiveness of this advertising copy as persuasive description.

USING NARRATION TO PERSUADE

Deliver a two–four minute speech or write a short essay of 200–400 words in which you tell a story to persuade. Describe the material in enough detail to create a mental picture for the reader or listener. Develop your material informally, with emphasis on details of action. An interesting story is an excellent means of reinforcing or clarifying your ideas.

Delivery: If you present this assignment orally, it should be delivered extemporaneously. An audience will expect you to have almost total eye contact when talking about your own experience. The more spontaneous and relaxed you are, the more your audience will enjoy your presentation.

Sample Main Ideas

1. Seat belts save lives.
2. Drinking and driving don't mix.
3. It pays to be courteous.
4. Never buy anything sight unseen.
5. Never judge a person on the basis of your first meeting.
6. Keep dangerous products out of the reach of small children.

CHAPTER 5

Persuasion

OBJECTIVES

After studying this chapter, you should be able to:
1. Define persuasion.
2. Explain the three characteristics of personal proof.
3. Identify nine specific suggestions you can use to enhance your image as a person of competence, integrity, and goodwill.
4. Explain the relationship between good or bad self-image and credibility.
5. Distinguish between inductive and deductive reasoning.
6. Determine the reliability of generalization, causal relation, and analogical reasoning in persuasion.
7. Identify fallacies in inductive and deductive reasoning.
8. Explain the difference between attitudes and motives.
9. Recognize the use of physical motive appeals in persuasion.
10. Recognize the use of social motive appeals in persuasion.

Never before in our society has the technique of persuasion been so important or profitable. Advertising ranks among our nation's billion-dollar enterprises. Political candidates pay staggering amounts to public relations firms to insure election. Motivational researchers make millions telling manufacturers how to sell their product. Few in our society are paid more than the effective salesperson. As a result of this, we are constantly bombarded with appeals to "get with it," to "come alive," to enjoy a new "taste sensation." We are the unceasing target for those who would persuade us to buy their product, to accept their viewpoint, or to support their cause. It is obvious, therefore, that because of the intensity of this competition for our money, our time, or our support, we must have an understanding of persuasion if we are to choose wisely.

A WORKING DEFINITION

Persuasion is *the conscious attempt to influence the thought or behavior of others through the use of personal, logical, and psychological appeals.*

The emphasis on persuasion as a "conscious" attempt to influence is important. The more aware you are of exactly what you want done, the more likely you are to be successful. Persuasion must be intentional. A good informative speech or paper may also persuade, but if its primary aim is to inform, then the persuasion is accidental. The persuader must deliberately attempt to influence.

However, you don't have to sell your product immediately to be successful. You don't have to change someone's mind on the spot. Persuasion can be a long-range process which modifies thought or behavior a little at a time. In some cases it might take a series of speeches, editorials, and meetings to change an existing policy or law.

Suppose that shortly after getting a driver's license you want to use the family car. If your parents say, "No, you're not ready yet," you must convince them that you are. Although you might point to your success in passing the driver's test, or an "A" in a Driver's Education course in school, convincing your parents that you are ready to take on this new responsibility will probably involve your driving the car a number of times while one of them is with you. Since you know that each time you do a good job you are influencing them to respond in the way you desire, you are careful to do your best when your mother or father is your audience. In this case, as you can see, it will take a series of these demonstrations of your ability to persuade them to see things your way.

In most cases you will be more successful in persuading your parents or friends than you will be in persuading others. This is because you have a better understanding of those you know; since you are sensitive to their likes and dislikes, you know how to handle them.

Now go back to the example above. You have convinced your parents that you should be allowed to use the family car for occasional dates, but you want it on a night when they were considering using it. Getting the car will be difficult. The first thing you must do is approach them when they are in a good mood. This might be after you have given your father his pipe and slippers and turned on his favorite TV program. Or you might choose a good moment to make your appeal to your mother. In any case, you are sensitive to the situation and attitudes of the person or persons to whom you are making the appeal. You are in effect a salesperson trying to sell yourself or your ideas. The cash register rings when the response is favorable. If you fail to make a sale, you learn from the experience and try a new approach the next time. As indicated in our definition, there are three appeals or types of proof you can use in selling your product more effectively: personal, logical, and psychological.

PERSONAL PROOF

Perhaps nothing is more important to a salesperson's success than the power of his or her personality. Over two thousand years ago the Greek philosopher, Aristotle, proclaimed that a communicator's character was the most powerful of all the means of persuasion. This same concept relates directly to your credibility as a speaker or writer. No factor is more important to your ability to persuade than the perception a listener or reader has of you as a person. This can involve two factors: (1) the impression the audience has of you prior to the communication, and (2) any change in your audience's perception of you, either favorable or unfavorable, during or following the communication. Ideally, you want your audience to see you as a competent person with integrity and goodwill.

Competence

Everyone admires the person who appears to know what he or she is talking about, the person who, because of education or experience, can get the job done. To be an effective persuader you must show your reader or listener that you have thought the problem over carefully, considered all the evidence, and decided on the best course of action. A well-organized, fluent presentation is the mark of a competent communicator.

Your audience also judges your competence by the language you use. The effective persuader chooses words that will convey his or her meaning accurately, grammatically, and forcefully. Words are chosen to communicate, not to display someone's vocabulary.

Integrity

Even though you are skilled in presenting your ideas, your audience must feel that you are worthy of their trust and respect. In today's society, with its credibility gaps and hypocrisy, the honesty of a writer or speaker is of major concern to an audience. Careful preparation and documentation will help to indicate your sincerity and honesty. Remember, you are judged by what you do and say. Be sure that your audience finds your comments and behavior desirable.

Goodwill

It is important that you indicate goodwill for your audience. When communicating to a reader or listener always be tactful, courteous, and respectful. A feeling of friendliness can often be projected with a good sense of humor. Whenever you can establish a common ground or interest with your audience, do so. Greet them with enthusiasm. Give them credit for having intelligence and ability.

In a March 23, 1775, speech to the House of Burgesses, Patrick Henry faced the difficult task of supporting a resolution of war against strong opposition by rich planters who feared an uprising even more than they feared oppression from the crown. Note how tactfully he compliments those with whom he disagrees.

MR. PRESIDENT:
No man thinks more highly than I do of the patriotism, as well as abilities, of the very worthy gentlemen who have just addressed the house. But different men often see the same subject in different lights; and therefore, I hope it will not be thought disrespectful to those gentlemen if, entertaining as I do opinions of a character very opposite to theirs, I shall speak forth my sentiments freely and without reserve. This is no time for ceremony. The question before the house is one of awful moment to this country. For my own part, I consider it as nothing less than a question of freedom or slavery. And in proportion to the magnitude of the subject ought to be the freedom of the debate. It is only in this way that we can hope to arrive at truth and fulfill the great responsibility which we hold to God and our country. Should I keep back my opinions at such a time, through fear of giving offense, I should consider myself as guilty of treason toward my country, and of an act of disloyalty toward the Majesty of Heaven, which I revere above all earthly kings.

The Image

Public relations people, advertisers, and motivational researchers are constantly involved in image building. They are acutely aware of the image of their product held by potential customers. They have come to realize that to a great extent it is this image which sells the product. In order for speakers or writers to gain acceptance of their ideas, they must project an image of themselves that will be favorably received by their audience.

Listed below are some specific suggestions you can use to enhance your image as a person of competence, integrity, and goodwill:

Competence

1. *Indicate your qualifications.* If you have special knowledge, education, and experience which qualify you to deal with your chosen subject, mention these at the beginning of your communication.
2. *Use correct grammar.* A reader or listener is apt to question the validity of your ideas if they are incorrectly written or spoken.
3. *Speak with confidence.* Whether you are speaking in front of a group, in an interview, or in group discussion, be positive in your approach.
4. *Organize clearly.* A reader or listener will react more favorably to your ideas if your material is logically developed.
5. *Be up-to-date.* Being current and well-informed is the mark of a competent person.
6. *Be fluent.* Expressing yourself fluently in writing or speech can best be achieved by allowing ample time for writing and rewriting or for practicing the speech.

Integrity

1. *Be fair minded.* By showing your audience that you can see both sides of an issue, you will avoid giving the impression that you are biased or subjective.
2. *Establish a common bond.* A reader or listener will respond more positively to a communicator who is seen as having similar problems, goals, values, and experiences.
3. *Dress appropriately.* The communicator whose grooming and dress conform to the expectations of the audience is much more likely to achieve a desired response.
4. *Indicate your motives.* If your audience feels that you are motivated to communicate with them unselfishly, your credibility will be enhanced.
5. *Be sincere.* Using a tone appropriate to what you are saying in either writing or speech is a must for establishing integrity. Even if they do not agree with you, readers or listeners will admire your conviction.
6. *Be prompt.* Whether you are turning in a report, delivering a speech, sending a letter, or arriving for an interview, being on time is the mark of a person with integrity.

Goodwill

1. *Show understanding.* Put yourself in the shoes of your readers or listeners, so that you can communicate to them that you are aware and appreciative of their viewpoint.

2. *Be respectful.* Treating your audience with respect is a must in establishing goodwill. Give them credit for being worthy and intelligent.

3. *Be diplomatic.* Whatever the communication situation, use courtesy and tact. If you do, the chances will be much better that you will succeed in your purpose.

4. *Use humor.* When used appropriately, humor is an excellent means of establishing goodwill with an audience. (This is especially true of humor directed at yourself.)

5. *Show enthusiasm.* Showing enthusiasm is an especially effective means of establishing goodwill with an audience, particularly in the speaking situation. Approaching your audience with enthusiastic movement and facial expression will show them that you're happy to be with them.

6. *Establish rapport.* Rapport is a French word for harmony or agreement. Whenever you can, make references to those in your audience. If you are on a first-name basis, by all means make use of this excellent way of showing goodwill.

Credibility

The better a person's image, the more likely we are to believe what he or she says. The term *credibility* refers to the extent to which we believe what someone tells us. A person who has a good image also has high credibility. Conversely, a person with a poor image has low credibility.

Image projection is a complex process. People form judgments about others on the basis of a variety of factors. Furthermore, these judgments can be made by evaluating what a person does and says, and what others say about him or her. Because of this complexity, the image that a person projects may or may not be an accurate representation of what that person actually is.

The society in which we live can often have a decided effect on the image that we develop. A person usually tries to develop an image of which others will approve, and the advertisers try to set the standards. We are told that "blondes have more fun," that a "thinking man" smokes a particular brand of cigarette, and that we should "grab as much out of life as we can," because we only go around once. And we respond. In 1983, the cosmetic industry in this country grossed over three billion dollars. Countless more billions are spent each year by Americans to keep in step with the latest fashion or style. It is "in" to belong to a certain group, and this group often determines a person's outward appearance, speech, code of ethics, and conduct. People try to be what the group wants them to be, and yet, in some cases, what they appear to be is not what they are at all.

Some psychologists feel that this projection of a false image has much to do with our high divorce rate. Two people are often attracted to each other because they believe they see traits that they admire. Then, when they get married, what they saw isn't actually there. The husband, who seemed considerate and charming, was actually selfish and dull. The wife, who appeared self-assured and insightful, was, in fact, withdrawn and insensitive. After the first few months of marriage, when their physical attraction no longer overshadows their daily routine, they find that the one they thought they married does not really exist.

As we have seen, a person often tends to evaluate what someone says in the light of his or her projected image. If the impression is good, credibility is high; if it is bad, credibility is low. The following cases indicate how credibility is related to this received impression.

Sue's Father

Sue's father, the owner of a small factory, is a highly respected member of his community. He goes to church regularly, contributes generously to charity, and belongs to several civic and fraternal organizations. He is considered by many people to be a man of intelligence, integrity, and goodwill, and consequently he enjoys a high degree of credibility with them. Sue, however, has a different image of her father. She has heard her father say that it was "good for business" to be seen at church on Sunday or to give to charity. She has heard her father brag about the "tax loopholes" and "payoffs" that he enjoys, and she strongly suspects him of infidelity on business trips. For this reason, Sue's father possesses little credibility in her eyes, particularly in dealing with issues regarding morality.

John and Harry

John and Harry both attend a small, Midwestern junior college. They share a small two-bedroom apartment and get along very well together although their style of dress and appearance is entirely different. John has shoulder length hair, a full beard, and wears levis, and an old army jacket. Harry, on the other hand, has a styled haircut, is clean shaven, and usually wears neatly pressed slacks and a sports coat. When dealing with fellow students who are little influenced by their manner of dress, their credibility is about equal. However, this changes markedly when speaking to their landlord, a middle-class businessman. Harry enjoys rather high credibility, while John's credibility is quite low. The landlord generally listens to Harry's opinions thoughtfully, while almost always dismissing John's as radical. He allows Harry to put up his "sister" over the weekend but threatens to call the police when John brings his girl home for a midnight snack.

Relationship of Image to Credibility

We have seen that what your audience thinks of you has a definite effect on their reaction to your persuasion. Sue's judgment of her father is based on knowledge that others do not possess. Because the landlord has a preconceived picture in his mind of both John and Harry, he is unable to react to them objectively. Although John had apparently done nothing to warrant it, the landlord responded negatively to him. He formed an image of John on the basis of outward appearance. The image *he perceives* of John is poor; therefore John's credibility is low.

You project an image to others by what you say and do, and by what others say about you. You have seen how important this image can be, how it, in effect, sells the product. Improve your image and you will sell yourself and your ideas more effectively. The first step toward improving your projected image is to improve your self-image. This can be accomplished by getting to know yourself better.

Personality Development

We develop our personalities largely as a result of our relationships with others. We learn to communicate by imitating those around us. Our views on life are shaped by those with whom we come in contact. We often mirror the attitudes and sentiments of our parents and friends. Our speaking habits are usually similar to the habits of those closest to us as we grow up. Problems like mispronunciation and unclear diction can usually be traced to parents or friends with the same difficulties.

The reaction of others to us as we are growing up also has an effect on our personalities. People tell us by their responses whether we are important or unimportant, good or bad, smart or dumb, and we develop a picture of ourselves accordingly. Furthermore, we tend to act like the person we conceive ourselves to be. Thus, a child who developed the self-concept of being unimportant because of his or her parents would probably respond by being withdrawn and unfriendly. The child who was thought of by classmates as being dull and a troublemaker would probably live up to this label.

The first step to personality improvement is careful self-appraisal. Obviously, the more accurate a picture a person has of himself or herself, the more clear it becomes how to improve, how to develop strengths and eliminate weaknesses. If, for example, John is strongly attracted to Jane but sees himself as being inferior to her in terms of personality and attractiveness, he is apt to communicate this attitude to her in uneasy, superficial, and, therefore, nonproductive conversation. On the other hand, if John can see his own strengths and weaknesses in their proper perspective and recognize his own self-worth, he will be more likely to communicate to Jane his interest in her.

The key to John's success with Jane is self-worth. Before anyone else can like you, you first have to like yourself. Communicate this attitude of self-worth to others by the careful preparation and practice of your speeches and the critical proofreading and rewriting of your papers and you will project a more effective image.

EXERCISES

I. Deliver a five–eight minute speech in which you demonstrate a technique or procedure. Pick something you enjoy doing and do well. In your introduction project an image of competency by telling your audience what qualifies you as an "expert" on your subject.

II. Deliver a two–four minute speech or write a short narrative of 200–400 words in which you relate a personal experience that gives your listener or reader a picture of you as a person of integrity. Describe the material in enough detail to create a mental picture for the reader or listener. Your actions in the story should depict you as being fair minded, moral, unselfish, or sincere.

PERSUASION TO ACTUATE

III. Write a 200–400 word appeal or deliver a two–four minute speech to persuade your audience to do something specific as a result of your communication. Make clear to your audience exactly what action you wish them to take. Your purpose is to get a physical response. You are asking your audience to act: to buy, to join, to vote, to help, to donate, to march, to sign, or to participate.

Suggestions

1. *Be realistic.* Make sure you know exactly what action you wish your audience to take, and be certain that it is reasonable. You can't expect an audience to do something which they are incapable of doing; e.g., most students could not afford to sponsor a child for $15 a month. Nor could you expect an audience to do something to which they are opposed, e.g., you could not expect your fellow students to drop out of school.

2. *Insure understanding.* Make clear to your audience exactly *what* they must do. You must point out such things as when they should act, what the exact cost will be, and whom they should contact.

3. *Be sincere.* Before you can get others to act, you must be sold on the suggested course of action. Be sure you believe that what you propose is in the best interest of your audience.

4. *Be accurate.* Make sure that what you are saying is absolutely true. Use only information that you have checked thoroughly.

Sample Main Ideas

1. Join the crusade to cure sickle cell anemia.
2. Install a smoke and fire detector in your home.
3. Work for the candidate of your choice in the forthcoming election.
4. Donate a life-saving pint of blood.

LOGICAL PROOF

We humans are rational creatures who take a great deal of pride in the fact that we have the ability to reason, to analyze, to think things out for ourselves. We are appreciative of intelligence and the ability to solve problems, and being adept at problem solving is important to us. Throughout our lives we use reasoning to decide what to buy, what to wear, what school to attend, or what to contribute in terms of time and money to our church or charity. In order to protect our self-image we must be able to justify our beliefs to others. We must rationalize our behavior to ourselves and defend it to our loved ones and friends. Therefore, an understanding of logical reasoning is imperative.

Argumentation

Reasoning is the process of drawing conclusions from evidence. When the relationship between the evidence and the conclusion is communicated to others in an attempt to influence belief, it is called argumentation.

In its simplest form argumentation consists of two statements, a premise and a conclusion drawn from that premise. The statements below are arguments in which the italicized conclusion is drawn from the premise.

1. John has been sent to the office three times this week for causing disturbances in class. Therefore, *he is a troublemaker.*
2. John is a member of a street gang. Therefore, *he is a troublemaker.*

Both of these arguments involve a premise–conclusion relationship. In the first example the conclusion was drawn from an examination of three individual situations: "John has been in the office three times. Therefore, he is a troublemaker."

When we examine individual cases and draw a conclusion, we are using *inductive reasoning*. The following situations involve the inductive process:

1. A poll predicting the winner in an upcoming election.
2. Tests conducted on a group of people to determine the effectiveness of a new vaccine.
3. The decision to put a traffic light on a street corner after a series of accidents.
4. A student deciding to become a college business major on the basis of previous interest and high school performance.

In each instance, the reasoning proceeds from specific cases to a general conclusion. In the first example, pollsters take a random sampling from a cross section of the voting population. On the basis of the results of this survey they conclude that the voting preference of the cross section will be typical of the vote of the entire group involved. The second example is similar: If the vaccine is effective for 95 per cent of the test group, it will probably be effective for 95 per cent of the total population. The third example—the decision to install the traffic light—also demonstrates movement from specific instances to a general conclusion. In the fourth case, the student considers experiences in his or her background before reaching a conclusion about the future. The movement in all of these cases has been from specific, individual experiences to a general conclusion.

Now let us return to the second of the two arguments concerning John: "John is a member of a street gang. Therefore, he is a troublemaker." It has been concluded that John is a troublemaker, not because he has been seen in individual situations in which he has caused trouble, but because membership in a certain group carries with it that label. You have come to some previous conclusion about members of street gangs being troublemakers. Since John is a member of that group, he, according to your stereotype, is a troublemaker. Reasoning in this manner, from a general rule to an individual (specific) case, is called deductive reasoning.

As you have seen, reasoning can take two forms—inductive and deductive. To test your understanding, indicate whether the following are examples of inductive or deductive reasoning.

1. I wouldn't eat that meat. It's been out of the refrigerator for days.
2. He couldn't be the burglar. He's a policeman.
3. I'll never learn to drive; I backed into the pool again.
4. I'm never playing cards again. I lost a bundle last night.
5. Don't trust him. He's a former CIA agent.
6. I'm never going to another opera. I can't stand the noise.

7. I'm never using that kind of fertilizer again. It burned out all my grass.
8. Don't go around with those Jones boys, son. Their father is an ex-con.

THE PROCESS OF INDUCTION

As a result of an examination of specific cases, the writer or teacher comes to a general conclusion on the basis of his observations. The three principal forms of induction are those of generalization, causal relation, and analogy.

Generalization

We generalize when we examine examples from a class and then draw conclusions about the whole class. We conclude that characteristics true of the cases examined are also true of similar cases not examined. For example, if we have had good service from three Buicks, we might come to the conclusion that a Buick is a good car to own. If we have done poorly in English throughout high school, we might conclude that English courses are not our "cup of tea."

As you can see, generalization is an often-used form of reasoning in our daily lives. Testing the reliability of generalization may be summed up in these questions.

1. Are the instances examined sufficiently large to warrant the generalization? The number of instances examined depends upon the proposition. For example, you might be justified, on the basis of only one or two observations, in concluding that obese men should avoid wearing shorts. Coming to a conclusion in this way is called an *inductive leap*, and in some instances it is warranted. However, if you were investigating the protective qualities of a new vaccine, you might have to examine thousands of people before you could justify a conclusion. If in doubt, a good rule of thumb is the more cases examined, the more reliable the generalization.

2. Are the instances examined typical? The examples in a generalization must be representative of those in the class which are not examined. For example, an adverse conclusion about teenagers based on a few newspaper stories would probably be slanted, since many newspapers generally deal with the sensational rather than the commonplace. All possible care should be taken to insure that the examples used are typical. The best method of doing this is to choose examples at random. A random sample is one selected entirely by chance, as in choosing the first and last name on every page in the phone book.

3. Is the information used true? We do not limit examples used in generalization to those we examine personally, but also include instances we hear or read about. In a court of law, hearsay evidence is usually inadmissible as testimony. It is important that the evidence used be accurate.

4. Are there any negative instances which invalidate the conclusion? A negative instance will not invalidate a generalization if it can be shown to be an exception to the rule. Suppose you conclude that people on welfare are living in extreme deprivation. Someone points out that a man receiving welfare payments was also working full time. If you can show that documented statistics indicate that less than 1 percent of welfare cases involve fraud, you will explain why the above case is an exception to the rule.

Causal Relation

Reasoning from causal relation is based on the principle that every cause has an effect. Causal reasoning may move from effect to cause or cause to effect. In either event, we reason from a known to an unknown. For example, in effect-to-cause reasoning, we see an increase in illegitimacy, and we infer an increase in promiscuity. We read of the high dropout rate for students at a particular university, and we infer that the school has rigid academic standards. We begin with a known effect and attribute it to a probable cause. In cause-to-effect reasoning, we read about a tax increase on beer and infer a rise in beer prices. We observe a new school being built in our district and anticipate an increase in next year's taxes.

Cause-and-effect relationships can be most clearly shown in a carefully controlled scientific experiment in which a control group is used to determine whether there are other causes operating in such a way as to contribute to the alleged effect. For example, suppose that researchers are interested in developing a vaccine for prevention of a new variety of Asian flu. They would use the control group method. Ideally, the control group should be composed of subjects matched in every pertinent way with those in the experimental group, except that the experimental group receives the vaccine while the control group does not. If the two groups are alike in every respect other than the isolated variable (the vaccine), we can conclude with some confidence that any effect in regard to immunity to this strain of flu is due to the vaccine.

When using cause-and-effect, be careful to include the important links in the chain of causation, or else your reasoning may be unclear. Notice how a series of events which develops a logical cause-and-effect relationship can be made unclear because of poor communication.

A student was late for his first hour class because he shut his alarm clock off and fell asleep.

When he finally re-awoke, he glanced in horror at the time, hurriedly dressed, and ran to his car.
In his rush to get to school, he exceeded the speed limit considerably.
He noticed a truck at an approaching crossroad too late to avoid a collision.
When questioned by the police as to why the accident had occurred, he replied, "Because I shut the alarm off and went back to bed."

Had the student explained the series of events as outlined above, his reply would have constituted a logical causal relationship. Instead, his brief reply, omitting essential links in the chain of causation, probably caused the police officer to wonder whether his reasoning had been affected by the accident.

Cause-and-effect relationships are more difficult to establish where strict controls cannot be implemented. This is especially true in the area of social problems, where causes may be so many that causal relation is almost impossible to define.

Analogical Reasoning

Use of analogy is a popular and colorful way of supporting a point. It assumes that if things are alike in known respects, they will also be alike in unknown respects. We conclude that a son who has been trustworthy when he was home will also be trustworthy when he is away at school. We reason that if there is discontent among ghetto area residents of one city, there will be discontent in the ghetto area of another city of similar size, population, job opportunity, and city management. For analogical reasoning to be persuasive, the points of similarity must clearly outweigh the points of difference.

It is important to examine carefully the essential comparative features in the analogy. Remember, the strength of the similarity is more important than the number of similarities found. As was true in regard to cause-and-effect relationships, it is difficult to make valid comparisons between people and between groups of people, because of the complexity of the problem. For example, in the analogy that a student will be unsuccessful in college because she got lower than average grades in high school, suppose that the student spends a number of years working before she enters college, and is thus highly motivated to succeed. This significant difference might outweigh the similarities and render the analogy invalid.

THE PROCESS OF DEDUCTION

Deduction is that form of reasoning which proceeds from a general truth to a particular conclusion. It is typically expressed in a three-step pattern known as the *syllogism*. The three statements are so arranged that the last can be inferred from the first two. They are known as the major premise, minor premise, and conclusion. The three most common types of syllogism are the conditional, the alternative, and categorical.

The conditional syllogism is based on an if-then relationship, such as "If I don't study, I won't pass the test." When stated formally, the conditional syllogism appears as follows:

Major Premise: If I don't study, I won't pass the test.
Minor Premise: I have to pass the test.
Conclusion: Therefore, I must study.

The alternative syllogism limits the number of choices in the argument to two. To come to a conclusion you must make one choice or another. The three statements are arranged this way:

Major Premise: Either she's not studying or she's stupid.
Minor Premise: She's not stupid.
Conclusion: Therefore, she's not studying.

The most often-used syllogism is the categorical syllogism. It gets its name from the fact that the major premise states a general proposition about a category of "things" (animals, people, religions, political parties, and so on). A typical categorical syllogism would be:

Major Premise
(general proposition
about a category)   All cows eat grass.
Minor Premise
(falls within the
category)   Bessy is a cow.
Conclusion
(what is true of the
category is true of
all parts of the category)   Therefore, Bessy eats grass.

How do these ideas relate to the persuader? The idea is to get your audience to agree with your premises. If they accept the premises as true, and if the premises are set up properly, then they must logically accept the conclusion.

Faulty deduction often occurs when people accept generalizations about classes of people as being general truths. Such generalizations are called stereotypes and are generally wrong when used as the major premise in a categorical syllogism. We develop stereotypes of the "conservative," "liberal," "communist," "Catholic," "Protestant," "stockbroker," "college instructor," and so on. The following stereotypes are stated as general rules from which people have reasoned incorrectly:

All politicians are dishonest.
All effeminate males are homosexuals.
All college professors are intellectual.
All members of street gangs are troublemakers.
All teenagers are rebellious.

FALLACIES

Fallacious reasoning can be the result of faulty induction or deduction, or the acceptance of misleading argumentation. Some of these fallacies occur so often that they have been isolated and labeled. The most common of these are treated below.

Unwarranted or Hasty Generalization

A generalization is fallacious when it is based on insufficient or unfair evidence, or when it is not warranted by the facts available. For example, "All hippies are dirty," "All welfare recipients are lazy," and so on.

Errors in Causal Induction

Fallacy in causal induction occurs when there is no logical relationship between a cause and an effect. Two most common cause-and-effect fallacies are *post hoc* (after this, therefore, because of this) and *non sequitur* (it does not follow).

Post Hoc   *Post hoc* is the fallacy of thinking that an event which follows another is necessarily caused by the other. Thus, you might conclude that the Democratic Party promotes war, that television viewing increases juvenile delinquency, and that an easing of censorship causes an increase in immorality.

The error in post hoc reasoning occurs because the reasoner ignores other factors which may have contributed to the effect. A survey of former college debaters revealed, for example, that they were considerably more successful in their chosen field of work than their nondebating counterparts. To assume from this that their experience as debaters was the cause of their success would be fallacious. Other factors must be considered: Students who become debaters usually possess superior verbal ability, have keen analytical minds, and are highly motivated by competition. No doubt these factors, which led them into debate, also contributed to their success.

Non Sequitur   In this fallacy the conclusion reached does not necessarily follow from the facts argued. The argument that because a man is kind to animals he will make a good husband ignores the possibilities that the man may make a bad husband, drink excessively, cheat, or beat his wife.

Begging the Question

An argument begs the question when it assumes something as true when it actually needs to be proven. For instance, the declaration that "these corrupt laws must be changed" asserts the corruption but does not prove it, and consequently the conclusion is not justified.

Begging the question also occurs when we make a charge and then insist that someone else disprove it. For example, to answer the question, "How do you know that the administration is honest?" would put the respondent in the position of trying to disprove a conclusion which was never proven in the first place. Remember, whoever makes an assertion has the burden of proof.

Ignoring the Question

Ignoring the question occurs when the argument shifts from the original subject to a different one, or when the argument appeals to some emotional attitude which has nothing to do with the logic of the case. An example of the first would be a man replying, "Haven't you ever done anything dishonest?" when accused of cheating on his wife. He ignores the question of his infidelity by shifting to a different argument.

An argument that appeals to the emotional attitudes of the reader or listener would be the statement, "No good American would approve of this communistic proposal."

False Analogy

To argue by analogy is to compare two things which are alike in germane known respects and to suggest that they will also be alike in unknown respects. This method is accurate if the things being compared are genuinely similar: "George will do well in graduate school; he had an excellent academic record as an undergraduate." It is likely to be fallacious when they are dissimilar: "There's nothing to handling a snowmobile; it's just like riding a bicycle."

Analogies are more difficult to prove when the comparison is figurative rather than literal. In a political campaign, the incumbent might admonish the voter "not to change horses in the middle of the stream," while the opponent replies that "a new broom sweeps clean."

Cartoon by Sanders © Used with permission of The Milwaukee Journal.

Either/or Fallacy

The either/or fallacy is reasoning that concludes there are only two choices to an argument when there are other possible alternatives. A tragic example would be the reasoning that escalated the Vietnam war. The argument was: either we fight and win in Vietnam or all of Southeast Asia will fall to the communists. Of course, we didn't win and all of Southeast Asia didn't fall to the communists.

Ad Hominem

In this fallacy the argument shifts from the proposition to the character of the opponent. Unfortunately, this abuse often occurs in politics, and the voters who fall for it wind up casting their votes against a candidate rather than for one. "I wouldn't trust him. His best friend is a homosexual," or "You're not going to believe a former convict?" are examples of this fallacy.

Red Herring

The red herring is similar to the *ad hominem* fallacy but does not attack the opponent's character. It gets its name from the superstition that if you drag a red herring across your path it will throw any wild animals following you off the track. Information is introduced which is not relevant to the question at hand in the hope that it will divert attention from the real issue. In politics an opposing candidate is pictured as being overly religious, ultrarich, or divorced. If the trait has nothing to do with the way he or she will perform in office, the argument is a red herring.

Ad Populum

The *ad populum* argument appeals to the theory that whatever the masses believe is true. Make no mistake; popularity is not always an accurate determiner of truth. Consider the landslide victory of Richard Nixon in 1972. A typical *ad populum* fallacy is: "Unconditional amnesty is wrong, because most people are against it."

EXERCISES

I.   Give an example other than those mentioned in this chapter of the following fallacies: (1) hasty generalization, (2) error in causal relationship, (3) begging the question, (4) ignoring the question, (5) false analogy, (6) either/or, (7) *ad hominem*, (8) red herring, (9) *ad populum*.

II.   Select an editorial or short essay which supports or criticizes an organization, program, or policy. Comment on its effectiveness as persuasion. Indicate whether the reasoning used is inductive or deductive.

III.   Deliver a two–three minute speech or write a 200–300 word essay in which you support or refute a stand taken on a controversial campus issue. Develop your communication inductively or deductively.

PERSUASION TO CONVINCE

Deliver a three–five minute speech or write a 300–500 word essay supporting one point of view in regard to a controversial subject. Analyze the audience beforehand to determine their attitude toward your point of view. People take great pride in the fact that they are rational creatures. They have a high regard for intelligence and problem-solving ability. Appeal to your reader or listener's desire to know the truth in order to modify existing attitudes. Rely chiefly on logical materials to obtain mental agreement from your audience.

Suggestions

1. Don't attempt to do too much in this assignment. You will be successful if you change, even if only the slightest degree, the attitudes and opinions of your audience.
2. Present your material objectively. An audience will react negatively to a reader or speaker who is overly biased.
3. Show that there is need for a change.
4. Show that your proposal is practical.
5. End with a statement of support for your proposal.

PSYCHOLOGICAL PROOF

Logical proof appeals to the reason of the audience. Psychological proof, on the other hand, makes its appeal to the audience's attitudes and motives. People do things as a result of two factors, motive and desire. We are predisposed to act in certain ways because of goals, attitudes, sentiments, and motives which we have developed as part of our personality. When the desire to satisfy this "inner drive" becomes strong enough, we act.

ATTITUDES

Through learning and experience we build up reaction tendencies, which cause us to respond in predisposed ways to situations, people, values, and events. These reaction tendencies are called *attitudes*. Our attitudes are developed from our own experiences and from information handed down to us by parents, teachers, and friends. Thus, we form attitudes toward religion, LSD, mothers-in-law, sex, liquor, and so on. These attitudes give direction to our behavior, causing us to react in positive or negative ways. Keep in mind the fact that attitudes direct behavior—motives stimulate it. The following example should help you to see the difference between attitudes and motives:

A young girl is attacked by a man wielding a knife. She is stabbed repeatedly while a number of people watch. When the knife-wielder leaves, one or two run forward to aid the dying girl. The others hang their heads, ashamed that they stood by while this horror occurred. All of the people who watched had attitudes which were in sympathy with the victim. Why didn't they help? Probably because they were held back by motives related to their own safety which were stronger than those motives which would have caused them to act.

MOTIVES

As you have just seen, *motive* is the inner drive or impulse that stimulates behavior. If we look at attitude as the directive force of behavior, we can call motive the driving force. All of us have certain physical and social desires and wants. The inner force which moves us to satisfy these wants is called a motivating force. Motive is defined, therefore, as an impulse or drive which causes a person to act in a certain way. There are two basic types of motives: (1) physical motives—hunger, thirst, self-preservation, shelter, and sex; and (2) social motives—security, approval, popularity, success.

Physical Motives

All of us have essentially the same basic physical wants. We try to eat when hungry, rest when tired, and protect ourselves when threatened. The more money we have, the more we spend to achieve the greatest possible comfort. We put money aside to escape heat in the summer and cold in the winter. We buy heated swimming pools, air-conditioned cars, and remote-controlled appliances to insure the comfort and protection of our most priceless possession, ourselves. We are, to a considerable degree, creatures of the body. Few could imagine how many business deals or sales have been made to clients who have been put into the right mood with a steak dinner and all the trimmings.

Hunger and Thirst   Although one and a half billion people in the world exist on a starvation diet, few Americans know what it is to go hungry. Therefore, advertisers do not attempt to satisfy the hunger or thirst of an audience, but to create desire which will cause them to want to eat or drink. In short, the persuader attempts to stimulate the appetite of his audience in order to sell the product. We read of a product's "delicious goodness," "enticing aroma," "frosty freshness," or "tantalizing taste," and if we are sufficiently motivated, we buy.

A typical ad shows a group of men working in the heat of the summer sun. Near them, on a table in the shade, is a tray with four ice-cold schooners of beer.

The caption reads:

It's hot and sticky and you've been working hard. You need a little lift and you know nothing will cool you off the way the refreshing taste of _____ beer does. So get with it. Grab a taste of gusto and cool off.

Self-Preservation   No drive is stronger in people than the drive for survival. Any account of the unbelievable horror and pain that people have endured in prison camps, in hospitals, or on the battlefield in an effort to stay alive testifies to the strength of this drive. The persuader who appeals to this basic want tries to create a need on the part of the reader or listener. Slogans like "Drive carefully; the life you save may be your own," and "Stop smoking; it's a matter of life and breath," direct themselves to establishing this need.

Sex   No appeal is used more widely in advertising than the appeal to the sex drive. Our society is supersaturated with sex in advertising to sell everything from spark plugs to corporate image. The degree of subtlety employed in advertising based on sex appeal depends upon the specific audience the ad is intended to reach.

A typical TV commercial shows a skinny, bespectacled young lad approaching a football stadium in his new car. He is met by a campus beauty walking arm in arm with a football player, a magnificent physical specimen who appears to be the hero of the game. When the girl sees the car, she pushes the hero aside and hops into the front seat with love in her eyes. Moral: When you buy Mustang, you buy sex appeal.

Shelter   While some in our society live under deplorable conditions of poverty, most of us live in relative comfort. For this reason, advertisers make their appeal to our drive for shelter in terms of the "desire for comfort" which is evident among most Americans. An air-conditioned restaurant on a sweltering July day might be more inviting than a sign promising excellent cuisine. The additional cost of building a fireplace in a new home is offset by the thought of sitting in front of its warm blaze on a chilly evening.

There are, however, times when the persuader must make an appeal on behalf of those who are in such desperate circumstances that the audience, having little experience of hardship themselves, would lack a basis for grasping fully the seriousness of the problem. It is then up to the persuader to make the situation as real as possible for the audience.

Putting one's self in another person's place is called empathy. When we cry or are saddened because of another person's grief, or when we are happy because another person is happy, we are responding empathically to that person. In order to get your reader or listener to respond in a desirable way, you must make your description real enough to produce empathic response.

Social Motives

The physical drives we have talked about thus far are called basic drives and are common to all higher forms of animal life. However, while animals conform only to the law of the jungle, men and women are social beings and must live within the framework of the group. Even in the most primitive society, people have values, mores, and customs to which they must adhere in order to avoid the condemnation of their peers. If they would live in harmony within their society, people must satisfy their physical drives in socially acceptable ways.

Early in life you learned to conform to certain rules if you wanted to maintain the approval of those around you. As you grew older and came in contact with more people you found that this "code of conduct" became more complex. In order to achieve satisfaction and still conform to the rules, you developed a set of secondary, social motives. We list these motives as security, approval, popularity, and success. They seldom operate singly, but frequently combine to effect behavioral response.

Different groups within the society have different codes of expectations. Therefore, in discussing values and customs we will be talking about those common to most Americans. It is our belief that, in order to survive, every free society must have a common set of values to which most of its members ascribe.

Security   Foremost among our social motives are those that provide for our survival. These include desire for money, property, health care, provision for loved ones.

The force of this drive for security is clearly evident in today's world. The effect that it has on us and our loved ones shapes our consideration of the war and the draft. Our appraisal of birth control is made in terms of our own sentiments, our religious attitude, and the health factor. The specter of pollution is a threat to our very existence. We attend college to assure ourselves a better future; we "go steady" to insure a dependable date; we buy insurance to provide for health care or income protection. In this world of violence and uncertainty, no generation of Americans has been as security-minded as this one.

Approval   Some of you are probably attending college now because you want to maintain the approval of your parents, friends, or employer. You might even dress in a style which is not particularly becoming to you because it is the "in" thing to do. Any store that promises the latest styles is selling approval along with its product. The drive for approval is particularly forceful. A person might spend months building a recreation room or weaving a fancy tapestry for the reward of being able to say, "I made this myself." The young hoodlum might risk a prison sentence to impress his fellow gang members with a particular daring crime. Approval is achieved by living up to or exceeding the expectations of others. It can be gained for a desirable personality trait or for some skill or ability. Most people admire such character traits as honesty, dignity, integrity, courage, and morality, and those who demonstrate these traits to others generally win their approval.

Probably the approval that means more to you than any other is approval of yourself. The poem below aptly points out how important self-approval is to you:

When you get what you want in your struggle for self,
    And the world makes you king for a day;

Then go to your mirror and look at yourself;
    And see what that guy has to say.

For it isn't your father or mother or wife,
    Whose judgment upon you must pass;

The fellow whose verdict counts most in your life,
    Is the guy staring back from the glass.

He's the man you must please, never mind all the rest,
    For he's with you clear up to the end;

And you've passed your most difficult, dangerous test,
    If the man in the glass is your friend.

You may be like little Jack Horner and "chisel" a plum,
    And think you're a wonderful guy;

But the man in the glass says you're only a bum,
    If you can't look him straight in the eye.

You can fool the whole world down the pathway of years,
    And can get pats on the back as you pass;

But your final reward will be heartaches and tears;
    If you've cheated the guy in the glass.

                              Author Unknown

Popularity   Close to our desire for approval is the drive for popularity. If approval means to be "liked," popularity means to be "well-liked."
It is strongest among young people, where being in the right group,
learning the latest dance step, having a lot of dates, getting many year-
book signatures, and being well-liked are major goals.

The success of dance studios, charm courses, and books on personality development attests to the large number of older people who also
have this need. This motive is closely linked to the sex motive. The American public is assured popularity if they buy the right deodorant, go to
the right school, drive the right auto, and wear the right undergarments.

Success   The desire for success can be called the great American
dream. The man who starts out on a shoestring and amasses a fortune,
the beauty who becomes a star overnight, and the local rock group that
wins national acclaim with a hit record are all forms of this dream.

For some, the drive for success can be so strong that it overshadows
all others. People have lied, cheated, stolen, and even killed for the sake
of personal ambition. Some have endured years of hard work and deprivation in an attempt to develop an artistic or musical talent. Others have
sought success by keeping up with the Joneses or living in the right neighborhood. Advertisers use the success appeal to sell products ranging from
razor blades to real estate. Ads promising sartorial splendor, palatial ele-
gance, and prestigious luxury appeal to this motive.

One major toothpaste commercial shows a young boy, Tommy, who
repeatedly finishes second best to his friend George. Tommy sits on the
bench while George quarterbacks the team to victory. George's ninth in-
ning homer wins the ballgame after Tommy's error permitted the opposition to tie the game in the eighth. George presses his lips to those of the
campus queen in the back seat of the car while Tommy presses his nose
to the windshield, straining to see out into the storm.

But finally the tables are turned. George, a member of the control
group in an experiment conducted by _____ toothpaste, has a mouth-
ful of cavities. Tommy, our new hero, is a member of the experimental
group that has conquered tooth decay. Moral: Buy the right toothpaste
and be a success.

It should be pointed out that because they are abstract, the four social motives discussed above can mean different things to different people. To some, success might mean achieving wealth, power, or prestige.
To others, success could be gaining membership in an "in" group, expe-
riencing self-actualization, or doing something to be proud of, like raising
a well-adjusted family.

Perhaps you see achieving wealth as a matter of security, attaining
prestige as a reason for approval, and gaining membership in the group
as an indication of popularity. In any event, be assured that whatever you

see security, approval, popularity, and success as being, they motivate people's lives.

EXERCISES

I Below is a list of social motives common to the field of psychology. These are variously titled human wants, human motivations, or motive appeals. Indicate which of these could be considered security, approval, popularity, or success motives. Be prepared to defend your choice.

Social acceptance	Good health
Creativity	Getting along well
Long life	Status
Status	Group belonging
Companionship	Fame
Prestige	Membership
Education	Acquisition of property
Power	Self-esteem
Pleasure	Altruism
Knowledge	Being accepted
Self-actualization	Imitation
Possession	Invention
Welfare for others	

II Arrange the following words in some reasonable order and defend that order orally or in writing as your instructor directs.

Fame	Ability
Integrity	Honesty
Charity	Affluence
Courage	Wisdom
Intelligence	

III Write an appeal similar to the one on page 72.

PERSUASION TO REINFORCE

IV Deliver a three–four minute speech or write a 300–500 word essay to reinforce. Persuasion to reinforce seeks to increase an audience's concern with a problem or course of action. The persuader should rely chiefly on psychological proof. He or she will appeal to the audience's emotions, motives, attitudes, and sentiments. The persuader must determine which appeals can be used to gain the desired response from the audience, so careful audience analysis is a necessity.

Delivery: This speech should be delivered extemporaneously. The speech to reinforce attempts to arouse the enthusiasm of the audience. The listener must feel that the speaker is sincere. Spontaneity and directness are fundamental qualities of such a speech.

Sample Topics

1. Seatbelts save lives.
2. Be honest with yourself.
3. Be proud of your school.
4. We *are* our brother's keeper.

CHAPTER **6**

Supporting
Your
Ideas

OBJECTIVES

After studying this chapter you should be able to:
1. Explain how supporting detail helps make ideas clearer or more persuasive.
2. After selecting a specific topic for a communication, choose appropriate and interesting examples to support your main idea.
3. Determine how much detail to include in an example for a given audience.
4. Explain how statistics can be made more interesting and meaningful.
5. Define testimony as a type of supporting material and explain how to use testimony effectively in a communication.
6. Explain the differences between figurative and literal comparison and contrast.
7. Give an example of each of the following forms of explanation and explain how these forms can be used effectively:
   a. Definition
   b. Analysis
   c. Description
8. Locate relevant sources from the card catalogue, the *Reader's Guide*, the *Guides to Books in Print*, the *Biographical Dictionary*, or the *New York Times Index*.
9. Prepare an accurate bibliography card.
10. Prepare an accurate note card.
11. Write footnotes correctly for a research assignment.
12. Arrange a bibliography for a research assignment.

The main idea statement, supporting points, and supporting materials form the content of your composition or speech. Supporting materials (examples, statistics, testimony, comparison/contrast, explanation) serve to clarify or reinforce your supporting points. In turn, these supporting points develop the main idea.

In most cases, you must use supporting detail to make your ideas clear or persuasive to others. For example, in a communication to inform intended to give your audience an understanding of George Washington's performance as a general, you might choose from a variety of supporting techniques. You might relate a few of his experiences on the battlefield (examples). You might describe the hardships he and his men faced or analyze his battlefield strategy (explanation). You might quote significant military experts or historians who have commented on his competency as a general (testimony). You might liken him to other generals (comparison). Finally, you might cite the number of his successes and failures on the battlefield and the odds he faced (statistics).

These same five techniques can also be used in communication to persuade. In persuasion they usually appear as evidence, supporting a positive statement or assertion.

Suppose, for example, that a student wants to convince her reader that the solution she proposes for the case problem below is correct. She might use any of the five supporting devices to support her assertion:

Question: Don and Alice are required by law to take a blood test before marriage. During the examination it is discovered that Don has had a venereal disease. When questioned about it he does not answer. What should Alice do?

Answer: Alice should tell Don to get lost.

Explanation: If Don does not answer when Alice asks him to explain, Alice will have nothing but trouble ahead of her if she marries him. Had he said, "I don't want to talk about it, it's too embarrassing," or something similar it would be a different story. Not to respond at all is unacceptable.

Example: Even if Don had said, "I don't want to talk about it," allowing this to go unchallenged could lead to future problems. Suppose that six months after they are married Don goes out bowling on a Friday night and comes home the following Sunday. When Alice asks him where he was, all he'd have to say was, "I don't want to talk about it."

Comparison: Don's refusal to answer Alice is like Alice disappearing for a full week while the two of them are engaged and not replying when Don asks her about it.

Testimony: According to Dr. J. Ross Eshleman, Chairman of the Department of Social Psychology at Wayne State University, "Although there are a multitude of reasons given for divorce, such as adultery, drunkenness, sexual problems and the like, in most cases these are behaviors caused by an inability of the marriage partners to communicate with each other."

Statistics: The U. S. Department of Health, Education, and Welfare's figure for divorces in 1982 was 2,430,000. This was the highest total ever recorded in the United States. If this trend continues at the present rate, 55% of all marriages will end in divorce by the 1990s.

As you have seen, supporting material may be divided into five classes:

1. Examples
2. Statistics
3. Testimony
4. Comparison/Contrast
5. Explanation

EXAMPLES

An example can be thought of as a "specific instance," a sample chosen to show the nature or character of the rest. Examples can be either abbreviated or detailed. One might cite the skateboard as an example of a fad; *Jesus Christ, Superstar* as an example of rock opera; the late Vince Lombardi as an example of the power of positive thinking; or the high unemployment rate as an example of the government's inability to cope with domestic problems.

When preparing for a particular speech or essay, look for appropriate and interesting examples that fit the subject, arouse curiosity or concern, avoid wordiness, and make a point.

The amount of detail included in the example is often dependent upon your audience. If the example you choose is familiar to your readers or listeners, you need only cite it briefly. If it is unfamiliar to your audience, you must develop it in enough detail so that its point is made clear to them.

Sometimes a speaker or writer will keep his examples brief so that he can present them in groups. Note how the frequency of the examples in the article below seems to strengthen the writer's point that many hospital emergency rooms are "overcrowded, incompetently staffed, and inadequately equipped."

Americans Take Big Chance in Hospital Emergency Rooms

The oft-repeated myth by the American Medical Association that while costs are the highest, Americans receive the best health care in the world, took another solid blow to the chin last week as a result of a most revealing article in the Wall St. Journal entitled "Grim Diagnosis." After citing incredible cases of medical bungling, the article says: "This kind of horror story is being told with increasing frequency these days. As the shortage of doctors becomes acute, more and more Americans are turning to hospital emergency rooms for injuries or illnesses of all types. And often, authorities say, the emergency rooms they turn to are overcrowded, incompetently staffed, and inadequately equipped.

STUDIES ARE QUOTED

"Two studies in Baltimore bear out that contention. Research published last year by two specialists at the Johns Hopkins University School of Hygiene and Public Health found that less than one-third of a group of patients showing up at a big-city hospital emergency room with nonemergency complaints were treated adequately.

"Shortly after that, another medical team at the school reported that more than half of a group of auto accident victims who died from abdominal injuries 'should have had a reasonable chance for survival' had not hospital errors in diagnosis and treatment occurred."

Here are some typical examples cited in the article:

George McGraw considered himself a lucky man.

PATIENT SENT HOME

To all appearances, he had emerged from a serious automobile accident near Baltimore recently with only a scraped elbow and a cut on one ear. Or at least, that's what he was told by the hospital emergency room physician who examined him and sent him home.

But for some reason the physician didn't have any X-rays made, and George McGraw walked out of the hospital door with a fractured neck and skull.

On the ride home from the hospital, bone fragments sliced into Mr. McGraw's brain and spinal cord. Today, the 58-year-old construction worker from New Freedom, Pa., is paralyzed for life.

EXAMPLE IS GIVEN

In New York, a 35-year-old unemployed man went to a hospital emergency room and complained of stomach pains. He was given a painkiller and sent home. He died 24 hours later, in another hospital, from massive hemorrhaging of stomach ulcers.

A Dallas nurse is still haunted by memories of an episode in a local hospital one night. An accident victim brought to the hospital was admitted as dead on arrival, on the word of the ambulance attendants. The emergency room was so crowded that night, according to the nurse on duty, that no one bothered to examine the man.

Several hours later, the supposed corpse coughed. The victim survived, but with serious brain damage apparently caused by the delay in treatment.

In a shocking number of cases, blatant incompetence by medical people is indicated. In Tennessee a few years ago, for instance, a teenage boy died of a ruptured liver after interns in a crowded emergency room diagnosed him as drunk and sent him away.

Nurses in Mississippi ignored a man who was bleeding to death. Near Chicago, a college football player broke his leg during a game. The general practitioner on duty at the hospital emergency room put the cast on so tightly that the boy's leg later had to be amputated above the knee.

Hence, it's not surprising that recent studies suggest a significant portion of the 700,000 medical and surgical emergencies that occur in the United States every year are mishandled in some way that often result in preventable death or permanent injury.

AMPUTATION FOLLOWS

In the emergency room of one Chicago private hospital, a 12-year-old boy with an open fracture of the right arm had to wait so long for treatment that gas gangrene developed in the wound and his arm had to be amputated.

The Milwaukee Labor Press, Oct. 21, 1971. Reprinted by permission.

At other times it may be more effective to communicate one example in detail. Detailed examples usually take the form of stories, which are easy to organize, since they are developed in chronological order. These stories may take the form of personal experiences, allegories, anecdotes, parables, or fables. They are excellent devices for clarifying and reinforcing ideas, and can often give the reader or listener a clear mental picture of the characters, setting, and action. For this reason, they are sometimes called word pictures, or *illustrations*. These detailed examples may be real or hypothetical, humorous or serious. They should be completely relevant to the point or moral principle being illustrated. One good example of a story that illustrates a moral principle is the Parable of the Good Samaritan, found in the tenth chapter of Luke in the Holy Bible. In response to the question, "Who is my neighbor?" Jesus replies:

A certain man was going down from Jerusalem to Jericho when robbers attacked him, stripped him and beat him up, leaving him half dead. It so happened that a priest was going down the road; when he saw the man he walked on by, on the other side. In the same way a Levite also came there, went over and looked at the man, and then walked on by, but a certain Samaritan who was traveling that way came upon him, and when he saw the man his heart was filled with pity. He went over to him, poured oil and wine on his wounds and bandaged them; then he put the man on his own animal and took him to an inn where he took care of him. The next day he took out two silver coins and gave them to the inn keeper. "Take care of him," he told the inn keeper, "and when I come back this way I will pay you back whatever you spend on him." And Jesus concluded, which one of these three seems to you to have been a neighbor to the man attacked by the robbers?

From *Today's English Version of the New Testament.* Copyright © American Bible Society, 1966, 1971.

STATISTICS

When used properly, statistics provide an excellent means of clarification or support. However, when handled clumsily, they confuse and discourage understanding. Few readers or listeners would struggle to pay attention to an uninteresting and complicated set of statistics. Therefore, if you want to be effective, make them interesting and meaningful. Here are some suggestions you should consider in using statistics.

You may use charts, tables, graphs, or pictures to help your audience grasp what is being presented. A student used the bar graph shown below in a research paper to show more clearly the small percentage of women in the medical profession of this country.

If you wanted to make use of this graph in a speech, you would either have to enlarge it so it could be seen easily or make enough copies for each listener. Using a chart too small to be seen by everyone in your audience would be ineffective, and passing one around through the audience would be distracting.

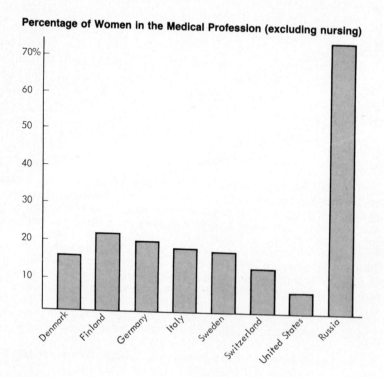

Percentage of Women in the Medical Profession (excluding nursing)

Dramatize Your Statistics

Whenever possible, your statistics should be stated in terms which relate to the interest and experience of your listener or reader. If you can form a mental picture for your audience by presenting your statistics in some dramatic form, they are more likely to be understood and remembered.

In this letter to the editor the writer relates the statistics she uses to the experience and interests of her readers.

To the Editor:

The cartoon in the November 2–22 issue depicting welfare recipients as lazy people who don't work but choose to sit home all day, drink beer, and watch TV is offensive, misleading, and in poor taste.

It is especially insensitive to the many single mothers attending MATC with the long-term goal of getting off of welfare.

According to the Department of Health, Education, and Welfare, 64% of the people on welfare are incapable of working, mostly because of age. Thirty-four percent of people on welfare are under 14 years of age, 18% are 65 years or older, 5% are disabled, and 7% are in school, aged 14 or older.

Of the remaining 36%, 24% work and 12% do not. Of this 12% who do not work, 11% are females, the vast majority of whom are at home and caring for young children (which, by the way, is work—but that is another issue).

Thus, only 1.4% of all those on welfare are abled-bodied unemployed males, many of them lacking skills and many of them living in areas of high unemployment.

Your cartoon grossly misrepresents the welfare system and does an injustice to people who receive aid. Could you summon at least a smidgen of the same outrage at truly a more horrendous fraud? Each year, every Milwaukee voter gives an average of over $3,000 in taxes to finance the military.

Between 1981 and 1985, the average family will give $22,000 in taxes to finance the military. The 1983 federal budget calls for more than $300 billion to fund military and military-related programs, more than three times what it calls for spending on all human service programs.

I would like to see articles in future issues of the MATC

Times showing what it is really like for a single mother at MATC struggling to keep her family together, going to school, working, and coping with an inhumane welfare system. The myth that being on welfare is a picnic is exactly that—a myth.

AMY WEISBROT

With permission of the *MATC Times*. From the December 9, 1982 edition of the *Times*.

Round Off Your Statistics

Whether you are writing or speaking, when dealing with large numbers it is a good idea to round them off. Instead of saying that the 1970 census lists the population of New York City as 7,792,892, round it off to an approximately 7.8 million. The shorter figure is easier for the reader or listener to understand and remember. In the excerpt below the student-speaker rounds off the statistics he uses to support his proposition that federal aid to education has not suffered during the first two years of the Reagan administration.

When Ronald Reagan became president in 1980, it was generally assumed that he would drastically reduce federal aid to education. This, however, has not been the case. Although he wanted to limit the growth of Guaranteed Student Loans, the GL budget has practically doubled from $1.6 billion in 1980 to $3.1 billion in 1983. He has tried but been unable to eliminate the National Direct Student Loan program, the State Student Incentive Grants, or the Supplemental Educational Opportunity Grants. In fact the overall federal higher education budget has risen from $11.7 billion in 1980 to $11.9 billion in 1983.

Document Your Statistics

Avoid using such vague phrases as "recent studies indicate" or "the last surveys show." Instead, indicate clearly when and by whom the statistics you are quoting were compiled. Chances are that some in your audience have been deceived in the past by statistics. Set their minds at ease by indicating exactly where the statistics came from.

This does not mean that you must document every statistic that you use. To do so would be both uninteresting and overly complicated. When the statistics you present are consistent with the general knowledge and experience of your audience, there is probably no need to indicate their exact source. Although none of the statistics in the student speech above are documented, few would question them, as they are widely known.

TESTIMONY

It is often wise for a speaker or writer to support his or her own ideas with the testimony of others. We live in a complex and technical age; ours is increasingly a society of specialists. The statement of an expert on a particular subject carries the weight of education and experience. Most of us would not quarrel with a doctor who recommended an emergency appendectomy or with a TV repairman who told us that our set needed a new vertical output transformer. Unless we doubted their competency or honesty, we would have little reason to question their judgment. If you want your audience to give credence to the authorities you cite, choose people they will consider well-qualified and objective. If the experts are unknown to your audience, give facts about them to establish their qualifications. William A. Nail, Public Relations Director of the Zenith Radio Corporation, uses this method of introducing Dr. Charles Keller.

Dr. Charles Keller, retired director of the John Hay Fellows program and retired professor of history at Williams College, goes around the country talking with teachers and young people in high schools. He has devoted the last years of his career in education to listening and sharing experiences with others—try to demonstrate what you learn, when you listen to others.

Dr. Keller listens continually to young people and their ideas. In a talk that he made to a meeting of librarians last year, he used a poem by a high school student that he had met in Portland, Oregon. I would like to share with you a part of this poem, which illustrates in a way the answer to the question—"What did you say?"

I found beer cans floating under dead fish,
and a forest converted to a chemical factory—
an image on the boob-tube
informed me of "100 percent chance precipitation"
and spoiled the surprise.
I looked for the moon and found Apollo 8, Telstar,
Halley's Comet and a Boeing 707.
Beauty is neither electronic nor man-made.
Stars are more silver than aluminum, and
wax fruit are blasphemous. Beauty is
that which is natural, original, and unexpected.
I am waiting for the day when computers
program themselves,
and leave us to ourselves, and
I am watching for the day that
the last blade of grass is removed
to make room for a missile factory.
I am waiting for a machine that can
fall in love, and
I am watching for an IBM card for God.

Vital Speeches, XXXVII:23 (September 15, 1971), 726.

The poem above is also a form of testimony. If someone else has said something in poetry or prose that you feel is particularly well related to your subject, quote him. Besides clarifying or reinforcing what you have said, this technique will add interest and variety to your writing or speaking.

Testimony is usually less effective as a support when you are dealing with a controversial subject. Experts tend to disagree on controversial issues. While one economist may believe in rigid price controls, another believes in none at all; one group of scientists advocates the use of unmanned rockets to explore space, another group defends our present use of manned rockets. Thus, experts who disagree may, in effect, cancel each other out.

When using the testimony of another, you can either quote that person verbatim or paraphrase what he or she has said. However, in most cases the testimony will be made stronger by direct quotation. When you quote an authority directly, your readers or listeners can decide the authority's meaning for themselves. They don't have to depend on the accuracy of your interpretation.

In this excerpt from an article in a student newspaper, the writer quotes an authority to give her readers a first hand explanation of some of the little known characteristics of wolves.

This is a story about eastern timber wolves, a man named Jim Rieder, and a society that wants to take the word "bad" out of the old phrase "big bad wolf."

Eastern timber wolves are being raised in captivity in Greendale (not far from the South Campus) by Rieder and the Timber Wolf Preservation Society. There are 18 wolves at the society, ranging in age from 18 months to 14 years.

These wolves are not tame or trained according to Rieder. "You don't train wolves. You condition them," he said. "Wolves will tolerate affection, but you don't ever want to forget they are wild animals."

When working with the wolves, you never want to make any sudden moves, Rieder explained. A mutual respect must be formed by entering into a relationship slowly. "They tolerate me as long as I'm cool," said Rieder.

In captivity, the adult males will weigh about 150 pounds and the adult females grow to a weight of about 100. Their counterparts—wolves in the wild—have a much shorter life span, and the males will weigh only 100 pounds with the females weighing 100 pounds full grown.

Wolves are monogamous, choosing a mate for life, said Rieder. The female maintains the monogamous relationship, and if her mate is killed, the female will take another mate only after two or three years have passed. If the female is older, she may never take another mate.

While male wolves participate in the monogamous relationship, they will mate after a short period of mourning the lost mate. Older males, however, will pine away and die shortly after the death of a lifetime mate, said Rieder.

Wolves in the wild travel, hunt, and survive in packs and, according to Rieder, the packs are all descendants.

"Female wolves reach maturity at two years, while the males are not mature until the age of three. Wolves mate within the pack, but do not mate with brothers or sisters from the same litter." said Rieder.

Wolves in the wild are the kind of predators that have no enemies except man, said Rieder. "In the wild, wolves feed off small mammals and rodents 60% of the time, and when hunting in a pack, they will eat moose or caribou, about 40% of the time," explained Rieder.

By Alice Jensen, with permission of the *MATC Times*. From the February 1, 1983 edition of the *Times*.

COMPARISON AND CONTRAST

You might describe your history teacher as an intellectual Phyllis Diller, your new boy friend as a chubby Richard Harris, or your parents as the Mr. and Mrs. Archie Bunker of Roseville, Ohio. Comparison/contrast can be used in an exacting manner, e.g., a statistical comparison of the infant mortality rate in civilized countries, or rather casually, e.g., your description of last night's date as "the battle of Bunker Hill revisited."

You were probably first introduced to comparison/contrast as a child. One of the best ways to teach the new or unknown to someone is to compare it to what is known. In answer to his child's question, "What does a zebra look like?" the parent replies, "Like a horse in striped pajamas." A teacher introducing her class to the concept of food as energy might compare food with the gasoline put in a car to keep it running.

Comparison

You would probably compare Shelley and Keats (romantic poets of the same period) and contrast farm life with city life. Comparisons may be *literal* or *figurative*. A literal comparison describes similarities between things in the same category. Comparisons between infant mortality in America and infant mortality in Sweden, between unemployment rates in 1985 and 1987, between Republican and Democratic candidates are literal comparisons. When we describe the similarities between things in different categories, we call this figurative comparison.

Examples of figurative comparison would be the comparison of communism to an ant colony, an occupied country to a canary in a cage, or a union-management bargaining session to a game of chess. Like all supporting devices, comparison can be used in communication to inform, entertain, or persuade. In his textbook *How a Writer Works*, Roger Garrison uses the technique of comparison to give the reader a clearer understanding of the writing process.

In northern New England, where I live, stone walls mark boundaries, border meadows, and march through the woods that grew up around them long ago. Flank-high, the walls are made of granite rocks stripped from fields when pastures were cleared and are used to fence in cattle. These are dry walls, made without mortar, and the stones in them, all shapes and sizes, are fitted to one another with such care that a wall, built a hundred years ago, still runs as straight and solid as it did when people cleared the land.

Writing is much like wall-building. The writer fits together separate chunks of meaning to make an understandable statement. Like the old Yankee wall-builders, anyone who wants to write well must learn some basic skills, one at a time, to build soundly.

Roger Garrison, *How a Writer Works* (New York: Harper and Row, Publishers, 1981) p. 4.

Comparison is often used as a technique in persuasion. How many times have you heard or used arguments similar to these? "John's parents are letting him go and he's even younger than I am." "Oh, come on and try it. Everyone else is doing it. Why miss out on all the fun?"

It is also frequently used in combination with other supporting devices. The excerpt below from a student essay combines comparison, contrast, statistics, and explanation in an attempt to persuade the reader that in an inflation the rich get richer and the poor get poorer.

One of the more painful aspects of inflation is the fact that in an inflationary economy the rich get richer and the poor get poorer. Nowhere is this more apparent than in the area of housing.

Figures released on April 10, 1977, by the Census Bureau and the Department of Housing and Urban Development showed that the median price of a single family home rose from $17,100 in 1970 to $47,500 in 1977, an increase of nearly 180 percent. During this same period, the median income for homeowners rose only 53 percent from $9,700 to $14,800. This placed the value of a single family home at about three times the income of its owner. When you add to this the cost of financing, it makes it virtually impossible for the average wage earner to purchase a first home.

The fact that inflation actually benefits the rich becomes apparent when one studies the report further. The report states that the housing/income ratio varies considerably accordingly to income level. While owners with incomes of $6,000 or less lived in housing valued at an average of four or five times that amount, the value of homes of those earning $25,000 or more was an average of less than two times income.

Furthermore, while renters paid about 25 percent of their annual income for rent in 1977 according to the study, the lower-income renter paid an average of 38 percent for rent, and the higher-income renter gave less than 10 percent of his earnings to landlords.

With permission of the writer, Joyce Jackson.

Contrast

While comparison points out similarities, contrast emphasizes differences. For example, there is an extreme difference between life in free and in totalitarian countries, between opera and rock, or between male and female (vive la différence!). The writer of the following editorial emphasizes the seriousness of our skyrocketing medical costs by contrasting a hospital visit in England with one in the United States:

What a Difference

A New York writer was in England last summer with his family. His four-year-old son became seriously ill, spent three nights in a private room in a hospital, had numerous tests and intravenous feeding. The boy's parents were given a room near him in the hospital.

Total cost was $7.80, for the parents' meals.

Foreigners in England are eligible, in emergencies, to receive the same treatment Britons get under their national health service.

On the other side of the coin—and the Atlantic—an Englishman visiting here last year was stricken and was rushed to a New York hospital. The hospital refused to admit him until it received a financial guarantee (he naturally had no private American health insurance coverage).

He died 16 days later. His wife received a bill for $12,000.

One point is not so much that a citizen of another country was treated shoddily here, bad as that is, but that many Americans would be in the same boat he was. The other point is that there are such things as health systems under which you can afford to get sick.

The Milwaukee Labor Press, November 18, 1971. With permission.

Contrast can be an effective attention-getter. Our language provides thousands of words which invoke striking contrasts. Life and death, love and hate, pleasure and pain, rich and poor, strong and weak, and fast and slow are just a few of the combinations that you have seen or heard. Charles Dickens uses the technique of sharp contrast in the opening paragraph of his novel, *A Tale of Two Cities:*

It was the best of times, it was the worst of times, it was the age of wisdom, it was the age of foolishness, it was the epoch of belief, it was the epoch of incredulity, it was the season of Light, it was the season of Darkness, it was the spring of hope, it was the winter of despair, we had everything before us, we had nothing before us, we were all going direct to Heaven, we were all going direct the other way— in short, the period was so far like the present period, that some of its noisiest authorities insisted on its being received, for good or for evil, in the superlative degree of comparison only.

EXPLANATION

As a student you are probably involved more with explanation than any other supporting device. The textbooks that you read are, for the most part, written for the purpose of making ideas clear. Your teachers are primarily explainers. The answers that you give in class or in essay examinations are explanations.

Definition

Explanation can take several different forms. It can include definition, analysis, or description. One of the necessities in communicating is to be understood. If you plan to use a term that may be unfamiliar to your audience, either define it yourself or choose an appropriate definition by someone else. Do not fall into the habit of always using dictionary definitions; they are sometimes inappropriate for your specific context. If you can, keep your definition brief, clear, and geared to your audience's level of knowledge and experience.

For example, the definition of a "spinner" as "a cap that fits over the hub of an airplane propeller" would be more communicative and interesting to most people than the more technical definition of a spinner as "a fairing of paraboloidal shape which is fitted coaxially to the propeller and revolves with the propeller."

Malcolm X uses definition to clarify the word "revolution." Notice that in his definition he contrasts what revolution is with what it is not:

> This is a real revolution. Revolution is always based on land. Revolution is never based on begging somebody for an integrated cup of coffee. Revolutions are never based upon love-your-enemy and pray-for-those-who-spitefully-use-you. And revolutions are never waged singing "We Shall Overcome." Revolutions are based upon bloodshed. Revolutions are never compromising. Revolutions are never based upon any kind of tokenism whatsoever. Revolutions overturn systems. And there is no system on this earth which has proven itself more corrupt, more criminal, than this system that in 1964 still colonizes 22 million African-Americans, still enslaves 22 million Afro-Americans.

Quoted in George Breitman (ed.), *Malcolm X Speaks,* p. 50; copyright © 1965 by Merit Publishers and Betty Shabazz. Reprinted by permission of Pathfinder Press.

Analysis

Analysis is the technique of breaking an idea down into its parts and explaining each part separately. It is essentially a process of answering such questions as: Who? What? Why? When? Where? How?

You use analysis when you demonstrate how to do something. While organizing a speech on "Swimming More Effectively," you might divide your speech into three parts: (1) the crawl stroke; (2) the body position; and (3) the flutter kick. An essay on how to plant a tree would probably be organized according to the steps involved: (1) digging the hole; (2) preparing the soil; (3) placing the tree correctly; (4) covering the roots and watering them down.

Evaluation is a form of analysis. The following student newspaper review uses the technique of analysis to comment on the musical group, the Jazz Machine.

One of the posters promoting a "Tribute to Ben Baldewicz" last month included the term, "The Jazz Machine."

What is the Jazz Machine?

Many thoughts ran through my mind. A large computerized music-making device, maybe? Perhaps some music students formed a group in honor of their former instructor?

The curiosity overwhelmed me, so toward the C Building Auditorium I went. There I found the Jazz Machine.

A light, easy jazz sound greeted me as I approached. Poking my head in, I spotted four men jamming away.

The Jazz Machine, I learned, is four of Milwaukee's premier studio musicians: Jack Grassel, guitar; Andy LoDuca, percussion; Rich Crabtree, piano, and Tom Pieper, bass.

Magical is an excellent way of describing the music this combo produced.

A small but obviously appreciative crowd was treated to about 40 minutes of jazz tunes from artists like Chick Corea and John Coltrane. Some lesser-known jazz composers had their songs played by the foursome, and there was even some original work from Grassel.

It wasn't long after I arrived that the concert seemed to take on the feel of a jam session—each musician playing off the others' lead. The musicians appeared to be enjoying the show as much as the crowd.

Grassel explained why the musicians were laughing at times during the show—he said they were playing the music at a faster tempo than normal and had fun trying to keep up.

As the crowd got more and more into the jam session their responses grew louder and louder. There was a genuine disappointment noticed when the Jazz Machine announced its last number.

For those in the crowd who love jazz, the show was a golden opportunity to see and hear highly polished pros jamming and having some relaxed fun. For those who were new to jazz, the show was an excellent introduction and a chance for a light and easy break in the day.

For those of you who missed the concert, don't slit your wrists—the Jazz Machine will be back. Watch for announcements.

By David Abresch, with permission of the *MATC Times*. From the December 9, 1982 edition of the *Times*.

Description

A third form of explanation, description, has been treated in Chapter 4. It makes use of the sensory appeals to give the reader or listener a clear picture of what is being communicated. The job of the writer or speaker who uses description as a form of support is to decide what to include and what to omit. Too much detail may bore your audience; too little may not communicate the picture you want conveyed.

For this reason, description is often included along with other supporting detail to make a writer's ideas clear or more persuasive to others.

EXERCISES

I. Choose one of the following statements and support it with a short example of each of the supporting devices:

"Wear a seat belt. The life you save may be your own."
"The U.S. should have a standard drinking age of 18."
"Give yourself a break and quit smoking."

MODEL

The U.S. should adopt a system of national health insurance.

Comparison. National Health Insurance does the job in Denmark; it will also work in the United States.

Example. Fred Feldman's wife entered the hospital in January and died six months later. The next day Fred was given a bill for $27,000.

Statistics. According to a 1970 survey by the U.S. Department of Health and Welfare, the average American pays over $1,000 per year in medical bills.

Testimony. The U.S. Surgeon General warns that unless something is done to halt the spiraling cost of health care, only the rich will be able to afford it.

Explanation. If we had compulsory national health insurance, we could control doctors' fees and standardize practices for more efficient service.

II. Find an ad that combines explanation and statistics to sell its product. Analyze this use of supporting material. Are the statistics documented? Who compiled them? Are they accurate?

III. Indicate an authority that most of your classmates would respect as an expert in each of the following fields: education, pollution control, space exploration, crime prevention, medicine, professional football, and politics.

IV. Find an example of effectively used statistics in a current newspaper. Indicate why you think the statistics are effective.

GATHERING SUPPORTING MATERIAL

No doubt, for much of your writing and speaking you will gather supporting material from your own personal experience. However, there will be times when you will be asked to rely on other sources to insure the accuracy or objectivity of your papers and speeches. Research, the systematic gathering and documenting of this material, takes place mainly in the library. The pages which follow will deal with using the library, taking notes, and writing footnote and bibliography entries.

The Library

Your college or community library is the best place to go to gather supporting material for a speech or writing assignment. Because of the vast amount of information available today, libraries are becoming increasingly complex. Not only are more books available than ever before, but there is an increase of information being stored on microfilm, records, and video cassettes. Therefore, the more you know about how your library works, the more efficient you will become in gathering supporting material.

The Card Catalog   The card catalog consists of cases of drawers containing three-by-five inch cards. These cards list all of the books in the library alphabetically under three headings: title, author, or subject. Therefore, *What Did You Say? Third Edition* by Koch and Felber, can be located in at least three separate card trays. It can be found in the W's after *What*, the first significant word in the title; in the K's under Koch, the first listed author; and under English and/or Communication Skills.

The card catalog also lists the date the book was published, the publisher and place of publication, the edition of the book, and the call number of the book.

While works of fiction are usually filed alphabetically by the author's name, nonfiction books in the library are arranged on the shelves according to call numbers. Libraries organize these books in either of two different ways—the Dewey Decimal System or the Library of Congress System.

Dewey Decimal System   The Dewey Decimal System, as the name suggests, is divided into ten general categories:

000–099	General Works	500–599	Pure Science
100–199	Philosophy	600–699	Technology
200–299	Religion	700–799	The Arts
300–399	Social Sciences	800–899	Literature
400–499	Language	900–999	History

Each of these general categories is further subdivided by tens:

600–609	Technology	650–659	Business
610–619	Medical Sciences	660–669	Chemical Technology
620–629	Engineering	670–679	Manufacturing
630–639	Agriculture	680–689	Other Manufactures
640–649	Home Economics	690–699	Building Construction

Library of Congress System   Library of Congress Classification numbers are arranged alphanumerically. The major categories are:

A.	General works	M.	Music
B.	Philosophy, Religion	N.	Fine Arts
C.	History (General)	P.	Language and Literature
D.	History (Old World)	Q.	Science
E.	History (American & U.S. General)	R.	Medicine
F.	History (U.S. Local & American)	S.	Agriculture
G.	Geography, Anthropology	T.	Technology
H.	Social Sciences	U.	Military Science
J.	Political Science	V.	Naval Science
K.	Law	Z.	Bibliography, Library
L.	Education		Science

Subject Guide to Books in Print   A second tool to use to locate books
is the *Subject Guide to Books in Print,* which lists by subject all the books
currently published in the United States, except fiction, poetry, drama,
and bibles. The advantage to using this guide is that it lists *every* book
presently in print in a particular subject area. If the library you use does
not have a particular book in its collection, you can ask them to borrow
the book from another library.

Periodical Indexes   Probably the best place to find short, current articles on a narrow subject is in a magazine or periodical. The most efficient way to search these publications is to use one of the available index-
ing services. Of these, the *Reader's Guide to Periodical Literature* is the most
popular. It covers articles in over a hundred journals, listing them by subject and author, and it is published monthly.

Your library will also offer a great many other periodical indexes,
specializing in such areas as photography, engineering, and applied technology. If you have a question about whether or not you are using the
best possible index, ask a librarian for help.

The New York Times Index   Since 1913 the *New York Times* has published a monthly index which lists, by subject, all of the articles that have
appeared in that paper. The index indicates the date, page, and column
of the article. Therefore, you can either look up the article in the *Times,*
or if the article is about an important event, use the date to locate a similar article in your local newspaper.

The Reference Room   Encyclopedias, dictionaries, atlases, almanacs,
biographies—all books of general information are kept on open shelves
in the reference section of your library. These books are labeled with an
"R" for reference. They are so important for research that they must be

used on the premises. Consult Winchell's *Guide to Reference Books* for the appropriate reference volumes. If you need help, don't be afraid to ask the reference librarian.

Bibliography Cards   If you are gathering your supporting material for research paper or speech, you should make one bibliography card for each source you will use. Use either a three-by-five or four-by-six inch card as your instructor directs. Your bibliography card should include the name of the author, the title, the call number of the book or periodical, the publisher, and the place and date of publication. You should also include a key number so your note cards can be "keyed" to the bibliography card.

Author's name (Last name first on bibliography card.)	Awad, Elias M. ⑬
Title, place, publisher, and date of publication	Automatic Data Processing: Principles and Procedures. Englewood Cliffs, New Jersey Prentice-Hall, Inc., 1970.
Call number	651.2 A 962

Taking Notes

If you prepare your notecards carefully and accurately, you will save valuable time. Here are some simple rules to follow in taking notes. Observe them carefully and you will save hours of time.

1. *Use either three-by-five or four-by-six inch file cards for notes.* Notecards which are of uniform size are easier to work with.

2. *Include only one idea per card.* Don't copy large sections of the material because you are not sure of what you want. Spend some time in deciding what particular point you want to make. Then jot it down.

3. *Put the same key number on the note card that appeared on the appropriate bibliography card.* Since the full bibliographical information is on one card you won't have to rewrite the information again.

Alphanumeric Data Representation

"... although the user is interested only in decimal numbers as output, the internal operation of electrical computers is based on digits in various binary forms."

p. 155

Sample Note Card

4. *Give each item a heading.* If you indicate the nature of the material with a topic heading, when you are ready to organize your cards into a paper, you can put them in piles according to topic.

5. *Follow the heading with information.* If the material is quoted exactly, use quotation marks. If you paraphrase, make sure you respect the author's meaning.

6. *Take accurate notes.* Be sure you have copied correctly the word order, punctuation and spelling of quoted material.

7. *Put down the exact page number from which your notes were taken.* You might have to refer to the source again to get a more complete statement. Besides you'll probably need the page number for your footnotes.

Footnotes

There are two types of footnotes, reference and content. Reference footnotes give credit to the author for direct quotations, facts, or opinions. Content footnotes provide a place for explanations and supplemental information which you feel are important but would impede the flow of discussion if they appeared in the body of the text. Footnotes appear either at the bottom of the page that contains an entry to be footnoted or in a section at the end of a research paper between the text and the bibliography. In either case, footnotes consist of two parts: the footnote number and the data.

The content footnote may be used to add comments or introduce additional information. The sample content footnote below appears as footnote 8 in the model documented essay at the end of this chapter.

In a reference footnote, the author, title, publisher, place and date of publication are given in the first reference to a book. When a bibliography is provided, the name of the publisher is sometimes omitted.

The key to effective footnoting is consistency. In order to make your footnotes consistent, you need to follow some conventional style. Below is a commonly used style of footnoting. Since footnoting styles vary, your instructor may ask you to use a different form.

Content footnote

[8]The word "omnicidal" comes from the Latin word *omnis* meaning "all" or "everything."

Reference footnotes

Book:
[1]George Soule, *The Theatre of the Mind,* (Englewood Cliffs, N.J.: Prentice-Hall, 1974), p. 7.

Periodical:
[2]George Adams, "Our Drug Culture," *Saturday Review* (January 20, 1978), pp. 48–50.

Newspaper:
[3]"Energy Crunch Continues," *The New York Times,* February 10, 1978, p. 4.

Subsequent References

When writing a research paper, you must often make subsequent references to a given source. For these references, you can use the author's surname and the page number provided that you are using only one book or article by that author. For subsequent references to newspaper or periodical articles, use the title (or shortened title) of the newspaper or periodical.

Examples:

[11]George Soule, *The Theatre of the Mind* (Englewood Cliffs, N.J.: Prentice-Hall, 1974), p. 7.

[2]Soule, p. 19.

[3]George Adams, "Our Drug Culture," *Saturday Review* (January 20, 1978), pp. 48–50.

[4]*Saturday Review,* p. 49.

[5]"Energy Crunch Continues," *The New York Times,* February 10, 1978, p. 4.

[6]*New York Times* or *Times.*

Following are some common rules for footnoting:

1. If you are entering your footnotes throughout the body of your paper, type a line 1½" long below the last line of the text to separate the footnotes from the text. Begin the line at the left margin and at least a double space below the last line of the text.

2. All footnotes should be single-spaced.

3. Footnotes should be numbered consecutively throughout the paper.

4. Footnotes are numbered with raised numbers placed one half space above the line of type. These numbers are not followed by a period.

5. A double space should be left between footnotes.

6. Unless they are placed at the end of the text, footnotes must appear on the same page as the reference to them.

7. Footnote items should be separated from each other with commas; a period appears at the end of each footnote.

8. In a footnote the author's name appears first.

9. Footnotes should run the full width of the page with the first line indented.

The Bibliography

A bibliography is a list of all the sources you have consulted in writing your paper. It is arranged in alphabetical order by author's last name. If there is no author, the source is listed by the first important word of the title. Since the bibliography is intended to show the reader where he can locate relevant material on the research topic, the first line is typed flush with the left margin (to make it more prominent) and the others are indented.

You can use the sample footnote and bibliography entries below as models. Make note of the major differences between the two.

A Book by One Author

Footnote:
   [1]William L. Rivers, *Writing: Craft and Art* (Englewood Cliffs, N.J.: Prentice-Hall, 1975), p. 205.

Bibliography:
Rivers, William L. *Writing: Craft and Art.* Englewood Cliffs, New Jersey: Prentice-Hall, 1975.

A Book by Two Authors

Footnote:
²Arthur Koch and Stanley B. Felber, *What Did You Say?* 3rd ed. (Englewood Cliffs, N.J., 1985), p. 109.

Bibliography:
Koch, Arthur and Stanley B. Felber. *What Did You Say?* 3rd ed. Englewood Cliffs, N.J.: Prentice-Hall, 1985.

A Book with More than Two Authors

Footnote:
³Anita Taylor et al., *Communicating* (Englewood Cliffs, N.J.: Prentice-Hall, 1977), p. 438.

Bibliography:
Taylor, Anita, et al. *Communicating.* Englewood Cliffs, N.J.: Prentice-Hall, 1977.

An Anthology

Footnote:
⁴Alan Casty, ed., *A Mixed Bag: A New Collection for Understanding and Response,* 2nd ed. (Englewood Cliffs, N.J.: Prentice-Hall, 1975), p. 220.

Bibliography:
Casty, Alan, ed., *A Mixed Bag: A New Collection for Understanding and Response.* Englewood Cliffs, N.J.: Prentice-Hall, 1975.

An Article in a Periodical

Footnote:
⁵A. F. Williams, "Social Drinking, Anxiety, and Depression", *Journal of Personality and Social Psychology,* March 1976, p. 693.

Bibliography:
Williams, A. F. *"Social Drinking, Anxiety, and Depression."* Journal of Personality and Social Psychology, March 1976, pp. 689–693.

An Article Without an Author

Footnote:
⁶"Campus '65," *Newsweek,* March 22, 1965, p. 49.

Bibliography:
"Campus '65," *Newsweek,* March 22, 1965, pp. 43–63.

An Unpublished Source

Footnote:
[7]Irwin Stranz, "Marijuana Use of Middle- and Upper-Class Adult Americans" (Unpublished Ph.D. dissertation, School of Public Health, UCLA, 1971), p. 11.

Bibliography:
Stranz, Irwin, *"Marijuana Use of Middle- and Upper-Class Adult Americans."* Unpublished Ph.D. dissertation, School of Public Health, UCLA, 1971.

A Newspaper Article

Footnote:
[8]"Americans Take Big Chance In Hospital Emergency Rooms," *The Milwaukee Labor Press,* October 21, 1971, p. 2.

Bibliography:
"Americans Take Big Chance In Hospital Emergency Rooms." *The Milwaukee Labor Press,* October 21, 1971, p. 2.

An Interview

Footnote:
[9]Interview with Joyce Jackson, Registered Nurse, Cudahy, Wisconsin, January 9, 1978.

Bibliography:
Jackson, Joyce. Registered Nurse, Ackerman Clinic, Cudahy, Wisconsin. Interview. January 9, 1978.

A Letter

Footnote:
[10]Dr. Niels Nojgaard, letter dated June 10, 1963.

Bibliography:
Nojgaard, Niels. Professor of Danish History, University of Kobenhavn, Denmark. Letter dated June 10, 1963.

EXERCISE

Use the card catalogue, the *Reader's Guide to Periodical Literature, The Subject, Author or Title Guide to Books in Print, The New York Times Index,* or other appropriate reference books to find the answers to the following questions in your local or school library. Along with your answers, indicate the source.

1.   What books has J. Paul Getty written?
2.   Who won the gold medal in women's figure skating in the 1976 Olympics?

3. What is the name of the Arthur Miller play concerning a salesman?
4. On what day in 1974 did Richard Nixon resign?
5. How many acts are there in the play *Macbeth*?
6. What were the names of the first men to land on the moon?
7. Which was the first country to be occupied by the Nazis in World War II?
8. From which college did Martin Luther King graduate?
9. Who wrote *Victory*?
10. How many books have been written about wolf children since 1962?

Assignments

1. Develop a 750–1000 word persuasive essay as your instructor directs.
2. Prepare a five–eight minute persuasive manuscript speech. Try to convince your audience to agree with the conclusions you came to as a result of your research.
3. Prepare a five–eight minute extemporaneous speech based on your research project.
4. Answer the following questions about your school library.
    a. Which system of classifying books does your library use?
    b. To how many newspapers does your library subscribe? List them.
    c. What hours is your library open?
    d. For what period of time can a book be checked out?
    e. What is the name and title of the person in charge of the library?
    f. Where is the *Subject Guide to Books In Print* located?
    g. What fines are imposed for overdue books or records?
    h. What is the procedure for examining a periodical?

Documented Essay To Persuade

Before It Is Too Late

If we divided the combined American and Soviet nuclear arsenals into bombs the size of the one dropped on Hiroshima and exploded one bomb a minute (or 1,440 a day), it would take two years and three months before the arsenals were emptied.[1] In spite of this fact, each day three to five nuclear warheads are constructed for these arsenals. A 20-megaton bomb, dropped on New York City, would incinerate every person within a radius of six miles of the blast's center and those within a radius of twenty miles would probably "either die instantly or suffer wounds from which they could not recover."[2] In spite of this, our government plans to spend $1.6 trillion on defense spending over the next five years. With each passing day, we are getting closer to the possibility of an all out thermonuclear war which mankind could not survive. We must change direction before it is too late. The United States must immediately negotiate an arms reduction agreement with the U.S.S.R.

An important reason for arms reduction is that the arms control talks between the United States and Russia are failing. For the past ten years, we have witnessed arms talks that are used as propaganda rather than forums of good faith. Time and again proposals are put forth which are unacceptable to the other side. For example, the Soviets will never agree to the Reagan "zero-option" plan because it puts them at a severe disadvantage.[3] In the next round of SALT talks, the United States will insist on this plan that would require the removal of the Soviet SS-20 rockets which threaten Europe along with their older SS-4s and SS-6s. In return we would not begin putting new missiles into Europe.[4] The Soviet response is, of course, that the only thing the United States is giving up is on paper.

They argue that this would involve disassembling missiles already in place in exchange for our not installing missiles which we haven't finished building as yet. Consequently, the Soviets and this nation continue the arms race and the saber rattling. The United States is cast as the "imperious, imperialist villain" by the Soviets while President Reagan warns evangelical

---

[1]H. Jack Geiger, "The Nuclear Threat," In Common, (Common Cause Report from Washington), August 1982, p. 45.

[2]Robert J. Lifton and Kai Erikson "Nuclear War's Effect on the Mind," The New York Times, March 15, 1982, p. 18.

[3]"Reagan's Nuclear Shell Game," The Progressive, December 1, 1982, p. 10.

[4]"Playing Nuclear Poker," TIME, January 31, 1983, p. 13.

church leaders in a March 7th speech to ignore "the aggressive impulses of an evil empire."[5]

Secondly, the probability of an accidental nuclear war is increasing. This risk increases as we increase the size of our arsenal and the number of those who have access. More than 100,000 people in this nation have access to nuclear weapons. More than three percent of them per year are removed from access for reasons ranging from drug abuse to evidence "of a contemptuous attitude toward the law."[6] A few months ago a nuclear technician created a major false alarm when he mounted a training film of a Russian rocket attack on a computer. The North American Air Defense Command reported 151 false alarms during one eighteen month period.[7] These false alarms should cause grave concern when we consider the limited time available to fire our missiles before they are destroyed. Computer failure is commonplace in every walk of life. It is not unreasonable to suggest that a computer failure could cause an accidental nuclear war. The risk of this happening increases with the improved sophistication of Soviet weaponry. While at this time we have almost thirty minutes to respond to a missile attack, this could easily be decreased significantly in a few years.

Finally, the first strike policy that the United States has adopted is omnicidal.[8] It states that we reserve the right to first use of nuclear weapons. However, what will happen when we do? The Soviets will, of course, fire their weapons, and a nuclear holocaust will take place that will destroy our planet. These consequences are so frightening that a new word had to be coined "omnicide": the destruction of our entire planet. In spite of this, the Reagan administration has initiated what critics called a "first strike policy" built around the development of the MX missile. Since the MX missile is not a counter-missile but an intercontinental ballistic missile its only value to us is a first strike weapon. In the words of a defense department report released in December 1982, "the 308 large Soviet SS-18 missiles are now deployed with warheads which with their large destructive power and accuracy are capable of destroying any known fixed target

---

[5]"Reagan condemns Soviet 'evil empire'," The Milwaukee Journal, March 8, 1981, p. 1.
[6]James E. Muller, "My Turn," Newsweek, March 1, 1982, p. 34.
[7]Muller, p. 33.
[8]The word "omnicidal" comes from the Latin word omnis meaning "all," "everywhere."

with high probability."[9] Consequently, the Russians could easily destroy our MX missiles unless they were used in a first strike attack. The logic of equating first use with deterrence in naming the MX missiles the "Peacekeeping Missile" is insane.[10]

The accelerating arms race carries the risk of the end of life as we know it. Imagine your city being turned into a 27 million degree furnace from an explosion that would incinerate every person within six miles of the center of the blast.[11] Imagine the few who survive walking around with bodies so horribly burned that the flesh appeared to be melted. These survivors are probably the unlucky ones because they have simply postponed their death. They would face a world of horror; a world of contaminated drinking water and food supplies; a world of people hideously affected by radiation, with no hospitals, ambulances, drugs, blood, or other medical supplies. Those not killed by radiation, would soon succumb to disease spread by insects and the millions of decomposing corpses. However, this does not have to be. Before these horrible imaginings become reality, we must change our direction. The United States must immediately negotiate an arms reduction agreement with the U.S.S.R.

---

[9]Herbert Scoville Jr. "First Strike," The New York Times, October 8, 1981, p. 34.

[10]John Somerville, "The Haig Doctrine: First Strike Policy," San Diego Newsline, April, 1982, Volume 5, Number 28.

[11]Geiger, p. 45.

Bibliography

Geiger, Jack H. "The Nuclear Threat." In Common, (Common Cause Report from Washington), August 1982.

Lifton, R. J., and Kai Erickson. "Nuclear War's Effect on the Mind." The New York Times, March 15, 1982.

Muller, James E. "On Accidental Nuclear War." Newsweek, March 1, 1982.

"Playing Nuclear Poker." Time, January 31, 1983.

"Reagan condemns Soviet 'evil empire'." The Milwaukee Journal, March 8, 1983.

"Reagan's Nuclear Shell Game." The Progressive, November, 1982.

Scoville, Herbert, Jr. "First Strike." The New York Times, October 8, 1981.

Somerville, John. "The Haig Doctrine: First Strike Policy." San Diego Newsline, April, 1982.

CHAPTER 7

Writing
and
Rewriting

OBJECTIVES

After studying this chapter, you should be able to:
1. List and briefly explain six considerations in preparing a rough draft of a composition.
2. Plan and write the rough draft of a composition.
3. Revise and rewrite a composition that is unified, coherent, concise, and complete.
4. Use standard correction symbols when revising your writing.
5. Write a composition in your own individual voice.
6. Recognize and correct errors in grammar, punctuation, and spelling.

WRITING AND REWRITING

The key to writing improvement is practice. This textbook will help you to plan and prepare a written communication with your subject, purpose and audience in mind. A concerned instructor will help you edit and revise what you have written by offering suggestions and giving direction. However, neither can do the writing for you. Like dancing and swimming, writing is a developed skill. And just as you learn to dance by dancing and to swim by swimming, you learn to write by writing. In order to give you as much time for practice as possible, the assignments listed at the end of this chapter can all be prepared from your own imagination, background or experience.

In the Peanuts cartoon on page 52, Charlie Brown is frustrated because he can only think of eight words for his one-thousand-word theme assignment. Even though an assignment of that length at Charlie Brown's grade level seems unlikely, the scene is familiar. We laugh because we can understand Charlie's plight. At one time or another each of us has faced a similar predicament: having to write something when we couldn't think of anything to say. While the situation didn't seem funny to us at the time, it does now. (Probably because it is Charlie sitting there instead of one of us.)

Knowledge and Interest

Unfortunately, the type of assignment lampooned in this cartoon is much too common. While "What I Did This Summer" is a subject the students know a lot about, the assignment ignores the fact that a writer has to be interested in a subject to write about it effectively. Take as an example a typical grade school class. Out of 25 students returning to school in the fall, how many would you guess have had a memorable summer vacation? Three? Four? If the class is typical, you can bet that even if there were that many, few of the other 21 have had vacations that would stimulate an enthusiastic response. The results of this kind of assignment are predictable—dull reading. It is pointless to try to make something that is uninteresting to you, interesting to others. As you can see, two key factors involved in motivating successful writing are knowledge and interest. In fact, writing on a subject you are knowledgeable about and interested in is half the battle.

Getting Started

At this point you might be thinking to yourself, "I've chosen subjects I knew about and was interested in and still found myself staring at a blank page." Well, when that happens, take a tip from the experienced writer. Instead of just sitting there in frustration like a Charlie Brown, get started on the writing process. Writing is not the result of inspiration but of hard work. You might have to force yourself to write. A professional certainly would. Here are some tips for overcoming the blank page syndrome:

1.   Write down random thoughts about your subject on a piece of paper. Try to think of specific details such as names, dates, places and the like. Any of these may trigger a response and get you on track. (If you are writing a longer paper, start on a paragraph or two somewhere in the middle or at the end.)

2.   Write down specific questions about your subject from the point of view of the reader. Put yourself in his or her shoes. If you were curious about this subject, what would you like to know? Where would you get information about this subject? Whom would you ask?

3.   Try the technique of brainstorming. Write down the thoughts that come to mind that even remotely relate to your subject. Jot them down in words, phrases or sentences as quickly as you can. Don't evaluate; just write everything down that you can think of in five minutes. Then stop. Start again and write for two minutes more.

4.   Try freewriting, a technique that involves sitting down and writing anything at all without stopping. You don't have to worry about subject or organization. Pay no attention to grammar, punctuation, or spelling. You don't even have to write complete sentences. The important thing is to keep writing. The purpose of freewriting is to get you to the point where you begin thinking and writing at the same time. You may begin writing gibberish only to end up writing sense.

The Rough Draft

Once you have gotten on track with your writing you are ready to begin your rough draft. The term "rough" should serve to remind you that this is just a first attempt to put on paper what you want to say. Very few writers can put down exactly what they want to say on the first try. Those who can are able to because they have done such a thorough job of planning and preparation that the paper practically writes itself. For the great majority of writers, however, the rough draft is the beginning of the most important stage of the writing process: revising and rewriting.

Because it involves discovering just how you will go about developing the ideas and information you want to communicate, this first writing has also been called the discovery draft. A highly successful writer of over one hundred books sees the discovery draft as the most exciting part of writing. "I never know what I'm going to come up with," he says, "until I see it written on the page." When writing the first draft, don't be overly concerned with grammar, punctuation or spelling. Although correctness is a must, you can deal with these considerations when you revise. Below are some specific suggestions to follow when writing your first draft:

1. Set aside a block of time in which to write. Effective writing requires continuity and concentration. There are some who can only write at a certain time of day and others who can write at any time. Experiment to find a time period best for you.

2. Find an appropriate place to write in an atmosphere that you find relaxing. For many this would mean a comfortable, well-lighted area free from noise and interruption. Others cannot write without a stereo or radio playing. It's up to you.

3. Write your rough draft as soon as possible after you have finished the planning stage. This will allow you as much time as possible for revising and rewriting. A good rule of thumb is to allow at least as much time for revising and rewriting as you did for planning and writing your first draft.

4. When you write anything but the last draft, skip every other line and leave an ample margin. If you type, double or triple space. You need room on the pages to make additions, deletions or changes when you revise.

5. Try to write your rough draft as spontaneously as possible. Don't revise each sentence as you write it. You will sound more natural if you write out your ideas as if you were talking to friends.

6. Don't be afraid of writing too much. If you have had the chance to plan and prepare what you are going to write about in the pre-writing stage, you have already screened your material. If not, develop what comes from your own experience as fully as you can. You will be revising your material later. Keep in mind that it is easier to delete material than to add.

Revision and Rewriting

The process of revising and rewriting involves much more than hunting for errors, correcting them and then rewriting. More importantly, revision and rewriting mean making clear what you mean. As the foreword of this book suggests, they involve asking yourself, "What did you say?" from the point of view of your reader. Did you get your ideas across in an "easy-to-understand and interesting way?" Reshape your sentences and paragraphs in order to come as close to what you want to say as possible. Successful writers are continually revising and rewriting. Ernest Hemingway, for example, wrote the last page of his highly successful novel, *A Farewell To Arms,* 39 times before he was satisfied with it. This is an extreme example, but it points out that the process of writing involves hard work.

Before you have anyone read what you have written, read it aloud to yourself. The ear is by far the best editor. Even the most avid reader listens far more than he or she reads. Over the years you have unconsciously developed an ability to hear what sounds clear or unclear, natural or awkward. Therefore, your ears even more than your eyes are able to determine what has been said effectively. When speaking, each of us uses a variety of different voices. We use one voice when talking to friends, another with strangers, still another in formal conversation and so on. Our manner of expressing ourselves in writing is also called *voice.* It is our unique style of writing. In most cases, a plain simple style of writing will be more effective than one which is formal. The latter would be appropriate when writing a research or opinion paper. Above all, it is important to develop a voice in your writing which is natural to you. You can best do this by using words or phrases in your writing that come easily to mind. Write from your own vocabulary. One of the best compliments you can receive as a writer is for one of your readers to comment, "That paper sounds just like you." When you read your paper aloud, ask yourself, "Does this sound right?" If it doesn't, rework it until it does.

Remember, the ability to write is not something that you are born with. It is a skill that is learned through many hours of practice. Writing that seems to flow spontaneously is the result of careful planning, revision and rewriting rather than instinct or intuition. While there are no fixed set of instructions you can follow to write well, there are standards by which writing is judged. Good writing possesses certain qualities. Below is a list of those qualities to look for in your writing:

UNITY

The word unity comes from the Latin word "unus" meaning one. Effective writing has one controlling idea, and everything in the text relates to that idea. When reading your paper for unity, ask these questions: Does each paragraph help to develop the controlling idea of the composition? Does each paragraph deal with only one idea? Does each sentence in a particular paragraph deal with the one main idea of that paragraph?

COMPLETENESS

Often, beginning writers fail to support and develop their ideas adequately. You must be sure to provide your reader with enough information to fulfil the purpose of your message. When reading for completeness, ask these questions: Does my reader have all the information he or she needs to respond correctly to my communication? Are my ideas adequately supported? Do the paragraphs develop the controlling idea of the composition adequately? Is any new information needed?

CONCISENESS

While it is important that your writing contains adequate information, it must be as concise and to the point as possible. A good rule to follow when revising for conciseness is to give your reader all the information he or she needs in as few words as possible. Ask these questions when revising for conciseness: Do my paragraphs contain any sentences that are unnecessary? Can I change any sentence around to make it shorter and clearer? Is there any deadwood? Have I cut everything that can be cut? Is my paper short enough to hold the reader's attention throughout?

COHERENCE

The term coherence means "sticking together logically." Coherent writing moves from one sentence to the next in an easy-to-follow way. When reading for coherence ask these questions: Is my writing continuous? Do the ideas in my composition move in an uninterrupted sequence from start to finish? Do the sentences in each paragraph follow some pattern of development? Are there transitions or other links between my sentences and my paragraphs?

VOICE

Voice refers to the way you say things in writing. A reader will pay attention to a voice that is clear, natural and spontaneous. When reading your paper to search for exactly the right way to say something, ask yourself these questions: When I read my writing aloud does it sound like one person talking to another? Is my language personal and to the point? Is it appropriate to the subject and the audience? Is it my own? Does it lend itself to being read aloud?

CORRECTNESS

The last step in revising your composition is to read it carefully to catch and correct any errors in grammar, punctuation and spelling that may have survived previous revisions. Check each sentence carefully. Ask these questions: Are there any run-ons, comma splices or fragments? Do verbs agree with subjects and pronouns with antecedents? Are pronoun references clear and accurate? Are there any misspellings? Are sentences correctly punctuated? If you have any doubts as to what is correct, refer to a dictionary or the handbook at the back of this text.

A Student Paper

Below is a rough draft and revision of a medium-length paper written by John Dunham, a student in a first semester communications class at a two-year junior college. The draft, a true story written in narrative, took a little over one hour to write. Dunham wrote the draft in longhand trying to get the information down as quickly as possible. He concentrated on getting the facts down the way he remembered them occurring and spent little time revising during this first writing. After he finished the draft, he typed it in order to have a clean copy to revise. After letting the paper sit for a few days, Dunham revised it according to the suggestions in the following revision guide:

SUGGESTIONS FOR REVISING WRITTEN WORK

Revision is the key to effective writing. No paper should be turned in without at least one revision. Medium-length papers should be revised twice and longer papers three times. Below are specific suggestions for revising papers:

I.   Allow a cooling off period between revisions. Do not revise your rough draft for at least 24 hours.

II. Except for the final one, each draft should be double-spaced with ample margins for additional material or changes.

III. Make your revisions as easy to read as possible. Write legibly and if you use a pen when writing, revise with a pencil or a pen of a different color.

IV. Before you revise any draft, read it aloud without stopping, to get an overall impression of it.

V.   Depending on its length, read and revise the first and/or second draft thinking of the composition as a whole. Look for unity, coherence, completeness, voice and conciseness. Ask these questions:

   1. Unity—Do all parts of the paper relate to the central idea?

   2. Coherence—Does the paper make sense? Do the ideas flow smoothly?

   3. Completeness—Is the paper complete? Is there enough material to satisfy the purpose of the communication?

4. Voice—Have you picked words from your own vocabulary? Does it sound like you?

5. Conciseness—Have you used clear, to-the-point sentences? Have you said it as efficiently as possible?

VI. Read and revise the second or third draft to eliminate errors in grammar, punctuation and spelling. Check for those kinds of errors you have made in the past. Use the following guide:

1. Check the sentence carefully.
   a. Eliminate fragments, run-ons, or comma splices.
   b. Eliminate shifts in person, number and tense.
   c. Make verbs agree with subjects and pronouns with antecedents.
   d. Be sure pronouns refer to antecedents clearly.

2. Check all punctuation. Use commas only when you know they should be used.

3. Check spelling and capitalization. Use a dictionary.

An "a" for Mrs. K

~~I Never Liked English~~

Until I became a senior in high school ~~I never liked English. Of all the courses I took in~~ English was my worst subject. ~~school English was the worst, I could take~~ Grammar, punctuation, spelling and all the rest weren't that bad ~~but I hated to write,~~ writing probably ~~I guess it was~~ because I just couldn't ~~write~~ do it well. ~~When~~ While the other students were writing I would just stare out the window or at my blank page, unable to ~~I couldn't~~ think of anything to say. ~~Have you ever sat~~ I would sit there half the class period or more with my ~~your~~ mind a complete blank? until ~~I would.~~ ~~Finally~~ Then the teacher would poke me, or I'd look at the clock. ~~So~~ I'd ~~hurry up and~~ frantically write something down and turn it in. Without fail, my papers would come back with an ~~We got our papers back and mind would be a~~ "F" or "D," on it. In spite of this ~~I was doomed to failure. But~~ I'd do well enough on the tests and ~~grammer quizes~~ to pass the course.

~~Then I got Mrs. K. Mrs. K looked like a typical English teacher. She was tall thin and fortyish and wore horn-rimmed glasses. She had greyish blond hair pinned tightly to her head in a bun. She never wore dresses but always dark plain suits usually brown or navy blue.~~

~~When I first saw her I thought she'd be like all the others but I was wrong.~~

On the first day, She introduced herself as Mrs. Kurszewski ~~and~~ but told us that her friends called her Mrs. K and we could too. Then she wrote on the board, ~~She walked up to the board, picked up some chalk and wrote the following words:~~ "Writing is Rewriting," ~~After~~ and ~~that she~~ sat down and ~~explained how the class would be run.~~ I remember thinking at the time, "How can you rewrite what you haven't written?" For the rest of the period Mrs. K talked to us. She didn't lectures she just talked. She told us we could ask questions at any time.

Mrs. K ~~She~~ told us that for the next 10 weeks we would be working on both writing and rewriting. She said ~~told us~~ that we could ~~she would let us~~ decide on the subject, ~~determine the~~ purpose and ~~choose the~~ length of our paper but we would have ~~writing. She could expect us~~ to have at least one conference with her during the planning stage and another ~~at least one other~~ for each draft. The topics we chose were to come ~~She said that we should choose topics~~ from our own experience so we wouldn't ~~couldn't~~ have to spend time looking up ~~going out to get~~ information. The number of drafts we wrote would be ~~was~~ up to us ~~she said because only we could tell which one was the final one. She said we would~~ but we had to turn in two ~~papers at~~ drafts to be graded for the mid-semester ~~the end of 10 weeks which we felt were our two best final~~ final marking period. ~~drafts. This would be our 10 week grade.~~ I remember thinking even two was too ~~2 was to~~ many.

For most of the ~~whole first~~ week I sat wasting time. Finally on Friday, I went up to Mrs. K's desk for a conference, bringing ~~I brought~~ a list of subjects which as usual I put together at the last minute ~~as usual~~. I thought ~~knew~~ she'd ~~would~~ be mad, but she ~~Mrs. K~~ looked at my list, smiled and said, "I hear you're ~~your~~ a hockey freak." ~~freek.~~ I couldn't believe my ears. ~~it. I had been playing hockey since I was six year old.~~ Most of the ~~other~~ kids ~~in class~~ knew ~~it~~ I played hockey and had been ~~because~~ my picture ~~was~~ in the paper a couple times ~~as a member of the sport's club little league team.~~ Mrs. K was the only teacher who had ever mentioned it ~~I couldn't believe it.~~ She said that ~~she thought the rest of the class~~ would like to learn more about the game, and thought the rest of the ~~she knew she would.~~

class would, too. I was hooked.

~~I thought she might be lying but I thought I'd give it a~~
~~try anyway.~~

It took me a week and two conferences to finish re-
writing my first draft. *During our conferences,* ~~When we had a conference~~ Mrs. K

let me do most of the talking. Once in a while she would ^coh^
say something ~~make a comment~~ like, "Would this be clear to someone ^awk^

who never saw a hockey game?" or "~~Its clear when your~~ ^wdy^

~~sitting here explaining it to me.~~ *"Perhaps* ~~Mabey~~ you should write

the way you talk."
Then one day, she
^coh^ ~~After my third draft,~~ Mrs. K suggested that I read
third draft
my ~~paper~~ to ~~the rest of~~ the class during *our* ~~sharing time,~~ ~~a~~
I did and everyone seemed to like it.
~~period, once a week when anyone who wanted to could~~

^coh^ ~~read their paper. When I read my paper most of the kids~~
I revised that draft and wrote one more to turn
~~liked it. I did to, I was hooked.~~ I wrote five drafts in all
in
~~and submitted the last one~~ as one of my ~~two~~ papers to be
and that made me feel proud.
^unity^ graded. I got an "A", ~~I was really proud but I felt that it~~

~~would, I had spent alot of time on it.~~
In fact, Mrs. K gave me an "A" for the semester. She
~~I finished Mrs. K's course with an "A". I gave her an~~
deserved one too. She taught me. She taught me ^sp^
"A" to ~~because I learned alot from her.~~ I learned that
But she taught me
what I had to say was worth something, ~~and I learned~~
something even more important: that writing can give you
~~that writing isn't all that bad if you work at it.~~
a lot of satisfaction if you know how to go about it.

As you can see, the draft was triple-spaced to allow ample room to
revise. We have included correction symbols on this revision to label the
errors that Dunham corrected. They appear on the inside back cover of
this textbook. Correction symbols are standard all over the English
speaking-world and cover the most common errors in writing. You might
find it helpful to use them when you revise your own copy.

After Dunham read his first draft aloud, he realized that both the
title and the introduction had to be changed. Although he hadn't liked
English and hated writing before he got to Mrs. K's class, his attitude
changed. This turnabout is aptly expressed in his new title, "An 'A' for
Mrs. K."

Although he corrected several errors in grammar, punctuation, and
spelling, the majority of Dunham's revisions were made to improve unity,

coherence, voice, and conciseness. (Note, for example, the removal of an entire paragraph for the sake of unity.)

After completing this first revision, Dunham retyped it as draft number two. He brought this draft to the conference with his instructor who told him:

"Your paper is clear and interesting. It is short enough to hold the reader's attention and yet contains enough information to make your point. Your attitude toward Mrs. K and her class is obvious from the point of view you express. Your voice comes through as being individual and natural. For the most part, your paragraphs are unified and coherent. Besides correcting specific problems in grammar, punctuation, and spelling and reworking a few sentences that are awkward or wordy, I would suggest that you might develop your conclusion more fully. It seems to me that from what you have said, this very effective teacher was responsible for helping you to an even greater extent than you give her credit for. If you carefully revise and rewrite this second draft you should be well on your way to a well-developed and effective composition."

Following that conference, Dunham carefully revised the paper once again. The rewritten version of that second draft follows. Notice how, in the revision of the last paragraph, Dunham responded to his instructor's suggestion.

An "A" For Mrs. K

Until I became a senior in high school, English was my worst subject. Grammar, punctuation, spelling and all the rest weren't that bad, but I hated writing, probably because I couldn't do it well. While the other students were writing, I would be sitting staring out the window or at the blank page unable to think of anything to write. I would sit through half the class period or more, my mind a complete blank, until the teacher would poke me or I would look at the clock. Then I'd frantically write something down and turn it in. Without fail my paper would come back with an "F" or "D" on it. In spite of this, I would do well enough on the tests to pass the course.

Everything changed, however, when I was put in Mrs. K's English 12A class. I thought her class would be like all the others, but was I wrong. On the first day, she introduced herself as Mrs. Kurszewski but told us that her friends called her Mrs. K and we could too. Then she wrote on the board, "Writing is rewriting," and sat down.

(I remember thinking at the time, "How can you rewrite what you haven't written?") For the rest of the period, Mrs. K talked to us. She didn't lecture, she just talked. She told us to feel free to make comments or ask questions at any time. This was not your typical English class.

Mrs. K told us that for the next ten weeks we would be working on writing and rewriting and that what we wrote would be up to us. She said that we could decide on the subject, purpose and length of our paper but we would have to have at least one conference with her during the planning stage and another for each draft. The topics we would choose were to come from our own experience so we wouldn't have to spend time looking up information. The number of revisions we were to write would also be up to us but we had to turn in two final drafts to be graded for the mid-semester marking period. I remember thinking, "Even two are too many."

For most of the first week, I sat wasting time. Finally on Friday, I went up to Mrs. K's desk for a conference bringing a list of subjects which, as usual, I had put together at the last minute. I thought she'd be mad, but she looked at my list, smiled, and said, "I hear you're a hockey freak." I couldn't believe my ears. Most of the kids knew I played hockey and my picture had been in the paper a couple of times, but Mrs. K was the only teacher who had ever mentioned it. She said that she would like to learn more about the game and thought the rest of the class would too. I was hooked.

It took me one week and four conferences to finish rewriting my first draft. I almost stopped there, but I had my reputation as a hockey player to live up to. During our conferences, Mrs. K let me do most of the talking. Once in a while, she would say something like, "Would this be clear to someone who has never seen a hockey game?" or "Perhaps you should write the way you talk." When I finished the third draft, Mrs. K suggested that I read it to the class during our sharing period. I did and everyone seemed to like it. Believe it or not, however, I decided it needed one more rewrite.

I revised that draft and rewrote it to turn in as one of my papers to be graded. It got an "A" and that really made me feel proud. Mrs. K gave me an "A" for the semester and she deserved one too because I learned a lot from her. I learned that to write well I had to revise and rewrite over and over until I finally made what I wanted to say as clear and interesting as possible. I learned that choosing a subject I knew about and was interested in made the job of writing easier and more rewarding. But most important, I learned how satisfying it was to create a piece of writing I could be proud of.

Writing Activities

The writing activities on the following pages are designed to allow you to develop your writing and rewriting skills without having to go out and find information. All the material you need to complete them you already have, or have easily available, from your own experience for any of the assignments. Choose something you are concerned about, or have a genuine interest in. This will make it easier to reshape, rework, and revise your writing into what you want to communicate.

Personal Experience to Entertain

Write a short narrative telling about something interesting that happened to you on some occasion. The story can be exciting, amusing, suspenseful, or otherwise memorable. It can be entirely true, partly true, or completely fictional. Emphasize details of action and keep the story moving to hold the reader's attention throughout.

Sample Topics

1. I'll never forget falling asleep in _____.
2. Have you ever found your _____ missing?
3. It was just last year that I experienced my first _____.
4. There is nothing as exciting as _____.

Model

Love is a wonderful thing, but, like anything worthwhile, it often has its ups and downs. For about six years prior to our meeting, my husband had been sequestered in the religious life. I knew very soon in our friendship that I was stimulating his interest in women but I could also tell he wasn't very versed in the art of courting and when it came to kissing—YUK!!! Forget it!

His kisses started out as quick stolen little pecks on the cheek and progressed to quick stolen little pecks on the lips. As his kisses increased in length, I saw that some things had to change. First there was the pucker—now, puckers are fine for babies and grandmothers, but for me—No Sir! Well the pucker soon changed to the tight-lipped method—That was just as bad as the pucker. Another thing was his approach. He wasn't quite sure of whether to jump right in and grab or to slowly sidle up and nonchalantly start kissing. What he didn't realize then was that you don't just attack with a passionate kiss, but that you work up to the really big one with tender little loving kisses.

One particular evening we were standing at the kitchen counter, just talking and drinking iced tea. I figured there was no particular limitation as to time or place, and after all practice makes perfect, so I made the approach this time. Well right in the middle of this fit of passion, just as I was marveling to myself at his improvement, I heard a strange noise, the sound of an iced tea glass being slid—klunk klunk— across the tiled counter. So I opened one eye—and curled one lip from the full press—and quietly said "Did you want a drink of iced tea?" As you can imagine it completely broke the two of us up. It seems I caught him off guard and he was just trying to put the glass back so he could get a better grip. That was the icebreaker, because from that time on it was clear sailing for my Romeo.

Used with permission of the writer, Pat Kiley.

Personal Experience to Inform

Write a short narrative in which you relate a personal experience which helped to mold your image of yourself. How you saw yourself in the situation can be either positive or negative. The important thing is that the reader be able to perceive your reaction to the situation and to understand how that reaction gave you a clearer picture of yourself.

Sample Topics

1. I found out last week I was a born organizer.
2. When it comes to carpentry I'm all thumbs.
3. I found out too late that I'm not the marrying kind.
4. I wouldn't have believed how sensitive I am.

Model

I found out even before I started school that I was a tough kid. We lived in a downstairs flat on the east side, next door to a bakery. Across the street was a Catholic church and grade school. In the spring during recess, the boys would play baseball on the school grounds. Often, I would walk across the street and stand around while they were choosing up sides, hoping someone would pick me, but no one ever did. I guess it was because I was too small; I had just turned five. One day, after I had been passed over by these boys, as usual, I got mad and grabbed their ball. I told them that I would not give it back unless they let me play. A kid with a bat ran up to me and hit me over the head with it. I really hurt, but I gritted my teeth and fought back the tears. Angrily I threw the ball onto the school roof and stalked home.

As I walked up the front stairs, my mother, who had spotted me through the front window, rushed to the door. "Good Lord, what happened?" she screamed.

"Some guy hit me with a bat," I said casually.

She quickly pulled me into the bathroom, and as she was wetting a washrag, I looked into the mirror. I saw then why she had sounded so frightened. My blond head was bright red from blood which had begun to run down my face and ears. My mother cleaned me up and said she hoped I had learned my lesson, but the next day there I was, as usual, standing next to the boys on the playground waiting to get picked. Only now, I had a huge white bandage on my head.

Personal Experience to Persuade

Write a short narrative in which you relate a personal experience to persuade. Describe the situation in enough detail so that you create a mental picture for your reader. Your purpose is to show the reader what you learned from a particular situation. If the reader sees that what you learned was valid, he or she will learn the lesson with you. A personal story is an excellent way to prove a point.

Sample Topics

1. Seatbelts save lives.
2. Getting involved can pay off.
3. A knowledge of first aid could save a life.
4. Don't judge a person on the basis of your first meeting.
5. Hanging wallpaper is not as easy as it looks.

Model

I used to feel that a lot of what people learn in classes at school was unnecessary. I remember thinking that about a course in first aid that I had to take as part of my naval reserve requirement. That all changed one evening about four years ago. I was sitting in our living room with my uncle George, watching the fights on television. During a particularly exciting round I heard a thud. Looking around I saw that my uncle had fallen to the floor. I rushed over to him and found that he wasn't breathing. Remembering what I had been taught in first-aid, I immediately rolled him on his back, put his head on a pillow and to the side and loosened his collar. After I checked to see if he had anything in his mouth, I rushed to the phone and called the rescue squad. When I returned, I found that my uncle was not only not breathing but that his heart had stopped too. I began giving him mouth-to-mouth resuscitation and external heart massage at the same time. Almost miraculously I remembered the instructions for both as if they were being given to me by the instructor again. "Exhale into the person's mouth and push down sharply on the sternum, release, count to ten and begin again." Finally, after what seemed like an eternity, uncle George responded and began breathing. By the time the rescue squad arrived, some of the color had returned to his cheeks and he had regained consciousness.

To this day whenever I think of a course as being of doubtful value, I think of my uncle George and work at it a little harder.

The Humorous Story

Everybody loves a funny story, but not everyone can tell one well. If you have a favorite story or anecdote that you feel is genuinely funny, try your hand at writing it. Write in a conversational style, emphasizing characterization and details of action. The more clearly your reader can visualize what you describe, the more effective will be your story.

Suggestions

1. Use vivid colorful language to stimulate the senses of your audience.
2. Organize your story in a clear chronological order.
3. Keep your story short enough to hold the interest of your reader.
4. Read such authors as Art Buchwald, James Thurber, and Dorothy Parker to get an idea of effective style.

Model

An old Arkansas farmer once bought a mule that was supposed to be the fastest in the whole state of Arkansas. When paying for it, he was told that if he wanted the best possible results from the mule, he should treat it with kindness. So he took the animal home, fed it a hearty supper and bedded it down on fresh straw in a clean stall. The next morning he walked the mule to the field and hitched it to a plow. "Let's go, friend," he said in his most pleasant tone. But the mule didn't budge. Well, the farmer was prepared, and he reached into his overalls and pulled out an apple—and some sugar—and a turnip—but the only thing that moved on the mule was its mouth. This so infuriated the farmer that he stalked back to the house to call the "S.O.B." who had swindled him. Before the telephone wires had cooled off, the fellow who had sold him the mule arrived and headed for the field with the farmer at his heels. On the way, he picked up a big stick and when he reached the mule he let him have it right between the ears. Then he whispered, "Come on, pal; let's plow the field," and the mule took off like a race horse. The farmer stood shaking his head in disbelief. "That's gotta be the fastest mule in the world," he said, "but you told me he had to be treated with kindness." "He does," said the other fellow, "but you have to get his attention first."

Letter to the Editor

Write to the "Letters to the Editor" column of one of your local newspapers expressing a point of view. It will be helpful if you familiarize yourself with these columns in order to be aware of the rules and format to follow. A reader will judge you on your style and grammatical correctness. A simple, to-the-point style must still be interesting.

Suggestions

1. Write as if you were speaking in an informal, direct way.
2. Keep your letter as short as you can without leaving out necessary information.
3. Proofread your letter carefully to eliminate weaknesses in style and correctness.
4. Read your letter aloud to a friend or two.

To the Editor:

   I am writing about a problem that should not occur at this school, the problem of allowing teachers to assign textbooks which are not used in class. I am a third-semester student in the Medical Technology Program at this school. Up to now, I have had two courses where I bought a book that we never used in class, and one where we were assigned an 18 chapter book but only discussed two chapters. The total cost of those books was $62.50 but I got less than $25.00 for them when I sold them back to the bookstore. That means I paid almost $40.00 to cover two chapters. That's $20.00 a chapter! If a book is assigned for a class it should be used. Is this too much to ask?

Signed, Disgusted

The Personal Letter

The personal letter can be a stimulating and effective writing assignment. Perhaps no other form of writing gives the writer a clearer picture of his reader. The most common purpose for the personal letter is to inform. A letter home to parents or friends, a letter to a pen pal, a letter to a friend or loved one in another part of the country is usually filled with information about activities, health, and so on. Of course, there is that inevitable personal letter to persuade you send when you run out of money. Writing a personal letter to entertain can also be rewarding. It allows you to use your imagination, it gives you a chance to see what you can do with humor, and it offers you the opportunity to brighten someone's day when he or she reads it. The personal letter below was published in a national magazine and has given enjoyment to a great many readers.

Model

Dear Mother and Dad:

Since I left for college I have been remiss in writing and I am sorry for my thoughtlessness in not having written before. I will bring you up-to-date now, but before you read on, please sit down. You are not to read any further unless you are sitting down. Okay?

Well, then, I am getting along pretty well now. The skull fracture and the concussion I got when I jumped out of the window of my dormitory when it caught fire shortly after my arrival here is pretty well healed now. I only spent two weeks in the hospital and now I can see almost normally and only get those sick headaches once a day. Fortunately, the fire in the dormitory, and my jump, was witnessed by an attendant at the gas station near the dorm and he was the one who called the Fire Department and the ambulance. He also visited me in the hospital and since I had nowhere to live because of the burnt-out dormitory, he was kind enough to invite me to share his apartment with him. It's really a basement room, but it's kind of cute. He is a very fine boy and we have fallen deeply in love and are planning to get married. We haven't got the exact date yet, but it will be before my pregnancy begins to show.

Yes, Mother and Dad, I am pregnant. I know how much you are looking forward to being grandparents and I know you will welcome the baby and give it the same love and devotion and tender care you gave me when I was a child. The reason for the delay in our marriage is that my boyfriend has a minor infection which prevents us from passing our premarital blood tests and I carelessly caught it from him.

I know you will welcome him into our family with open arms. He is kind, and although not well-educated, he is ambitious. Although he is of a different race and religion than ours, I know your often-expressed tolerance will not permit you to be bothered by that.

Now that I have brought you up-to-date, I want to tell you that there was no dormitory fire, I did not have a concussion or skull fracture, I was not in the hospital, I am not pregnant, I am not engaged, I am not infected, and there is no boyfriend in my life. However, I am getting a D in History and an F in Science and I want you to see those marks in their proper perspective.

Your loving daughter,
Susie

Reprinted with permission of Forbes Magazine. Writer unknown.

Pet Peeve Paragraph

Write a paragraph of 100–150 words in which you criticize a person, policy, or organization. Pick a subject that really annoys you. Be forceful. Express your views in a direct, to-the-point manner; emphasize your annoyance with the language you use.

Suggested Topics

1. Welfare is another word for stealing.
2. When are we going to stop kidding ourselves about America being a free country?
3. Another name for Congress is a pack of thieves.
4. Nobody is meaner than my mother-in-law.
5. Let's end our hypocritical attitude toward (censorship, bussing, racism, religion, etc.)

Model

One of the things that really annoys me is being forced to buy a book for a class and then not use it. This has happened to me three times now. Just last semester I took a course where the book cost over twenty dollars. Even though we were assigned chapters to read, the instructor never discussed them. She said we would talk about them later but we never did. We ran out of time, and she said to just forget them. We were never even tested on those chapters. It was bad enough having to read the damned chapters for nothing, but I only got half my money back when I sold the book back to the bookstore. It burns me up whenever I think about it. The school should do something about instructors who assign a textbook and then don't use it. This stinks.

Poetry

The ability to write poetry is a special talent. Those who possess it should develop it as fully as they can. If your instructor permits, you might write a poem as an alternative to some other assignment. Below is a poem written by Gary W. Longrie about his mother. It captures an important moment in his life that will live on through the lines of the poem.

Voice Prints

(1)

The swirl of loving birches
surrounding the pale green house
bent under the rumbling raging storm
from the Northeast.
And you, diminutive,
under the strong tall pines
bent forward into the storm
clutching the mail
down the long drive
toward the house.
One of your last
defiant acts against

that more dangerous storm
inside you.
Your voice, strong, in and through
your whole being shouted love.
And we, standing scared at the back door,
applauded you.

(2)

From its vantage
on an old poplar
between the woodpile
and the road,
we moved the little sign
"chipmunk crossing"
to the oaks
outside your window.
The chipmunks moved
too!
From your chair
you watched them—
and the bluejays, chickadees,
dusty sparrows and squirrels,
on into the dusk
of evening waters
until your voice was tired
and consciousness ebbed.

Used with permission of the author, Gary W. Longrie.

CHAPTER **8**

Effective
Sentence
Structure

OBJECTIVES

After studying this chapter, you should be able to:
1. Classify sentences as simple, compound, complex, or compound-complex.
2. Distinguish among correct sentences, sentence fragments, and run-on sentences.
3. Recognize and correct errors in agreement of subject and verb.
4. Recognize and correct errors in agreement of pronoun and antecedent.
5. Recognize and correct errors in faulty parallelism.
6. Revise wordy sentences.
7. Revise sentences containing misplaced and dangling modifiers.
8. Analyze the sentence patterns found in *normal* sentences.
9. Expand the sentence patterns found in *normal* sentences through modification, coordination, and subordination.
10. Recognize and construct periodic, parallel, and balanced sentences.

SENTENCE VARIETY

The big league pitcher who threw nothing but fast balls would probably be batted out of the box in short order. A pitcher wants to keep the batter guessing, so he varies the pattern, throwing first a fast ball, then a curve, then a change of pace. The successful quarterback will, on occasion, throw the "bomb" when percentage dictates a power play into the center of the line. He, too, varies the pattern.

Sentence variety comes easily to the gifted writer. For those still striving to attain fluency, an understanding of different sentence classifications, both grammatical and rhetorical, will help to overcome the most common stylistic flaw in student writing—monotonous sentence structure.

GRAMMATICAL CLASSIFICATION

A clause is a word group containing both a subject and a predicate. A main clause (or an independent clause) makes sense when it stands alone. A subordinate clause is dependent upon, or subordinate to, a main clause within a sentence or between sentences. An understanding of these relationships will enable you to recognize four basic sentence types: *simple, compound, complex,* and *compound-complex.*

The *simple sentence* consists of one independent clause.

1. John went to a rock festival. (one subject, one verb)
2. John and Mike went to a rock festival. (compound subject, one verb)
3. John and Mike went to a rock festival and met some interesting girls. (compound subject, compound verb)

All three examples above are simple sentences. Don't be confused by compound subjects and compound verbs. If the sentence contains only one main clause, it is a simple sentence.

The *compound sentence* consists of two or more independent (or co-ordinate) clauses. In order for a compound sentence to be effective, the ideas expressed in the main clauses must be of equal rank.

1. The doorbell rang, and John answered it. The doorbell rang; John answered it. (two independent clauses, separated by a conjunction or semicolon)
2. "The hum of talk came to him dimly, his rage blood pounded in his ears, and he burst through and strode away." (John

Steinbeck, *The Pearl*) (three independent clauses, separated by commas and a conjunction)

Do not use compound sentences to express ideas of unequal importance.

Ineffective: John is a technical engineering student, and he has won a full-tuition scholarship.

Improved: John, a technical engineering student, has won a full-tuition scholarship. (*Note:* This is a simple sentence because it contains one independent clause.)

The *complex sentence* consists of one main clause and one or more subordinate clauses. Because it enables us to combine ideas of unequal rank in the same sentence by subordinating one idea to another, it is the sign of a sophisticated writer.

1. My brakes are defective.
2. I don't have any money to replace them.
3. I won't be able to drive home between semesters.

We could coordinate these three independent clauses in a single compound sentence, but that would only result in three parallel strands with nothing emphasized. The best solution would be to subordinate the first two clauses to the last in a complex sentence.

Because my brakes are defective and I don't have the money to replace them, I won't be able to drive home between semesters.

The *compound-complex* sentence combines the principles of coordination and subordination; consequently, it consists of two or more independent clauses and one or more subordinate clauses. Used too frequently, the compound-complex sentence can result in a cumbersome style, but, on occasion, it is an effective means of connecting interrelated ideas.

1. Get dressed and have your breakfast while we load the gear.
   (two independent clauses)   (one subordinate clause)

2. When we went on our picnic, I left my camera in the car and
   (subordinate clause)   (two independent clauses)

   Mike went back to get it.

EXERCISE

Indicate whether the following sentences are: (1) simple, (2) compound, (3) complex, or (4) compound-complex. Be prepared to explain your answers in class discussion.

1. When he smashed up his car, his wife became angry and the company cancelled his insurance.
2. Janet closed her eyes and rested her head on his shoulder.
3. George said he would return with the tickets, but I haven't seen him since noon.
4. My repeated attempts to talk him out of dropping English have fallen on deaf ears; nevertheless, I shall try again.
5. When the bell rings, leave quickly.
6. George Hays, the tallest player in the Conference, was dropped from the basketball team because of poor grades.
7. Before you report for your job interview, have your hair cut short and borrow your roommate's suit.
8. Jim's car, for which we couldn't obtain parts, had to be junked.
9. Before being wheeled into the operating room, the patient was given an anesthetic.
10. Being the only male in a class of nursing students must have its disadvantages, but I can't think of any.

Frequent use of complex sentences and an occasional compound-complex sentence can effectively link ideas of unequal importance. Our discussion of rhetorical classification will provide other equally effective techniques for achieving sentence variety. But before we proceed to this discussion, it would be well to pause and reflect upon the most basic type of sentence error: the inability to distinguish among complete sentences, run-on sentences, and sentence fragments.

Think back to your writing experiences in high school. Have your teachers ever commented on your inability to distinguish between a sentence and a nonsentence? Do you recall such symbols as *frag.* (sentence fragment) and *R.O.* (run-on sentence) in the margins of your compositions? If so, you may have a writing problem serious enough to affect adversely your chances for college and vocational success. Now is the time to resolve to correct that problem. Unless you plan to obtain remedial instruction, this will probably be your last classroom opportunity to learn to write a correct English sentence.

The following diagnostic test will measure your ability to distinguish among correct sentences, sentence fragments, and run-on sentences. If you achieve a score of 17 or better (out of a possible 20), you may skip the discussion of sentence fragments and run-on sentences and continue on page 161, beginning with *Agreement of Subject and Verb: Language Harmony.*

DIAGNOSTIC TEST

For each of the following word groups, indicate *C* for correct sentence, *R* for run-on sentence, or *F* for sentence fragment.

1. When the moon comes over the mountain.
2. The moon comes over the mountain.
3. Don't worry, we will work it out somehow.
4. Hoping to hear from you soon.
5. Go!
6. Sam Jones, who is the oldest student in the class and the best swimmer in the school.
7. While running to the bus stop, I fell.
8. After buying her one ounce of fine French perfume and taking her to the best restaurant in town.
9. Then we arrived at our destination.
10. The books were neatly arranged, however, papers were scattered all over the floor.
11. Jogging for two miles before breakfast was his usual routine.
12. He quickly glanced to his right, then he sprinted for the finish line.
13. This car needs new brakes and new tires, nevertheless, it's a good buy for the money.
14. Working out on the parallel bars for three full hours each day.
15. My job, however, leaves much to be desired.
16. Leaving his place of employment promptly enabled him to avoid the rush hour traffic.
17. Wondering whether the cute blonde in his English class would meet him later on for a sandwich and a coke.
18. The interesting scenery, however, makes the drive to school relaxing.
19. I just can't feel sorry for him flunking out of school was his own fault.
20. Rereading the chapter increased his understanding.

The Sentence Fragment

The word *fragment* means a part broken off or detached. A sentence fragment is a part of a sentence, as in the following examples:

Fragment: 1. Martha did poorly in her history examination. *Although she spent all of her time studying.*

2. *Because my parents and kid sister are driving up for a visit.* I won't be able to have dinner with you tonight.

Explanation: Although both italicized examples contain subjects and verbs, they are incomplete. The words *although* and *because* introduce subordinate clauses which require main clauses to complete the context.

Combining the subordinate clause with a related main clause produces a grammatically correct, complex sentence.

Correction: 1. [Martha did poorly in her last history examination.]
                                         main clause

[although she spent all of last week studying.]
                                subordinate clause

2. [Because my parents and kid sister are driving up for a visit,]   subordinate clause

[I won't be able to have dinner with you tonight.]
                                main clause

Review: Use the following subordinate clauses in complex sentences:

1. After we finished our dinner.
2. Even though summer jobs are very scarce.
    Note: The subordinate clause may precede or follow the main clause.

Fragment: *Controlling exhaust emissions of the internal combustion engine.*

Explanation: Phrases, unlike clauses, are word groups which do not contain subjects and verbs; therefore, they are not complete sentences.

A phrase can, however, function as the subject of a complete sentence.

Correction: [Controlling exhaust emissions of the internal combustion engine] is one way of combating air pollution.
phrase as subject

Review: Use the following phrases as subjects of complete sentences:
1. Watching televised football in color.
2. Studying for final examinations at the end of a busy day.
3. To play chess well.
4. The best dancer in our group.

Fragment: *To prevent loss of fuel vapors.*

Explanation: A phrase can modify a main clause.

Correction: [To prevent loss of fuel vapors,] [the gas tank should
                   phrase as modifier   main clause
always be tightly capped.]

Review: Use the following phrases to modify main clauses in complete sentences:
1. In order to decide which extracurricular activities to participate in.
2. Working as quickly as he could.
    Note: The modifying phrase may precede or follow the main clause.

Fragment: 1. *Hoping to hear from you soon.*
                 2. *Walking in the rain.*

Explanation: A phrase can be converted into a main clause by adding a subject and a verb.

Correction: 1. I hope (am hoping) to hear from you soon.
                   2. I am walking in the rain.

Review: Convert the following fragments into correct sentences:
1. Giving my best whenever I compete.
2. Looking for a mutually satisfactory solution.

Fragment: *Jimmy Smith, the overwhelming choice for all-conference center.*

Explanation: We have a subject, *Jimmy Smith,* and a modifying phrase, *the overwhelming choice for all-conference center,* but a verb is lacking.

If we add a verb, perhaps as part of a complete predicate, our sentence would be complete.

Correction: [*Jimmy Smith*,] the overwhelming choice for all-con-
subject

ference center, [has received] an offer to play pro-
verb

fessional football.

Review: Convert the following fragments into correct sentences:
1. Deciding what to do next Saturday night.
2. Discussing yesterday's lecture with two of his classmates.
3. The new Student Union, a massive combination of steel and concrete.
4. Mr. Halloway, the best English teacher I ever had.

On occasion, you may find professional writers using fragments punctuated as complete sentences. Grammatical rules, like most other rules, have their exceptions. An accomplished writer will sometimes *knowingly* write a sentence fragment in order to achieve a particular stylistic effect. When a student *unknowingly* punctuates a fragment as a complete sentence, he tells his reader that he is unable to distinguish a sentence from a nonsentence.

It is generally a good idea to avoid fragments early in your college writing career. Once you have achieved a measure of linguistic sophistication, you may feel ready to deviate from some of the rules.

The Run-On Sentence

A *run-on* sentence contains two or more complete sentences punctuated as a single sentence. The two types of run-on sentences discussed in this section are the *fused* sentence and the *comma-splice*.

Run-on: Wait here we will see whether Tom is in his office.

Explanation: Two sentences are said to be *fused* when appropriate punctuation is omitted. This type of run-on sentence can be corrected as follows:
1. Place a period after the first sentence and begin the next with a capital letter.
2. Use a semicolon instead of a period if the two clauses are closely related.

3. Formulate a compound sentence by separating main clauses of similar rank with a conjunction.

4. Formulate a complex sentence by changing one of the main clauses into a subordinate clause.

Correction:

1. Wait here. We will see whether Tom is in his office.

2. Wait here; we will see whether Tom is in his office.

3. Wait here and we will see whether Tom is in his office.

4. If you wait here, we will see whether Tom is in his office.

Review:

Correct the following fused sentence by using each of the four methods identified above:

I purchased my cassette recorder many years ago it still gives me trouble-free service.

Run-on:

Wait here, we will see whether Tom is in his office.

Explanation:

When a comma is used to separate two complete sentences, the result is a *comma-splice,* another type of run-on sentence. The comma is not a terminal mark of punctuation; therefore, it cannot take the place of a period or semicolon. A comma, like a yellow traffic light, is a signal to pause and proceed with caution. Periods and semicolons are the "red lights" of punctuation; they are used to stop sentences from running into one another.

Correction:

In order to correct a comma-splice, follow the same procedure previously indicated for the fused sentence. (If the two main clauses are not of similar or equal rank, do not use the third technique involving connection with a conjunction.)

Review:

Correct the following comma-splice. Attempt to use each of the four methods indicated above.

Let's have dinner at the Nantucket, they serve the best Kansas City strip steak in town.

Run-on:

This semester I am taking a reduced program, therefore, I must take two additional courses in summer school in order to graduate.

My suitcases are already packed, however, I still have a few things to take care of before we leave.

Explanation: These two comma-splice sentences illustrate a particularly troublesome type of run-on sentence. The sentences can be corrected as follows:

1. Separate the two main clauses by placing a period after the first sentence and beginning the next with a capital letter.

or

2. Use a semicolon instead of a period if the two clauses are closely related.

Correction:

1. This semester I am taking a reduced program. Therefore, I must take two additional courses in summer school in order to graduate.

2. This semester I am taking a reduced program; therefore, I must take two additional courses in summer school in order to graduate.

3. My suitcases are already packed. However, I still have a few things to take care of before we leave.

4. My suitcases are already packed; however, I still have a few things to take care of before we leave.

Additional Explanation: The words *therefore* and *however* in the above sentences perform similar functions. Because they modify or qualify the first main clause and relate it to a second clause, they are called conjunctive adverbs. Some common conjunctive adverbs are:

therefore   besides   consequently
however   then   furthermore

Sometimes a comma-splice sentence containing a conjunctive adverb can be corrected by placing a conjunction before the conjunctive adverb:

First we plan to have dinner together, and then we will see a play.   conjunction, conjunctive adverb

Do not confuse the conjunctions *and, but,* **and** *or* with conjunctive adverbs:

Correct: The tree in our yard is huge, *but* it doesn't provide much shade.

Incorrect: The tree in our yard is huge, *however,* it doesn't provide much shade.

Correct: The tree in our yard is huge; *however,* it doesn't provide much shade.

Conjunctive adverbs separate main clauses. When words such as *however* and *therefore* appear *within* main clauses, they are separated from the words they modify with commas:

Correct: Most rules, however, have their exceptions.

Correct: The train was four hours late. The team, therefore, forfeited the game.

Review: Make the needed corrections in the following:

1. I lost my notes, therefore, I cannot study for the following examination.
2. I have enough money to last until payday, however, I cannot afford to spend any of it foolishly.
3. I have enough money, however, to last until payday.
4. The game was dull, besides, the weather was terrible.
5. Rachel studied these pages carefully, consequently, she will do well on the following post test.

POST TEST

For each of the following word groups, indicate *C* for correct sentence, *R* for run-on sentence, or *F* for sentence fragment.

1. After inviting him to dinner two consecutive Sundays and buying him a watch for his birthday.
2. Walking to Bill's apartment in this blizzard is folly.
3. Then we were ready to leave.
4. Losing his balance unnerved him.
5. Your directions were impossible to follow, otherwise I would have been here hours ago.
6. The extra money, however, paid for his tuition.
7. Jim Gibbons, who is the best punter and the fastest runner on the squad.
8. Because you aren't permitted to operate this machine without permission.
9. You aren't permitted to operate this machine without permission.
10. Conscientiously taking his medication after each meal enabled him to keep the problem under control.
11. Leaving me in charge of the automotive shop for the next three days.
12. Leave!

13. Try again, I'm sure you will be able to master the procedure shortly.

14. He said he would clean up after he finished the job, however, the house was a mess when he left.

15. Wishing you were here with me.

16. He checked his instruments and adjusted his helmet then he waited for the race to begin.

17. My plans, however, are still subject to change.

18. I hear the movie is excellent, besides, the concert has been sold out for more than a week.

19. Attempting to revise his plans so that he could visit his friend before the end of the semester.

20. Skating around the rink for the first time in years, I was surprised at how well I did.

Agreement of Subject and Verb: Language Harmony

Some years ago, a local department store advertised its annual sales event with the slogan: *Capacity Days Is Here.*

Some local partisans of grammatical purity were offended. How can the singular verb "is" be used with the plural noun "days"? The advertising agency responsible for the slogan rose to its own defense. They argued, quite logically, that while Capacity Days does, in fact, extend over a period of days, the term refers to *one* sale, the big sale of the year. Therefore, since Capacity Days refers to a single sale, the singular verb "is" is perfectly proper.

Certain elements of the population weren't convinced. The plural noun "days" followed by the singular verb "is" just didn't sound right. Rather than alienate prospective customers, the store compromised and adopted a modified slogan: *Capacity Days Is/Are Here.*

The basic rules of subject and verb agreement are simple and logical: Singular subjects require singular verbs; plural subjects require plural verbs. However, as we saw from the foregoing example, application of the rule can sometimes be troublesome. Let us take a closer look at a few of the more difficult situations:

Which verb form would you select in each of the following?

1. Jane, together with the other students in our English class, (was or were) offended by the instructor's sexist remarks.

2. Every student and faculty member (has or have) to carry an identification card at all times.

3. Neither Rachel nor the other bowlers on the squad (is or are) likely to finish the season with a 175 average.

4. The jury (is or are) still deliberating.

5. The value of the committee's decisions (is or are) open to question.

6. An anthology of short stories (is or are) what Maggie would like for her birthday.

7. His height and agility (make or makes) him an ideal candidate for the basketball team.

8. Basic Economics (is or are) required for an Associate Degree.

9. Each of us who (is or are) enrolled in Communication Skills must write six papers this semester.

Now, let us see how well you did.

1. The subject is *Jane.* Don't be confused by the phrase beginning with "together with." When constructions such as *together with, as well as,* and *in addition to* intervene between the subject and the verb, the verb still agrees with the subject. *Jane . . . was* offended by the instructor's sexist remarks.

2. The indefinite pronouns—*each, every, everybody, nobody, neither, either, no one*—generally require singular verbs. *Every* student and faculty member *has* to carry an identification card. . . .

3. In either/or and neither/nor constructions, the verb agrees with the closer of the two subjects. Neither Rachel nor the other *bowlers are* likely. . . .

4. A collective noun—team, jury, class, public—requires a singular verb when the group is represented as a unit, a plural verb when the members of the group are acting as individuals. The jury *is* deliberating, but the jury *are* unable to agree on a verdict.

5. The subject is *value.* Don't be misled by *decisions,* the object of the preposition. Since the subject, *value,* is singular, the value *. . . is* open to question.

6. Our subject is *anthology. Short stories* is the object of the preposition. Since the subject, *anthology,* is singular, an anthology *. . . is* what Maggie would like. . . .

7. Our compound subject—*height and agility*—requires a plural verb. Notice that while nouns generally add an *s* to form the plural, verbs frequently drop the *s* to form the plural. His height and agility *make* him an ideal candidate. . . .

8. Nouns that are plural in form but singular in meaning agree with singular verbs. Basic Economics *is* required.

9. The relative pronouns—*who, which,* and *that*—agree with singular or plural verbs, depending on their antecedents. Each of *us who are* enrolled in Communication Skills must write six papers. . . . The relative pronoun *who* refers to the antecedent *us,* which is plural; therefore, we use *are,* the plural verb form.

EXERCISE

Select the correct verb form in the following sentences:

1. Two weeks (is or are) too short a time for an annual vacation.
2. Neither my brothers nor my sister (is or are) as tall as I.
3. *Rocky III* is one of the five movies that (have or has) been nominated for an Academy Award.
4. Mike, along with two of my other friends, (is or are) planning a trip to Florida during the spring recess.
5. Each one of us (is or are) entitled to be treated with respect.
6. Five dollars an hour (is or are) good money for inexperienced and un-trained workers.
7. The committee (recommend or recommends) that the present policy be changed.
8. The worth of my photography courses (is or are) already evident.

Agreement of Pronoun and Antecedent: More Language Harmony

Which is correct? An antecedent is (a) the predecessor of the Honda Civic, (b) a long-lost aunt, (c) a small, blood-sucking insect, (d) the word to which a pronoun refers.

Effective Sentence Structure

Just as subject and verbs must agree to achieve language harmony, so too, must pronouns and antecedents:

Singular: *Carol* enjoyed *her* dinner very much.
            antecedent   pronoun

Plural: The *children* lost *their* way in the darkness.
            antecedent   pronoun

Supply the correct pronoun form(s) in the following sentences:

1. Each person in this class should put forth (   ) best effort.
2. Every man and woman should do what (   ) can to con-serve electricity.
3. (a) The team enjoyed (   ) position in first place.
   (b) The team took (   ) seats on the bench.
4. Either Rachel or her friends may miss (   ) bus.

A singular pronoun is generally used with such indefinite anteced-ents as *each, every, everyone, everybody, someone, somebody, either, neither,* and *no one.* Traditionally, when the antecedent included those of both sexes, a masculine singular pronoun was used. Therefore, a traditional grammarian would correct Examples 1 and 2, above, as follows: 1. *Each* person in this class should put forth *his* best effort. 2. *Every* man and woman should do what *he* can to conserve electricity.

The above problems of agreement of pronoun and antecedent illustrate the sexist nature of our language. Even though men and women are involved in both situations, the masculine singular pronoun form has been identified as "correct" by the traditionalist. Language specialists have long deplored the fact that we have no word in our language that means *his* or *her.* Accordingly, you would be well advised to include alternate masculine and feminine pronoun forms or reword your sentence in the plural, as follows:

1. (a) *Each* person in this class should put forth *his* or *her* best effort.

    (b) *Students* should put forth *their* best efforts.

2. (a) *Every* man and woman should do what *he* or *she* can to conserve electricity.

    (b) *Men* and *women* should do what *they* can to conserve electricity.

In informal English, the plural pronoun form is becoming increasingly commonplace: *Every* man and woman should do *their* best.

3. Collective nouns agree with singular pronouns when the group acts as a single unit: The *team*, therefore, enjoyed *its* position in first place. When the members of the group act as individuals, the pronoun should be plural: The *team* took *their* seats on the bench.

4. When a pronoun refers to two antecedents, one singular and one plural, the pronoun agrees with the closer of the two: Either Rachel or her *friends* may miss *their* bus.

Let us examine a few additional pronoun reference problems.

1. Jim told his friend that he would ace the exam.
2. Do not leave your machine unattended. This is an unsafe practice.
3. When one is ill, you should notify your supervisor as soon as possible.

In sentence 1 the antecedent of *he* is unclear. Does Jim mean that he will ace the exam? Or, does he mean that his friend will ace the exam? One way to clarify such sentences is to insert the proper reference immediately after the pronoun: Jim told his friend that he (Jim) would ace the exam.

In sentence 2, although the meaning of "this" is apparent, the pronoun reference is awkward because the antecedent is not specifically stated. Reword the sentence: Leaving your machine unattended is an unsafe practice.

Sentence 3 makes a needless shift in person. When *one* (third person) is ill, *you* (second person) should notify your supervisor. The pronoun shift from third to second person is awkward and unnecessary. When one (third person) is ill, (he or she) should notify (his or her) supervisor as soon as possible. Needless shifting should be avoided, not only within sentences, but within longer communications. If you are writing a narrative and you begin by relating an experience in the first person, try to follow through with the first person whenever possible.

EXERCISE

Correct any errors in agreement of pronoun and antecedent that appear in the following sentences:

1. Every member of this class should turn in his or her technical report before the end of the month.
2. After the delivery men removed the refrigerator from the crate, they discarded it in the village dump.
3. The class was making good progress with their semester project.
4. When one works and goes to school, I find it difficult to do justice to both.
5. Each member of the committee have specific responsibilities.
6. If a person wants to see your federal government in action, they should visit Washington, D.C.
7. If you don't remove the rat from the trap soon after the catch, it will start to smell.
8. I left Sam convinced that he lacked understanding.
9. Neither Bill nor the other members of the crew volunteered to work on their day off.
10. I rush to the refrigerator every time a commercial appears on the screen. That is not the way to stay trim.

Parallelism: "One of These Things Is Not Like the Others"

One reason for awkward sentences is lack of parallel structure. What do we visualize when the word "parallel" is mentioned? Some of us see railroad tracks; some see parallel bars in a gym; some see two parallel chalk lines on a blackboard. Whatever we visualize, the parallel elements are of the same length and the same material. When we have words or groups of words side by side in a sentence, they should be constructed the same way. This sentence, for example, lacks parallel structure:

(1)   (2)   (3)

He likes to play cards, to swim, and listening to music.

We don't even need to know any grammatical terminology to figure out what's wrong here; in the words of the Sesame Street song, "One of These Things Is Not Like the Others." The groups of words numbered (1) and (2) consist of *to* plus a verb, while (3) is an *ing* construction. To correct the faulty parallelism, we must make all three alike. We can say:

	to play cards,			playing cards,
He likes	to swim, and	OR	He likes	swimming, and
	to listen to music.			listening to music.

EXERCISES

The following sentences are awkward because of faulty parallelism. In each sentence identify the element that is not like the others. Then rewrite the sentences to eliminate the faulty parallelism.

1. The professor's lectures are dry, disorganized, and they are difficult to follow.
2. Super Woman is a beauty, can cook, and is also an electrical engineer.
3. I admire people who are honest, who are outspoken, and sticking to their principles is also admired.
4. To eat, drinking, and to make money are his goals.
5. Riding a motorcycle requires skill, coordination, and one has to have courage.

Supply the missing elements. Sometimes you may supply words, sometimes groups of words, but in any case your finished sentences should have perfect parallel structure.

1. I wish I had a job that _____

_____

_____

2. My idea of a fun evening is _____

_____

3. TV programs would be better if _____

_____

4. I disapprove of _____

_____

5. Students who are doomed to failure are those who _____

_____

Economy: Clearing the Air

The need for clarity is obvious. If a sentence isn't perfectly clear, if it doesn't make sense to the reader, what good is it? One of the enemies of clarity is wordiness. Too many unnecessary words may prevent the reader from getting the sense of the sentence—or at least getting it as quickly and easily as he should. But note the word "unnecessary." We aren't saying that sentences should be brief, short, or skimpy. We are merely saying that sentences should be stripped of useless verbiage and pretentious language.

Consider, for example, the following sentence: "I find myself in a state of regret because my present financial situation is so depleted that I will be unable to have the pleasure of accompanying you on your jaunt to the cinema." How much more quickly we get the point if the writer says, "I'm sorry I haven't enough money to go to the movie with you."

EXERCISES

Revise the following sentences, removing "deadwood" and pretentious language.

1. With regard to the high cost of transportation, I believe we should affiliate ourselves with a car pool whenever such an arrangement is feasible.

2. In my opinion I believe that the President has done a good job of leading the country in his first year in office.

3. By virtue of my interest in numismatic concerns, I recently purchased a subscription to *Coin World* for a period of three years.

4. The sizable and unexpected high cost of repairing my vehicle thwarted my plans for a relaxing and restful vacation in the vicinity of the Caribbean Islands.

5. She faithfully reads the newspaper *The Milwaukee Journal,* which is widely distributed throughout the State of Wisconsin.

Write sentences that are deliberately wordy. Exchange your sentences with those of a classmate. Now rewrite each other's sentences, getting rid of the "deadwood," without changing the original meaning.

Modification: The Case of the Misplaced Modifier

Another enemy of clarity is faulty word order. Words should always be near the words they modify; when they are not, the result is awkwardness and ambiguity. (If something is ambiguous, it has two or more possible meanings.) Now granted, particularly in poetry, we may want something to be interpreted on two levels, but when we speak of ambiguity we are talking about a variety of possible meanings that tend to confuse the reader or listener.

Consider, for example, the following sentence: "Tonight there will be a panel discussion about drug addiction in the student lounge." Does the writer mean that the discussion will be held in the student lounge, or that the discussion will concern drug addiction that is evident from student behavior in the lounge? If we change the word order and write, "Tonight in the student lounge . . ." we have the meaning that the writer probably intended. But the reader shouldn't have to juggle and guess.

Sometimes, in the case of what we call dangling modifiers, the words that the modifiers describe are not even present in the sentence. Consider the following: When only five, my father taught me how to swim. The words "when only five" are next to father, but when father was only five he obviously was not a father, nor was he capable of teaching swimming. To make the sentence make sense, we must insert the missing words: When I was only five, my father taught me how to swim.

EXERCISE

In the following sentences, the intended meaning is unclear. Revise these sentences so that all possible ambiguities are removed.

1. The fight was broken up before further damage was done by the security guard.

2. Hurrying to class, my wallet was lost.

3. A ham sandwich was in my lunch bag which I ate eagerly.

4. The milk spilled all over the kitchen floor that I had intended to drink for breakfast.

5. Jogging around the campus for forty minutes, my appetite increased.

6. He was carried out of the smoke-filled building by two attendants on a stretcher.

7. Discouraged by the score, the stadium began to empty.

8. I placed the chair in the corner of the room that I had recently purchased.

9. After sitting there awhile, it began to snow.

10. He gave the sweater to the girl that he had won in track.

RHETORICAL CLASSIFICATION

We have seen how the use of subordinate clauses in complex and compound-complex sentences helps add variety to our writing. Our discussion of rhetorical classification will provide other equally effective techniques for achieving sentence variety. Sentences may be classified rhetorically as *normal, periodic, parallel,* and *balanced.*

The Normal Sentence

The *normal sentence,* so called because it occurs more frequently than any other type, consists of variations of the following subject-verb patterns.

Subject-Verb (S-V)   In this sentence pattern the verb is *intransitive,* meaning it does not require an object to complete the predicate.

1. The boy fell.   (S-V)
2. The boy fell (down the stairs).   (S-V-M)
3. Rachel sang.   (S-V)
4. Rachel sang (beautifully).   (S-V-M)

Modifying phrases or words do not change the basic sentence pattern.

Subject-Verb-Direct Object (S-V-O)   In this pattern the verb is *transitive,* meaning that it requires an object to complete the predicate.

1. Bill hit a home run. (S-V-O)
2. Janet bought a sweater for her boyfriend.   (S-V-O)

The modifying prepositional phrase, *for her boyfriend,* does not change the basic sentence pattern.

Subject-Verb-Indirect Object-Direct Object (S-V-IO-DO)   Sometimes S-V-O sentences also contain indirect objects. When this is the case, the indirect object follows the verb, but precedes the direct object.

1.   Mom bought Dad a new suit.
      S   V   IO   DO
2.   Janet bought her boyfriend a new sweater.
      S   V   IO   DO

Subject-Verb-Complement (S-V-C)   In this pattern a linking verb connects the subject to the complement. A complement functions like a direct object, but it always follows a linking verb.

1.   Janet is a dental assistant.   (S-V-C)
2.   Mary is beautiful.
3.   Jim felt bad.

To *be* is the most common linking verb. Other verbs often used to connect subjects to complements are *to become, to feel, to taste, to touch, to smell, to sound, to grow, to appear, to seem, to remain,* and *to become.* If in doubt about whether the verb is linking, try to substitute a form of *to be* for the verb in question. If the meaning of the sentence remains essentially the same, the verb is linking.

1.   The swimming pool became (was) rusty.
2.   The hamburger tastes (is) great.

Two other commonly employed normal sentence patterns are the *expletive* and the *passive.* The *expletive sentence* begins with *there,* and the verb precedes the subject.

1.   There *is a stranger* at the door.
         V   S
2.   There *have been* no more *tickets* available for two weeks.
         V   S

The *passive sentence* is a variation of the S-V-O sentence in which the subjects and objects are interchanged.

1.   Bill hit the ball.   (S-V-O)
2.   The ball was hit by Bill.   (Passive)

3. Tom met Mary at the dance. (S-V-O)

4. Mary was met at the dance by Tom. (Passive)

Modifying phrases do not change the basic sentence pattern.

EXERCISE

Basic patterns may stand alone in simple sentences or be combined in compound, complex, and compound-complex sentences. Using the following abbreviations, identify each of the roman patterns.

S-V   S-V-O   S-V-IO-DO   S-V-C   E   P

1. Players from both sides swarmed onto the field.
2. Some players become nervous before a game; others keep their cool.
3. There are twenty students in class, *and* all of them seem to be shouting at once.
4. The house had been sold by Mr. Potter, *but* the agent didn't know the selling price.
5. If you give him the ball, he will make the first down.
6. Ernest Hemingway's novels brought him international fame.
7. A sentence containing a subordinate clause and a main clause is complex.
8. There are many good motels in town, *but* the Elgin is the best.
9. When anyone asks Jim a question, he becomes hard of hearing.
10. Our cousins from New York arrived by plane this afternoon.

Effective sentence combinations illustrate variations of these basic sentence patterns. Three rhetorical devices—modification, coordination, and subordination—help us to expand these basic patterns.

Modification   Two of the eight traditional parts of speech, adjectives and adverbs, function as modifying elements in the sentence. In addition, phrases and clauses also function as modifying elements. This principle has been illustrated in various examples of basic sentence patterns. Modification is an effective means of avoiding the choppy, monotonous sentence structure that makes for ineffective writing.

Weak: Dick Person is the first baseman for the Oshkosh Outlaws. He hit a home run on August 3. It was the longest home run ever hit in People's Stadium.

Improved: On August 3, Dick Person, the first baseman of the Oshkosh Outlaws, hit the longest home run ever hit in People's Stadium.

Weak: I have a new dog. His name is Willy. He is very intelligent.

Improved: My new dog, Willy, is very intelligent.

Coordination   Just as we combine independent clauses in a compound sentence, we utilize this same principle by coordinating subjects, verbs, objects, complements, and modifiers in any sentence to achieve economy of expression.

Weak: My new dog, Willy, is very intelligent. He is a beautiful animal.

Improved: My new dog, Willy, is intelligent and beautiful.

Subordination   As previously defined, subordination provides us with the means of linking ideas of unequal rank in the same sentence.

Weak: My brother is home on vacation. He attends the Milwaukee Area Technical College.

Improved: My brother, who is home on vacation, attends the Milwaukee Area Technical College. (Or, depending on which idea is emphasized: My brother, who attends the Milwaukee Area Technical College, is home on vacation.)

Weak: My new dog, Willy, is intelligent and beautiful. He is not as good a watch dog as Rusty. Rusty is my friend's dog.

Improved: Although my new dog, Willy, is intelligent and beautiful, he is not as good a watch dog as my friend's dog, Rusty.

EXERCISES

Combine each of the following sets of sentences into one sentence by coordinating, subordinating, and modifying the various elements.

1. My little sister went to the store. She forgot to chain her bike to the railing. Her bike was stolen. She was afraid to tell my father.

2. Our regular English teacher is Mr. McCarthy. He is ill with the flu. Mr. Longrie is a substitute teacher of English. He has been temporarily hired to teach senior English until Mr. McCarthy returns.

3. My older brother lives in New York. His name is Ken. He is an engineer with Arco Industries. Last year we flew to New York to see him. We traveled via Northwest Airlines.

4. It was raining very hard. My windshield wipers were defective. My vision was severely hampered. My car swerved into the guard railing. I received a severe whiplash and I also broke my arm.

The Periodic Sentence

A *periodic sentence* must contain the rhetorical effect of building to a climax through a series of words, phrases, or clauses. Although the main idea of a periodic sentence is always withheld until the end, not every sentence in which the main idea is withheld is periodic. This somewhat confusing distinction might best be explained by example.

Not Periodic: When you go to the store, bring back some beer. (Although the main clause is withheld, the rhetorical effect of building to a climax is not present.)

Periodic: If you like authentic rock music, a sandy beach, picturesque Southern architecture, and lovely girls, you will love Fort Lauderdale.

Periodic sentences must be well-planned and properly executed if they are to be effective. They should be used more sparingly than any other rhetorical device if they are to add variety, rather than monotony, to your writing. The Reverend Martin Luther King, Jr., concluded his memorable *I Have a Dream* speech with the following periodic sentence:

And when we allow freedom to ring, when we let it ring from every village and hamlet, from every state and city, we will be able to speed up that day when all of God's children—black men and white men, Jews and Gentiles, Catholics and Protestants—will be able to join hands and to sing in the words of the old Negro spiritual, "Free at last, free at last; thank God Almighty, we are free at last."

Douglas MacArthur's 1961 speech commemorating Philippine Independence Day provides the following example:

In the effort to build a world of economic growth and solidarity, in the effort to build an atmosphere of hope and freedom, in the effort to build a community of strength and unity of purpose, in the effort to build a lasting peace of justice, the Philippines and the United States of America have become indivisible.

Shakespeare proves that a periodic sentence need not be lengthy to be effective.

To die, to sleep; to sleep, perchance to dream;
Aye, there's the rub. . . .

The Parallel Sentence

A *parallel sentence* is one which emphasizes coordinate elements—single words, phrases, or clauses—usually in a series. Anytime a coordinating conjunction (and, or, but) appears in a sentence, an element of parallelism is present. But for the purpose of our definition, a rhetorical effect different from that of a normal sentence must be achieved.

> . . . and that government *of the people, by the people, for the people,* shall not perish from the earth.
>
> —Abraham Lincoln

> *We hold these truths to be self-evident, that all men are created equal, that they are endowed by their Creator with certain unalienable Rights, that among these are Life, Liberty and the pursuit of Happiness.*
>
> —Declaration of Independence

> "Duty," "honor," "country"—those three hallowed words reverently dictate *what you want to be, what you can be, what you will be.*
>
> —Douglas MacArthur

Frequently, the effect of parallelism is achieved by intentional repetition of key words or word groups through a series of sentences or paragraphs. Emphasis by repetition can be effective, if it is not overdone.

> *Dreyfus is innocent.* I swear it. I stake my life on it. I stake my honor. In the presence of this Court, the representative of human justice, before all France, before all the world, I now solemnly swear that *Dreyfus is innocent.* By forty years of work, by the authority it has given me, I swear that *Dreyfus is innocent.* By the name I have made, by my contributions to the literature of France, I swear that *Dreyfus is innocent.* May all the results of my life melt away, may my work perish, if Dreyfus is not innocent. *He is innocent!*
>
> —Emile Zola

The Balanced Sentence

A *balanced sentence* emphasizes contrasting coordinate elements, usually two main clauses. It is similar to the parallel sentence in that it emphasizes coordination, but with one important distinction: the key to the balanced sentence is contrast. The conjunction "but" frequently serves as the fulcrum of the two contrasting ideas.

> The world will little note, nor long remember, what we say here, *but* it can never forget what they did here.
>
> —Abraham Lincoln

> The true test of civilization is
> not the census,
> nor the size of the cities,
> nor the crops,
> no,
> *but* the kind of man the country turns out.
>
> —Ralph Waldo Emerson

Survival is still an open question—not because of environmental hazards, *but* because of the workings of the human mind.

—Adlai Stevenson

Notice how the elements of *parallelism* and *balance* are combined in the following example:

It is time that we see this doctrine of guilty by association for what it is: not a useful device for detecting subversion, *but* a device *for subverting our constitutional principles* and practices, *for destroying our constitutional guarantees,* and *for corrupting our faith in ourselves and our fellow man.*

—Henry Steele Commager

A simple but striking method of achieving sentence variety is to vary sentence length. The paragraph from Zola given above is an excellent example. The sentences vary from three to twenty-six words. The shorter sentences at the beginning and end of the paragraph ring with finality. The longer periodic sentences in the middle build up to the same spirited conclusion—"He is innocent!"

We have touched on but a few of the many ways in which a writer may vary sentence structure and thereby improve his or her writing. Because the sentence is our basic unit of communication, we have analyzed it, both grammatically and rhetorically, in the belief that this knowledge will enable the student to develop a fluent and distinctive style.

EXERCISE

Examine a recent issue of *Vital Speeches*. Locate at least two examples each of periodic, parallel, and balanced sentences. Then, construct two original examples of each type.

CHAPTER 9

Effective
Paragraphing

OBJECTIVES

After studying this chapter, you should be able to:
1. Write paragraphs that are unified, complete, and coherent.
2. Identify seven different patterns of developing a paragraph.
3. Write paragraphs that are organized according to any of the seven organizational patterns.
4. Analyze paragraphs, identifying the topic sentence and the organizational pattern.

Short story writers and novelists utilize similar techniques in developing a narrative. Similarly, the planning and execution of paragraphs and longer compositions have much in common. For this reason, the paragraph has been referred to as a composition in miniature. Because of its brevity, the paragraph is an ideal subject for careful analysis. The techniques of careful paragraphing to be developed in this section apply to longer compositions as well.

PURPOSEFULNESS: A PLAN OF ATTACK

The principles of purposeful communication have already been detailed. Once your primary purpose is clear to you and you have tentatively selected your subject, you are ready to tackle the job of proper restriction. The brevity of most paragraphs makes adequate restriction particularly important. A subject not properly restricted invariably results in superficial writing. Having arrived at an adequately restricted subject, you should then formulate the main idea of your paragraph. Generally, this main idea is specifically stated in the paragraph; at times, however, it may be implied. The main idea of a paragraph is called the *topic sentence*. Here are some sample topic sentences:

1. Paperback textbooks are inexpensive and convenient.
2. A good dictionary is the most useful of all general reference books.
3. The phenomenal success of the instant 126 cartridge camera is due to its simplicity of operation.

UNITY: THE GUIDING LIGHT

We are often told that a topic sentence will assure unity in a paragraph. We are told that a topic sentence is the simple summary of ideas expressed in the paragraph, that it may come first, last, or at some convenient place within the paragraph or may be omitted entirely.

The beginning writer will find it wise to have a topic sentence in each paragraph, because unless she has fixed clearly in mind the central thought she wishes to develop, she may ramble off in different directions. She frequently begins her flight with uncertainty, pursues her course as if chasing a will-o'-the-wisp, and ends in a bog of confusion.

In the following paragraph, notice how the writer rambles from point to point. He apparently meant his first sentence to be his topic sentence, but it did not keep him developing in a steady line. As a result, he did not stress one central thought throughout the paragraph.

The Battle of Bunker Hill showed that the Colonists were brave men. They fearlessly stood their ground as the Redcoats charged up the hill. Bunker Hill is in Charlestown, Massachusetts, near Boston. Nearby is Breed's Hill, which was part of the same battle. Bunker Hill is famous as one of the first major battles of the American Revolution. Paul Revere made his brave ride a couple of months before the battle. The Colonists were under General Prescott. It was Prescott who said, "Don't fire until you see the whites of their eyes!" His men waited until the English soldiers under General Howe were right in front of them and then fired point blank. Their deadly volleys broke the advancing ranks of the Redcoats three times. The battle took place on June 17, 1775. General Gage was in command of the English, and he learned that the Americans meant to defend their principles. The Redcoats finally took the hill. The battle was the real start of the Revolutionary War. The war came to an end when Cornwallis surrendered at Yorktown on October 19, 1781.

The topic sentence of the above paragraph seems to have suggested to the student a number of ideas associated with the Revolutionary War. He talks about Bunker Hill, Cornwallis, the surrender at Yorktown, brave men, the battle, the principles of the Colonists, General Gage, and other things. He fails to realize that he should discuss only one idea in the paragraph, and he does not even recognize the one idea that the topic sentence, as he has worded it, seems to stress. What he should have developed was the idea "brave men" in terms of "the battle of Bunker Hill." The paragraph as written has good details, but since it lacks unity, it fails to be clearly developed.

Until we learn how to start with a definite idea and stick to it as we develop a thought, we should not ignore the only signpost that can give direction to our journey. Until we become experienced, we should include a topic sentence in the paragraph.

What, then, is a good topic sentence? It is a sentence that contains the topic or idea that the paragraph is to develop. Emphasis must be placed upon the words "topic" or "idea," for the paragraph will usually be about the "idea." In the topic sentence, "The Battle of Bunker Hill showed that the Colonists were brave men," the important idea is "brave men." The paragraph should be about that one idea. The rest of the topic sentence tells under what circumstance the men were brave, but the idea "brave men" was the writer's chief concern.

Such a topic sentence is rather general. The idea "brave men" permits the writer to use whatever details, illustrations, and reasons he believes will support his point. Sometimes, however, it may be well to word the topic sentence so that the basic idea is more limited. Instead of only "brave men," it may say "brave men despite every disadvantage." The paragraph will still be about the "brave men" at Bunker Hill, but the writer's chief concern now is to tell about the men who were brave "despite every disadvantage." Compare the original Bunker Hill paragraph with the following:

The Battle of Bunker Hill showed that the Colonists were brave men despite every disadvantage. Against superior numbers of Redcoats they held their ground on the heights. Against superior training they pitted their impromptu drills and primitive tactics. Against a seasoned officer like General Howe, they confidently backed their less experienced but courageous General Prescott. The colonial minutemen were limited in numbers and were poorly supplied with ammunition and provisions; the Redcoats were but a small part of the whole English army in and around Boston and could depend upon extensive reinforcement and adequate supplies.

All the material in this paragraph supports "brave men despite every disadvantage." The writer kept this idea clearly in mind and excluded from the paragraph everything that did not develop it. His paragraph, therefore, has unity.

We have just seen how an expression like "brave men" or a phrase like "despite every disadvantage" can be the basic idea of a topic sentence. Sometimes you may find that a whole clause is needed to express your basic idea; for instance, "The Battle of Bunker Hill showed that the Colonists were bravest when the odds were most against them." A paragraph developing this topic sentence would try to show that the Colonists were brave men during battle, especially "when the odds were most against them."

In writing a topic sentence, then, we should be sure that it contains a definite word, phrase, or clause that points out the chief idea of the paragraph. Sometimes the first written form of a topic sentence needs to be revised so that its chief idea is actually included or is given a place of greater prominence.

The difference between a topic sentence that contains a topic idea and one that does not is like the difference between a highway that is clearly marked and one that is not. Like the traveler, the writer (and the reader) needs a guide. Let us call this guide the *controlling idea.*

The controlling idea is the basic or topic idea which we have been discussing. There is a difference between a topic sentence as used by many students and a topic sentence containing a definite controlling idea. For a paragraph of average length, say about 150 words, many beginning writers would be satisfied with the following topic sentence:

Napoleon was one of the greatest generals in history.

With this as a topic sentence, they might proceed to discuss everything they could think of to explain the whole statement. They might tell how Napoleon led his men through several victorious campaigns, including the Battle of Austerlitz; how he was finally defeated at Waterloo and was banished to Elba; how he remained a heroic figure in the minds of his followers and of succeeding generations. They might even include examples of children in recent times who chose to be "Napoleon" while playing war.

What would such material, such a rambling discussion, actually make clear? What central idea could the reader get? True, all the statements would in some way be related to Napoleon, but really, what is the point behind them? When one is through reading them, what does one know of Napoleon as a general or a defeated leader, or an outcast, or an idol? Like the various foods in a supermarket, everything seems related, but there is no single purpose behind the selection, nothing like a specific picnic that prompts the choice of special foods. Suppose, on the other hand, a student had worded the topic sentence:

Napoleon proved to be a great strategist in the Battle of Austerlitz.

Such a topic sentence would limit what might be said about Napoleon to his abilities as a strategist alone. Furthermore, it would force the student to fix his or her attention upon "strategist" in terms of the "Battle of Austerlitz." Under such control, "strategist" in terms of the specific battle becomes the controlling idea of the paragraph. Finally, it is a far more suitable topic idea for a paragraph of some 150 words.

As we have seen, the controlling idea may be stated in a single word, a phrase, or a clause, depending upon what is needed to express the basic idea of the paragraph. It is the core of thought that is to be explained. Furthermore, the language expressing it is the guide to direct our thinking, the sign by which we choose this and that material from all the material available to us. In summary, *the controlling idea is stated in the word, phrase, or clause that announces the central idea that is to be explained in a particular paragraph.*

COMPLETENESS: WHAT DIDN'T YOU SAY?

Have your papers ever been returned with such comments as "support your judgments" or "further development needed"? Failure to support and develop your ideas adequately is an all too common characteristic of student writing. There are two main causes of inadequate development:

1. The writer *assumes* that his or her readers have knowledge about the subject that they do not, in fact, actually possess.
2. The writer *intends* to provide a more complete explanation, but because of laziness or the inability to support judgments, fails to do so.

During the planning, execution, and proofreading of your writing, consider your readers and provide them with sufficient information to receive your message. Whether you are relating an incident from personal experience or dealing with a subject you have researched, it is incumbent upon you, as the expert, to supply sufficient details. If you must err, it is better to provide too much detail rather than too little.

See Chapter 6 for a detailed treatment of the five major supporting devices: Examples, Statistics, Testimony, Comparison Contrast, and Explanation. It would also be desirable to review President Kennedy's televised speech concerning the Cuban Crisis for an analysis of how these supporting devices are incorporated into a finished manuscript. The preceding pages contain examples of student writing which illustrate adequate generalization—support development.

Depending upon your approach to your subject, you might decide to use a combination of supporting devices or only one extended example. The quality of a communication cannot be judged by the number of supports used. One well-developed example of a heavy smoker who developed lung cancer because of his habit might be far more effective than a series of statistics and explanations.

EXERCISE

The following paragraphs are incomplete. Indicate why. Revise either, supplying additional supporting details for the topic sentence in order to achieve completeness.

1. After attending college for two semesters, I finally have discovered the way I can best earn good grades. Besides taking good notes in class, keeping good attendance, and doing assignments promptly, I have learned a good method to study for exams. I still have much to learn about good study habits, but now higher grades come much easier for me.

2. Regular reading of *Ms. Magazine* is a must for every career woman of the '80s. It is one of the finest magazines for and about women on the American newsstands today. If you have not seen it, you should go out and buy a copy now.

COHERENCE: KEEPING IT ALL TOGETHER

Effective paragraphs must be coherent; that is, all of the sentences must "stick together." After all, they form a unit of expression—the paragraph—and therefore must be related to each other as parts of a whole. Each sentence must carry the reader to the next for smooth reading. A paragraph that is coherent is one with transitions, or links, between every sentence. A number of useful devices can aid a beginning writer in providing these links from sentence to sentence in a paragraph.

1. Use transitional words and phrases.
   Again, also, and, besides, furthermore, in addition, likewise, similarly, at the same time, but, conversely, however, in contrast, in spite of, nevertheless, on the other hand, yet, therefore
2. Use enumerative devices.
   A good student must have three essential skills. *First,* she must take excellent notes; *second,* she must be a good reader; *third,* she must be able to take exams well.

3. Use parallel structures in successive sentences.
   When you are loaded, *your friends* love you. *When you are* broke, *your friends* avoid you. *When you are* collecting debts, *your friends* don't know you.

4. Use a pronoun to refer to a word in the previous sentence.
   Joann knew she deserved a D in Communication Skills. What she did mind, however, was taking *it* all over again with the same instructor.

5. Repeat some key word from one sentence in the following sentence. For example, the direct object of the first sentence may be used as the subject of the second.
   Leonard did not want to admit his *drug addiction* to his wife. *Drug addiction* was not something he was proud of, but he was still unwilling to hurt his family with the truth.

6. Use the same subject in the successive sentences, employing identical words, synonyms, or pronouns.
   Alcoholism is not a crime. *Alcoholism* is a sickness.

EXERCISE

In the following paragraph, identify the devices used to achieve coherence.

Although the bodies of our cameras do the same job, the similarities end there. My parents' Instamatic camera is large and made of plastic. It's not all that rugged, and a good jar would leave it cracked or damaged. My camera, on the other hand, is small and compact. Its all-metal design makes it a strong, dependable piece of equipment. It also houses a film buffer assembly that holds the film on which the image is to be formed perfectly flat. The Instamatic has no such buffer; therefore, the image produced is not as sharp.

Since paragraphs are also part of a larger whole (the essay), they must also be linked together to show their relationship. The following suggestions will help us provide transition between paragraphs to attain a coherent essay.

1. Conclude a paragraph with a sentence that introduces the next phase of the action.
   Example: A week later, the students decided to take action and occupy an office in the "O" Building.

2. Use a connective or a transitional word or phrase in the first sentence of a paragraph: *furthermore, therefore, as a result, in addition, on the contrary*.

3. Begin a paragraph with a sentence that refers clearly to a statement at the end of the preceding paragraph or its topic idea.

Example: Many high schools, then, are not giving the students adequate preparation for college-level writing. Should this be ignored by the colleges, or accepted as a real challenge?
(The first sentence summarizes the idea of the preceding paragraph. The second sentence introduces the controlling idea of the paragraph.)

ORGANIZATION: SEQUENCE OF IDEAS

Unity, completeness, and coherence are further aided by a logical plan of development suited to the material. Each paragraph has its own order or sequence of ideas. An essay may take advantage of several types of paragraph orders to achieve variety. The examples of organization given below are taken from student writings.

General-to-Specific Organization

Effective communication involves adequate generalization—support development. When the topic sentence stating the generalization or main idea appears at the beginning of the paragraph and the supporting details follow the topic sentence, a general to specific organizational pattern is employed.

Of the four basic organizational patterns, the general to specific is by far the most popular. Why? If you begin with your topic sentence and remain conscious of your main idea as you develop and support it, it is almost impossible to stray from your purpose.

Main Idea

Supporting Details

Although at first glance a final exam appears to be nothing more than a series of sloppily mimeographed, vaguely worded questions, *it is really a conspiracy aimed at students everywhere.* It is a third degree with no safeguard against self-incrimination, a mismatch with no time out between rounds, a sentence to solitary confinement without bread or water, and a parachute jump without a parachute. While purporting to test a student's knowledge of subject matter, the final exam measures, instead, his ability to withstand the ill effects of poor ventilation and bad circulation in an overcrowded classroom. It forces the student to sit between a rhythmic sniffer and a compulsive cougher while being serenaded from behind by a nervous throat-clearer and carefully watched by a sadistic proctor. Temporary relief is just around the corner, but the establishment figure in charge views with suspicion the student who attempts to relieve the tension through the only avenue left open: a brief, but glorious visit to the john.

Main Idea   *Loving someone for a long period of time is like breaking in a new pair of denim jeans.* At first they are scratchy and stiff, constricting your movements, making you constantly aware of their presence. Very gradually they begin to loosen up; the color changes from intense navy to pale blue, more easy to live with; the material molds to your contour, becoming almost like a **Supporting** second skin. As you continue to wear them, they be-**Details** come inextricably linked to your experiences. You have spilled coffee on them, cried on them, and spit up on them. You have sat in them, crawled in them, and slept in them. Soon they are so much a part of you that you take them for granted, almost forgetting they exist. So, you have a brief fling with your designer jeans and feel flashy and attractive. But you always go back to the comfort and security of your blue jeans. You've spent too much of your life with that piece of denim to toss it away.

Specific-to-General Organization

At times you might attempt to achieve a specific stylistic effect by beginning your paragraph with a series of details which lead up to your generalization. When the main idea or topic sentence is withheld until the end of the paragraph, a specific-to-general organizational pattern is utilized.

Supporting Do you often take in a movie or watch television when you should be doing assigned reading? Do you **Supporting** enjoy having bull sessions with your friends into the **Details** early hours of the morning when you should be getting your rest? Would you rather tackle a ski slope on a winter afternoon than crack a novel assigned by your English instructor? Do you prefer a burger, fries, and a Coke to a well-balanced meal? Are you more interested in campus social life than you are in the pursuit of knowledge? Do you view a college degree as a passport to the good life? Have you puffed on an oc-**Main Idea** casional joint and given some thought to the hard stuff? Are you frequently bored and occasionally stimulated by class lectures? If so, cheer up; *like thousands before you, you're college material.*

One night in a fit of idiocy I counted the number of times I have moved. It came to twenty-one times in the twenty-three years that I have been on this earth! This,

Supporting Details   of course, does not include vacations and trips, of which there have been many. If I were to count all of the hours spent in preparation for travel, hours spent using some mode of transportation and hours spent readjusting to new surroundings, I am afraid I might become more than a little hysterical. It is best left untotalled and uncounted. Let us just say that I never want to move again, but I know I will. *I am very tired of it all; I have moved too much.*

Main Idea

Chronological Organization

When you employ a chronological pattern of development, you relate a series of incidents according to the order in which these events actually occurred. Narration and exposition are the two forms of discourse most frequently organized chronologically.

Narration   Just before sunrise I awoke, quietly dressed, shook Mike, my son, and went outside to start the coffee. A few minutes later Mike came bounding out of the tent raring to go. We had decided the night before to get some fishing in before breakfast. After shoving off we maneuvered our raft into the deep water. Mike got a bite almost as soon as his bait struck water. Seconds later, the tip of my pole went down under the weight of a catch at the end of my line. When I reeled in the line and started to pry the hook from the walleye's mouth, Mike started to laugh. As I looked up I noticed that we had drifted back to shore. The gentle breeze had carried our anchorless raft halfway across the lake. Mike baited my hook, as I paddled back to the deep water.

Our morning was busily occupied by the activities of catching fish, rebaiting, and paddling back to the deep water. After this cycle had been repeated many times, I noticed my wife waving us in to shore. As we headed for land, Mike and I held up our stringers of fish and Mike proudly hollered, "This should make a delicious breakfast." "Breakfast," my wife exclaimed; "it's time for lunch!"

Narration   The first move that I can remember took place when I was four years old. We moved by streetcar from one Chicago neighborhood to another. I don't remember caring much one way or another about the moving, but I was thrilled by the streetcar ride. I bounced gaily from seat to seat, gazed out of the windows, and tried to see everything. There were to be many moves following that one. Each one was both exciting and heartbreaking, but perhaps the most poignant was the last move we made as a family. We left the first real home we ever had to the wreckers who tore it down to make a larger football field for Marquette High School. A young woman drove her own car away from that house, and unlike the little girl on the streetcar, she did not gaze out the window, but stared straight ahead and tried very hard not to cry.

Exposition   *The phenomenal success of the instant loading 126 cartridge camera is largely due to its simplicity of operation.* First swing the back open and insert the cartridge into the camera. Then close the camera and advance the lever clockwise, repeatedly, until it locks. You are now ready for your first exposure. Compose your picture carefully, using either a horizontal or vertical format, whichever better suits your subject. Then squeeze the shutter release, taking care not to jerk the camera. Continue to advance the lever, compose carefully, and avoid excessive camera movement for your remaining exposures. Provided your lighting is adequate, a series of pleasing snapshots will be your reward.

Spatial Organization

An organizational pattern is spatial when the progression of details is arranged according to some logical arrangement in space. Placing gravel, plants, and ornaments in your new aquarium, arranging an attractive floral display, and describing a place with which you are familiar are subjects that would lend themselves to this pattern of development.

Main Idea   Tucked away on the north east corner of our unpretentious second story flat, *my 10' × 12' room houses all my possessions, treasured and otherwise.* As I enter the room my maple bed, placed adjacent to the north wall, is immediately evident. My matching nightstand, to the left of my pillow, supports my clock radio, a recent birthday gift, and a hand-me-down lamp with a battered pirate ship for its base. The remainder of the west wall surrounds the only window in the room, my window on the outside world. There I sometimes sit for hours watching the early morning traffic entering the city or the late afternoon traffic returning to suburbia, **Supporting Details** thinking thoughts, dreaming dreams of life styles so very different from my own. Beneath the window sits my desk, antiqued blue years ago by my father. The cigarette burns and chipped corners are usually hidden from view by the ever present textbooks and clutter of papers. Opposite the window my mirror-topped dresser is placed in the middle of the east wall, surrounded by the sports banners and autographed pictures of my youth. My black wrought iron bookcase, covering the two feet of wall space between the door and the closet of the south wall, is crammed with the paperbacks, magazines, and records that enable me to escape, if only temporarily, my commonplace surroundings.

Order-of-Importance Organization

News stories appearing in our local newspapers are generally organized by order of importance. Reporters know that when stories are cut, they are likely to be cut from the bottom up; therefore, it is important that the really significant information appear in the earlier paragraphs.

News stories are not, however, the only communications that are suited to order-of-importance organization. For a variety of informative and persuasive situations, you may find it advantageous to lead off with the most important evidence or argument, followed by others in descending order of importance. In the following example, the student lists reasons why he believes he should be exempt from the introductory courses in communication skills. Reason one, he surmises, might be sufficient to produce the desired result. However, since he has two other arguments, almost equally compelling, why not list all three in order of importance? The combined effect, he reasons, should enhance his chances of persuading the Dean to grant his request.

Dear Dean _____:

In support of my request for exemption from English 151 and 152, I offer the following reasons for your consideration:

1. I have completed two semesters of Freshman English and one semester of Introduction to Speech at State University with grades of "B" in all three courses. A copy of my official transcript is attached.

2. For the past two summers I worked for radio station WMTC editing news and filling in for announcers on vacation. Mr. Roger Stone, Station Manager, will be happy

to verify my competence in written and oral communication.

3. Should my request be granted, I intend to enroll in Technical Report Writing, a course which should be of great help to me since I plan to obtain a two-year degree in Photo Instrumentation Technology.

Sincerely yours,

_____

Pro-Con Organization

The pro-con pattern can be a very effective method of organizing persuasive communication. When you are for or against a proposal or when two or more alternative solutions to a problem are being considered, lead off with the arguments or solutions of your adversaries. If these arguments contain some advantages, summarize them honestly. Intentional distortion is unethical. Furthermore, such distortion weakens your credibility, particularly with a knowledgeable reading or listening audience. Conclude by pointing out weaknesses in opposing arguments and summarizing your position, presumably the best solution to the question under consideration. Think of the pro-con pattern as a method of "setting up" your opponent by summarizing his position first, then "knocking him down" with the weight of your point of view.

Proponents of the proposal to restrict our suburban high school's enrollment to children who reside in our district claim that their plan will save taxpayer dollars and maintain quality education. "Why," they argue, "should those of us who moved to the suburbs to insure better schools for our children subsidize those who remain behind?" They also point out that the overcrowded classrooms that could result will harm all children, suburban and city.

Should the open enrollment plan be adopted, the increased cost to suburban taxpayers would be minimal, only 75 cents per $1000 of assessed valuation. In return for this slight expenditure, we would provide increased educational opportunities for minority students who live in the city. In addition, we would give our children the opportunity to mingle with and befriend other children of varied backgrounds and life styles. Our children will become the new culturally disadvantaged if we restrict their contacts to their suburban counterparts.

The open enrollment plan I support has a built-in safeguard: out-of-district student enrollments would be limited to 40 students each year. Since our high school is operating at only 70 percent of capacity, the "overcrowded classroom" argument is merely a smokescreen aimed at keeping our schools racially segregated.

I urge all of you—for the sake of our cities, ourselves, and our children—to support the open enrollment plan.

Question-to-Answer and Effect-to-Cause Organization

Still another method of organizing your paragraphs involves answering a question asked at or near the beginning of your paragraph or stating an effect and then indicating its cause. The question-to-answer or effect-to-cause pattern is particularly suited to expository or persuasive communication. Notice how, in the following paragraph, the "fib" about the "funny-looking church" (effect) is clarified for the reader through effect-to-cause development:

Effect What happened in the "funny-looking church" with the hard benches, dark walls, and the stained glass windows, brought many changes to my life. It wasn't a church at all you see; it was a court room. It took many years to figure out why my **Cause** first mom and dad told a fib about the church. They weren't in the habit of lying to me; it just wasn't their way. Perhaps they were, in a sense, lying to themselves because they didn't want to believe what was happening. I had been theirs since I was ten days old and now four years later this was all to change. Calling it a church hadn't helped at all; the man in the long black robe just didn't see things their way. The woman who had given birth to me had not signed the papers, so their four years did not count for anything in this court of law.

The foregoing discussion is not intended to be inclusive of all patterns of development. As you become more proficient in your organizational ability, you may elect to vary some of the patterns. In general-to-specific organization, for example, you might restate your topic sentence at the conclusion of your paragraph. Or you might modify or qualify your initial statement with new insights. The patterns summarized above are guidelines for developing organizational skills, not gospel to be rigidly followed.

EXERCISES

Study the following essay. Identify the pattern of development employed in each of the paragraphs.

Why do I question my God and my religion? Why do I demand answers to a multitude of questions which plague my mind about my religion in my life? Perhaps it is my search for a convenient and unfailing crutch. Perhaps this crutch is the insecurity of the life I lead and the responsibilities I face. I often feel a strong and demanding desire to define all the reasons for my existence, my religion, and my purpose in this frustrating world.

I begin by asking myself why I practice the religion of my parents. I wonder what choice I had as an infant being baptized to decide my own faith. Upon reaching seven years old, I was promptly enrolled in a parochial school. Eight years of religion in this grade school were followed by four more years in a parochial high school. Parochial schools can give a very precise and unyielding point of view concerning God and religion. After leaving school, I first began to really evaluate and examine my religion.

And today, I have difficulty discussing my evaluations and thoughts with members of my own family. My father cannot seem to understand why his youngest son has turned into a heretic. My mother refuses to believe I could sustain any doubts about my religion and casts off my questions as typical of a "growing" stage. And of course my older brothers and sisters can't begin to answer my questions, so they turn their backs to me as if I've fallen victim to some sort of disease.

All this seems very amusing, I suppose, but consider my own feelings on Sunday mornings as I walk through the glass doors of my church. The light is very dim inside this house of God as I walk down the long center aisle towards the huge marble altar in the front of the church. The high walls on each side of me hold stained glass windows in the forms of saints and angels. The carved statues high on their pedestals along these walls seem to bow their heads in shame as I walk by. And most of all, the figure on the large wooden crucifix high above my head refuses to give me the answers I need, to feel as though I, too, belong in this church—this religion.

PARAGRAPH ANALYSES

Paragraph A

It is 6 a.m. of a winter Sunday in Putney, a crossroads town in southern Vermont. There is a foot of new snow, but lights go on in the houses as families arise and start to pack picnic lunches. Minutes later the lights go off, doors open and laughter fills the crimson dawn. Toddlers, kids and adults snap onto narrow touring skis and, bodies bent and arms swinging, glide off through the fields. As the sun rises and twinkles on icy peaks, more people join the parade. Children call to each other as they disappear into the silent forest, their voices muted by the powdery snow.

Excerpt from "The Magic of Ski Touring," by Jean George, *The Reader's Digest*, February 1972. Copyright © 1972 by the Reader's Digest Assn., Inc.

Analysis

1. Which organizational pattern is employed?
2. Locate a simple sentence, a compound sentence, and a complex sentence.
3. Locate a parallel sentence.

4. Show how two of the sentences in the paragraph illustrate the principle of modification.

5. Is the paragraph effective? Explain your answer.

Exercise: **Describe a seasonal scene, organizing your paragraph chronologically.**

Paragraph B

Frequently, some belligerent, anti-law enforcement elements of our society refer to police officers as "pigs." Obnoxious four-letter words are shouted at policemen, and the familiar chant, "Off the Pigs," meaning "Kill the Police," is a prominent cry wherever these groups assemble. Further, cartoons and publications depicting police officers as pigs are common fare, even for children. The ridiculous statement, "The only good pig is a dead pig," is a slogan of violent protesters. Such deplorable epithets can be gratifying only to little minds.

By J. Edgar Hoover. Reprinted with permission of the FBI Law Enforcement Bulletin.

Analysis

1. Identify the topic sentence and the organizational pattern.

2. Hoover describes policemen as "officers," a term having favorable connotation, while bemoaning the fact that certain elements in society refer to them as "pigs." Complete the following table, supplying favorable and unfavorable terms for the neutral words given:

Favorable	Neutral	Unfavorable
Officer	Policeman	Pig
_____	Teacher	_____
_____	Lawyer	_____
_____	Housewife	_____
_____	Student militant	_____
_____	Salesman	_____
_____	Politician	_____

3. How do connotative words reveal the attitudes and values of the communicator?

Exercise: **Write a paragraph giving your point of view about a word having a strong connotation, either favorable or unfavorable. Use either a general-to-specific or specific-to-general organizational pattern.**

Paragraph C

Fashions in what society considers proper fluctuate wildly. A number of words Chaucer used in the *The Canterbury Tales,* one of the great masterpieces of the language, couldn't possibly be printed today in a book like this one, and though they have only very recently again been permissible in contemporary fiction, they have also helped set off controversy about the "degeneracy" of the modern novel. In contrast, our Victorian forbears were "proper" in public to a degree that seems fantastic to us today. "Legs" were unmentionable, for instance. The decent word for them, especially on ladies, was "limbs," but it was no doubt preferable not to have to mention them at all. It was during this era that the "breast" of chicken became "white meat," to avoid any unpleasant suggestivity in mixed company. At about the turn of the century Owen Wister wrote a story entitled "Skip to My Loo," set in Texas, in which much is made of the disapprobation of the local people for names like "boar," "stallion," "rooster," and "bull," euphemisms being employed in their stead. I myself have heard an old-timer refer to a bull as a "he cow." (Incidentally, dancing was frowned on as quite sinful by the people in this story, though they enjoyed a game set to music, remarkably like dancing, which was called Skip to My Loo, and hence the name of the story.) I remember that during my boyhood something of this attitude lingered on in the more primitive backwaters of the West, where I was raised, and I was punished once for using the word "belly" and again for calling my younger brother a "liar." In this latter instance it wasn't my attitude toward my brother that was considered wrong—calling him a "storyteller" would have been all right—but the coarse, bald, ugly word "liar" itself.

Ray Past, *Language as a Lively Art* (Dubuque: Wm. C. Brown Co., 1970), p. 274.

Analysis

1. Identify the topic sentence and the organizational pattern.
2. Identify and illustrate the methods of support.
3. Explain the "controversy about the 'degeneracy' of the modern novel" referred to in the paragraph. Does this controversy extend into other art forms?
4. What is a euphemism? Give at least three examples not found in the paragraph.
5. How does the author's point about euphemisms relate to the preceding Hoover paragraph?
6. Give three examples (other than those mentioned in the paragraph) of words that have graduated to positions of respectability.

Exercise: **In a paragraph relate an experience, preferably personal, involving the changing nature of the English language. Employ whatever organizational pattern you deem appropriate.**

Paragraph D

Contrary to the widespread notion that people go through a divorce with a minimum of psychic disturbance, divorce is generally an emotionally, psychologically, and socially traumatic experience, which leaves its marks and scars on the personalities involved. To begin with, many individuals experience a sense of personal rejection, which is painful. Even when there is mutual agreement that the divorce is necessary, each may feel that he was not wanted or desired by the other. Furthermore, there may be a profound feeling of having failed in a personal sense. It is as though the couple "should have made it work" in spite of any obstacles in their path. The extent to which one is disturbed by a divorce is frequently increased when one member of the former marriage decides to remarry. For the remaining individual the remarriage of his former spouse may prove to be rather traumatic. This is particularly so when one member of the relationship continued to hope, as many do, that somehow even after the divorce "they would get back together." Sometimes these people become martyrs, waiting for the mate to return. In other instances they may desperately plunge into a new relationship prematurely in order to prove that they are still lovable and desirable.

Herman R. Lantz and Eloise C. Snyder, *Marriage: An Examination of the Man-Woman Relationship* (New York: John Wiley & Sons, Inc., 1962), p. 410.

Analysis

1. Identify the topic sentence and the organizational pattern.
2. Identify the principal method of support. Are any other supporting devices employed?
3. Do you agree that a "widespread notion that people go through divorce with a minimum of psychic disturbance" really exists? Discuss.
4. Define in context: *psychic, traumatic, martyr.*
5. Discuss the effectiveness of the foregoing paragraph.

Exercise: **Take issue with a commonly held belief, employing a general-to-specific organizational pattern.**

Paragraph E

In a troubled corner of the country, something vaguely subterranean is welling up. It seems, at once, an apprehension of the final catastrophe or the huge breathing of a vast organism, or perhaps the anonymous mobility of some mute ghost that yearns to make itself known. The American South—a land of labored fables, shared glories, soil, blood, brassy vanity and souls spun tight together in patterns of tradition—remains an intricate, fugal overlay of clashing passions: gentility and violence, humanism and hatreds, beliefs and brutalities, obscurities, incongruities, cadenzas of humor, Sweet Jesus and unknowable madness. Add to this an infinitude of traumas and small transformations, multiply by 38 million whites, 11 million blacks plus every possible variable of the past, the present, the climate and the terrain, and you extract today a place where nothing whatever is the same. Yet you draw from this, too, a people who in being forced to find pragmatic new realities of their own, may well forge prophetic insights into the very root of all human hearts.

With permission of Cowles Communications, Inc.

Analysis

1. Identify the topic sentence and organizational pattern.

2. As what part of speech is *welling* used in the first sentence? The word *well* is an excellent example of *functional shift,* meaning that a word shifts its function or part of speech in different contexts. With the help of your dictionary, indicate how *well* can be used as five different parts of speech. Then illustrate each use in a separate sentence.

3. Define in context: *subterranean, mute, fugal, humanism, incongruity, cadenza, pragmatic, prophetic.*

4. Identify and illustrate the methods of support.

5. State the purpose of the paragraph.

Exercise: **In a paragraph, give your impression of a place with which you are thoroughly familiar: a neighborhood, a favorite hangout, a vacation retreat, a school, a place of employment. As in the foregoing example, provide your readers with insights into the people who occupy the place you describe.**

CHAPTER 10

The Opinion Essay

OBJECTIVES

After studying this chapter, you should be able to:
1. Write an effective thesis statement.
2. Choose major points that will prove the thesis.
3. Write body paragraphs to develop each major point.
4. Write an introductory paragraph.
5. Write a concluding paragraph.
6. Select an appropriate title.

THE OPINION ESSAY

In an opinion essay, the writer presents an opinion and supports it with whatever material he or she feels is necessary to get the reader to understand or agree with it. Therefore, an opinion essay is a composition whose general purpose is to persuade.

In the preceding chapter, we referred to the paragraph as a composition in miniature. As you recall, the paragraph develops a main or controlling idea which is usually stated in a topic sentence. Like the paragraph, the essay also develops a controlling idea. This idea is stated in a sentence called the *thesis statement*. Here are some sample thesis statements:

1. Being a single parent is difficult.
2. This nation owes a debt of gratitude to black Americans.
3. Jogging is the ideal exercise.

As the three examples show, a thesis statement expresses the writer's opinion. This opinion is expressed in a one-sentence statement around which the entire essay is developed.

An essay is nonfictional and fairly brief, generally between 400–1200 words. It is divided into three parts: the introduction, the body and the conclusion. While the number of paragraphs in the body may vary depending on the scope of the essay, both the introduction and conclusion should be at least one paragraph long. Here is a sample student essay written on the thesis: Being a single parent is difficult.

Tough Sledding

A little over two years ago, my husband, Bill, walked into our bedroom at three o'clock in the morning and announced that he was leaving me and the children. "Don't blame yourself," he said. "It's not your fault. I'm just not the type who likes to be tied down." Then he picked up his suitcase and left. I haven't heard from him since. I have learned a lot since then. I've learned who my friends are. I've learned how depressing nights can be. But most of all, *I've learned being a single parent is difficult.*

Perhaps the hardest part is *that there is never enough money to pay the bills.* When Bill left us, he took what little money we had saved. By the time I filed for welfare and received the first check, we were already a month behind with the rent, and I owed my sister and her husband $200. Up until then, we had just managed to save a little on Bill's $400-a-week take-home pay. Now, I found myself having to make do on a welfare check that averaged $145 a week. No matter how carefully I shopped and budgeted, I seldom had enough money to last until the next check. Fortunately, we were able to move into a smaller, less expensive apartment, and now I just squeeze by.

Decide on Major Points

If you have chosen your subject wisely, it is one with which you are already familiar. This should make it possible for you to come up with several major points to clarify or reinforce your thesis. After all, the thesis is your opinion about something. There are, no doubt, a number of reasons that led you to form that opinion. What are they? When looking for major points to prove your thesis, ask yourself:

> How did I arrive at this opinion?
>
> What makes my thesis statement valid?
>
> What can I say to convince someone to agree with me?

Keep in mind during this stage, that it is the thesis statement that should determine which major points you select.

The number of supporting ideas you need to prove your thesis is up to you. For instance, while a 600 word theme might have three major points to prove its thesis, yours might be adequately supported by two or require as many as four.

Write Your Major Points as Topic Sentences

Since the major points will become the topic sentences for your paragraphs, they should be written out as complete sentences. Each should be stated clearly and emphatically so there is no doubt in the mind of your reader as to what your message is and what you are trying to accomplish. Here are some specific suggestions for developing major points for your essay:

1. They should be written as complete sentences.
2. They should cover your subject adequately.
3. They should reinforce your thesis statement.
4. They should be parallel both in importance and phrasing.

They should be written as complete sentences.

Writing your major points as sentences will enable you to carefully examine them so that you will be sure they relate to your main idea and accomplish your purpose. Then, when you write them down under your thesis statement in a brief outline, you will form a pattern that will help you determine whether your ideas are clear.

They should cover the subject adequately.

If your major points fail to cover the important aspects of your subject, you will leave your reader with too little information. It is important that you develop your subject fully enough to achieve the purpose of your essay.

They should reinforce the main idea.

The term "reinforce" means to strengthen. The thesis of your essay must be strengthened by major points which make it clearer and more forceful. These major points will, in turn, be strengthened by examples, statistics, explanation, testimony, and comparison.

They should be parallel both in importance and phrasing.

Although each of your supporting statements must be subordinate to the thesis of your essay, they should be coordinate with each other. This means they should be of equal importance. Supporting your thesis with two good points and one poor one could defeat your purpose.

It is also a good idea to word supporting ideas similarly, thereby emphasizing the fact that they are coordinate. One effective way of achieving parallelism of major points is to repeat key words.

Arrange the Thesis Statement and Topic Sentences in Outline Form

Below, in outline form, are some major points written as topic sentences supporting various theses. Note that they are written as complete sentences, cover the subject adequately, reinforce the main idea, and are parallel in importance and phrasing.

1. Thesis statement: This nation owes a debt of gratitude to black Americans.

   Topic sentence: Throughout our history, black men and women have contributed significantly to the growth and improvement of the United States.

   Topic sentence: Today's black leaders have done much to improve both the government and quality of life in our country.

2. Thesis statement: Swimming is beneficial to your health.

   Topic sentence: It conditions both mind and body.

   Topic sentence: It exercises most of your muscles.

   Topic sentence: It increases the capacity of your lungs.

3. Thesis statement: The art museum is an excellent place to visit.

   Topic sentence: There are fascinating traditional paintings on the first floor.

Topic sentence:	The second floor is replete with sculpture from classical to the modern.
Topic sentence:	The third floor houses an unbelievable collection of modern art.

4. Thesis statement: Iguanas make great pets.
   Topic sentence: They are clean.
   Topic sentence: They are inexpensive.
   Topic sentence: They are easy to care for.

5. Thesis statement: We should have a policy of open enrollment in our schools.
   Topic sentence: Some say open enrollment will result in overcrowding.
   Topic sentence: Some say open enrollment will result in higher costs.
   Topic sentence: The proposed plan will neither result in overcrowding nor cost more to implement.

6. Thesis statement: Our school should provide low-cost, adequate parking for students.
   Topic sentence: Students pay high prices for parking in lots near our school.
   Topic sentence: Overparking on the streets by students has resulted in an excessive number of tickets.
   Topic sentence: There is adequate space on our campus that has not been made available for parking.

Choose Appropriate Supporting Material

An outline can be a useful guide. It allows you to begin to see the shape of your essay. It will give you a good idea as to whether you have or can gather enough supporting material to write the essay. Consider, for example, outline number four which has as its thesis: Iguanas make great pets. A person writing an essay on the Iguana lizard has probably owned one. When supporting the topic sentence, "Iguanas are easy to care for," he or she would probably simply list what is common knowledge to an Iguana owner: Iguanas live very contentedly in a 10- or 15-gallon aquarium with a few tree forms to climb. Keep them warm and give them plenty of water and they'll be happy. Feed your Iguana lettuce, celery leaves, bananas, berries, and other plant material.

An essay developed from outline two, on the other hand, might require some research. Testimony, statistics, explanation, comparison, or example could serve to clarify and reinforce the thesis: Swimming is beneficial to your health.

Decide on a Logical Plan of Development

After you have gathered your supporting material you can develop a more detailed outline of your essay or begin writing your body paragraphs. Each paragraph in the body should include a topic sentence stating one of your supporting ideas. A more detailed outline for thesis number one follows:

I.   This nation owes a debt of gratitude to black Americans.

    A.   Throughout our history, black men and women have contributed significantly to the growth and improvement of the United States.

        1.   Blacks have helped to both develop this nation and defend it.

        2.   Blacks have served illustriously in the field of medicine.

        3.   Black contributions to art, music, and literature have been impressive.

    B.   Today's black leaders have done much to improve both the government and quality of life in our country.

        1.   Black public officials have become a viable force on the political scene.

        2.   Black religious and moral leaders have acted as the conscience of America.

        3.   The list of black leaders in the field of sports and entertainment is long and impressive.

In this chapter, we have started each sample body paragraph with the topic sentence. Although this is not an inflexible rule, it makes the pattern of the essay clear to both the writer and the reader. The writer states his topic sentence at the outset and then proceeds to back it up with supporting details, and the reader is clear as to what the writer is attempting to prove. Very often, the material you use to clarify or reinforce your topic sentence will determine your organizational pattern! The organizational pattern in the paragraph below, for example, is chronological. This pattern is almost always used when writing about history.

Throughout our history, black men and women have contributed significantly to the growth and improvement of the United States. As early as 1619, European explorers of the New World, the first to reach the shores of North America, were accompanied by blacks. A black pioneer named Jean Baptiste Dusable founded the settlement of Chicago. Mathew Henson, another black, was with Robert Peary when he discovered the North Pole. Over 5,000 blacks served in the Continental Army during the American Revolution. In 1770, Crispus Attucks, a black man shot by the British in the Boston Massacre, became the first of many black Americans to die for the cause of freedom. The list of blacks who have served with valor in the defense of our nation is long and distinguished. Nearly a quarter of a million blacks served during the Civil War. Twenty of these received the nation's highest medal for heroism, the Congressional Medal of Honor.

When linking your paragraphs together use the transitional devices discussed in chapter 9. A paragraph immediately following the one above, for example, might begin this way:

Blacks have also served illustriously in the field of medicine. Dr. Daniel Hale Williams, the first doctor to perform open heart surgery, was black. One of the world's foremost authorities on blood plasma, ...

THE INTRODUCTORY PARAGRAPH

After you have finished writing all of the paragraphs that will comprise the body of your essay, you are ready to write the introductory paragraph. The introductory paragraph of an essay should capture the reader's attention, and, in most instances, state the "thesis" or main idea of the essay. One effective technique when writing this paragraph is to make your thesis statement the last sentence of your introduction, thereby providing a smooth transition to the first body paragraph.

In order to capture the interest of your reader, you might begin with an attention-getting technique. Listed below are eight suggestions for beginning an essay effectively. Each is followed by a model.

1.   Begin with an appropriate quotation.

"God helps those who help themselves," is an ageless and familiar piece of good advice. Our student government has been left with a problem that to some seems overwhelming: the reduction by one-half of the money we formerly received from student fees. But while this will create a great deal of work for us, the problem is solvable. We must engage in a fund-raising effort to make up the difference. Ten years ago, when we were faced with a similar situation we held a Bratfest to raise the money. *I propose that our student government plan and hold a two-day Bratwurst Festival during the month of October to raise money for the student government.*

2.   Begin with a rhetorical question.

Do you know how much it would cost you to make an important contribution to humanity? Let me tell you. The price of a drive-in movie for you and your date plus a snack afterwards would pay for a month's supply of food for a family of four in Bangladesh. One less night out on the town would buy from 50 to 100 feet of water pipe, and the cost of an Easter vacation in Florida would provide a complete water system for a drought-stricken village in West Africa. How is this possible? Through a tax deductible contribution to CARE. *CARE is the most effective and efficient charitable organization in the world.*

3. Open your introduction with examples.

In a Madison drugstore, three customers and the owner are pistol-whipped and then executed by a crazed gunman. Two days later in the same area, a 30-year-old man taking his family shopping is shot to death in front of his wife and children. On the university campus, two young coeds are raped repeatedly at gunpoint. What do these crimes have in common? They were all committed with the aid of a handgun. *This country must pass a law to make the sale or possession of a handgun illegal for anyone but law enforcers.*

4. Use statistics to start your introductory paragraph.

A divorce rate of over 35 percent makes marriage a bad risk. Although almost two-thirds of those who get married stay married, I am frightened by the climbing divorce rate. My parents have their disagreements but still get along. However, some of my friends who have gotten married regret it already. It would be less of a problem if my parents would accept my living together with my boyfriend, but they're just too old-fashioned. I wish there was some way a person could be sure about marriage. It seems like the right thing to do, but the odds keep getting worse.

5. Begin with a startling statement or idea.

If two pounds of plutonium were distributed evenly among the world's population, every person on earth would be contaminated with a lethal dosage. Yet if present trends continue, by the year 2000, the United States will be producing 1,700 tons of the substance. We learned from Three Mile Island that the possibilities for a catastrophe exist. *Unless we create a foolproof system of safeguards, this country's nuclear energy program might contaminate us all.*

6. Begin with a statement that is exactly the opposite of your thesis statement.

When I was a girl, the unwed mother was the exception to the rule. Perhaps it was because of the stigma attached to it. If a girl got pregnant, her family would whisk her away somewhere until the whole ordeal was over. When she came back, few of her friends would risk the embarrassment of being seen with her. Today, however, things are different. It is no longer uncommon to see a young girl going to high school or even junior high in a maternity dress. *The alarming number of teenage pregnancies is a national disgrace.*

7. Begin with an anecdote or brief story that leads into your thesis.

The young girl awakens in fright to see a man standing at the foot of her bed with a butcher knife in his hand. He is tall and burly with a pale, bulldog face disfigured by an ugly scar. His leering lips are open to expose yellow, rotting teeth. She screams as he lunges at her with the knife, slashing her unmercifully again and again. Her screams fade to moans which end in a bubbling sound as she draws her last breath. Now the scene changes to a TV commercial but not before the two young children who have been watching the drama have begun to cry. This scene and others like it are repeated over and over again on prime time television throughout this nation. *We must put a stop to violence on television during children's viewing time.*

8. Begin with a definition.

Dr. C. Henry Kempe of the University of Colorado Medical Center, a noted authority on child abuse, has defined the victim of child abuse as "any child who receives nonaccidental injury or injuries, as a result of acts or omissions on the part of his parents or guardians." Last year, in the United States, an estimated one million children were abused or neglected, and over two thousand of them died needlessly and painfully. While every state in this nation has a law which requires its citizens to report suspected cases of child abuse, in many, the penalties for abusing animals are more severe than those for abusing children. Therefore, *the United States should enact a federal law which requires a minimal sentence of ten days in jail for anyone who knowingly fails to report a case of child abuse.*

CONCLUDING PARAGRAPHS

The conclusion of an essay should restate the main points already made in the body. New material should not be introduced in the conclusion. Included should be a summary of the essay's major points or a restatement of the thesis or central idea. Like the introduction, the length of the conclusion depends upon the length of the essay. A short essay of 400 to 500 words might require only two or three sentences while one twice as long will need a more fully developed paragraph. When writing your conclusion avoid using the overworked "in conclusion" or "in summary." Listed below are five suggestions for ending your essay effectively:

1. End with a summary of the major ideas developed in your essay. The essay that had as its thesis, "Paul was the perfect male, sensitive, kind, and considerate," might end this way:

As I pointed out, I found Paul to be the perfect male. His sensitivity to the beautiful things in nature, literature, poetry, music and art made him a fascinating person to be with. The kindness he had for others which he demonstrated in both word and deed never ceased to impress me. And the consideration with which he treated me has always made me feel special and loved and still does, for I married that perfect male.

2. End with a restatement of your thesis. The essay that had as its thesis, "The alarming number of teenage pregnancies in this country is a national disgrace," might be ended in this manner:

Finally, we must convince the parents of this nation of their responsibility to adequately educate their children about the dangers of premarital sex. We must establish an effective and comprehensive and continuing sex education program beginning at the lower elementary level in our schools. And we must make free contraceptive materials available to any teenager who requests it without notifying the parents. Until we do at least these three things the national disgrace of teenage pregnancies in this country will continue.

3. End with a call to action.
The essay that had as its thesis, "This country must pass a law to make the sale and possession of handguns illegal for anyone but those who enforce the law," might end like this:

And so I am asking you to write to your congressmen and senators and tell them to, "Get the guns off the streets." They can do it. They have to. We need a federal law to make it illegal to own or possess handguns. We need a law to protect the honest citizens of this nation who have a right to walk the streets safely and to carry out their business without being threatened by some criminal with a handgun. We need a law to prevent the increased slaughter of enforcers of the law killed in the line of duty by some punk with a handgun. We need a law right now that will "Get the guns off the streets."

4. End with a question.
The essay that began with the thesis, "Therefore, the United States should enact a federal law which requires a minimal sentence of ten days in jail for anyone who knowingly fails to report a case of child abuse," might end this way:

Besides the physical pain, we must consider the mental anguish of the child. Not only is the child afraid of the parent or other abuser, but also of the world in general for causing his pain. He feels rejected, helpless and alone. Because he feels no one values his existence, neither does he. The tragic result of child abuse is often the loss of potential for one of these children. Can America afford this?

5. End with a vision of the future.
If your thesis is expressed as a course of action to take, end with a prediction of what will occur if it is implemented. The essay that had as its thesis, "Our college should provide low-cost, adequate parking for students," might end this way:

With low-cost, adequate parking available, students will benefit financially from the savings they will realize in not paying the high prices of outside parking, and the fines they have incurred from being ticketed. Furthermore, students and faculty will benefit from the improvements in punctuality and attendance, and in morale, engendered by being able to park a convenient distance from the classroom. Finally, citizens in the community will benefit from having more space available for their own parking.

THE TITLE

Once you have completed your concluding paragraph, you should decide on a title for your essay which will gain the reader's attention, and relate to the main idea of your essay. The title of this book was chosen to attract the reader's attention and to emphasize the central idea of this book: that anyone who has anything to say has to ask himself the question, "What did you say?" before beginning to communicate. Three methods for developing a title are listed below. They are (1) the rhetorical question, (2) the use of key words from your essay, and (3) a two-part title which moves from the general to the specific.

Rhetorical Questions

1. Is a Bratfest the Answer?
2. Is TV Destructive?
3. Can Teenage Unwed-Pregnancy be Halted?

Key Words

1. Get the Guns off the Streets.
2. Child Abuse Must End.
3. Let's Not be Wasted by Nuclear Waste.

General-to-Specific

1. Care: A Gift Worth Giving
2. Black History: A Subject for Everyone
3. The Perfect Pet: An Iguana

Suggestions

1. Center your title about three spaces or one-and-a-half inches above the introductory paragraph.
2. Capitalize all the important words in your title.

3. Do not put quotation marks around or underline your title.
4. Spend some time and effort selecting your title. An imaginative title can be very effective.

CHECKLIST FOR DEVELOPING THE OPINION ESSAY

1. Choose and restrict an appropriate subject.
2. Write a thesis statement expressing your opinion.
3. Develop the major points which reinforce your thesis.
4. Write each of these major points as a topic sentence for your body paragraphs.
5. Outline these topic sentences in a logical sequence.
6. Choose appropriate supporting material to clarify and reinforce these major point topic sentences.
7. Decide on a logical plan of development for your body paragraphs suited to the supporting material.
8. Develop your introductory paragraph so that you capture your reader's attention and make the main idea of the "thesis" in your essay clear.
9. Write a conclusion that summarizes your essay's main points or restates its central idea.
10. Document with appropriate footnotes the sources for any published ideas or information in your essay.
11. List in a bibliography all of the sources you consulted when preparing your essay.
12. Choose an imaginative title.

THE DOCUMENTED OPINION ESSAY

When you want to reinforce your opinion with supporting material from outside sources, you must identify the source by documenting it in a footnote. There are three reasons for footnoting: (1) to back up what you have to say with supporting material from more "expert" sources, (2) to give credit to opinions you are expressing which are other than your own, and (3) to direct an interested reader to the source of your information.

Avoid overusing footnotes. Cluttering the bottom of your pages with references to material that is common knowledge or easily verifiable is a disservice to your reader. Furthermore, the thesis you have put forth in your essay is your own opinion. Too many footnotes makes it appear that you are merely stringing together the ideas of others rather than referring to other sources to back up your own.

There are, of course, circumstances in which it is wise to document more fully. The essay which follows, for example, was written by a student-jogger. The writer knew from experience that although many readers would agree with the importance of exercise, few would accept his opinion that jogging was the ideal one. Therefore, he cited statistics, testimony, studies, and examples to back up his opinion.

End your opinion essay with a bibliography, an alphabetized list of all the sources cited in your writing. A bibliography will show your reader where he or she can locate relevant material on your topic.

A documented opinion-essay written on the thesis: *Jogging is the ideal exercise* appears on p. 210.

The Life You Save

Jogging has been called "the ultimate exercise and man's healthiest activity."[1] It combines the achievement of physical fitness with the satisfaction of self-actualization. No age group is excluded from jogging. A child can begin when he or she is old enough to run safely, and an adult in good physical condition can jog virtually to any age. A case in point is the 78-year-old man who recently completed the grueling 26-mile San Francisco Marathon.[2] Jogging strengthens the heart, develops good emotional balance, and aids in removing unwanted fat. <u>It is the ideal exercise</u>.

<u>Jogging strengthens the heart.</u> The advantage of a strong heart is that it pumps blood more efficiently, working less and resting more. Jogging strengthens the heart in four ways: (1) it improves collateral (auxiliary) circulation; (2) it increases the efficiency of the heart in extracting oxygen from the blood; (3) it lowers the fat concentration in the blood; and (4) it lowers blood pressure. These benefits to the heart significantly reduce the risk of heart attack and stroke. A scientific study of the benefits of jogging administered to a group of Harvard graduates indicated that the rate of heart attacks for those who exercised the equivalent of twenty miles of jogging per week was a full 39 percent below those who exercised lightly or not at all.[3]

<u>Jogging develops good emotional balance.</u> Perhaps the most important prerequisite of emotional well-being is a good self-concept. A jogger almost always experiences a boost in self-confidence due to his or her improved physical condition. This is often accompanied by a feeling of fulfillment and self-worth. The emotional benefits of jogging are well-documented. A controlled experiment at the University of Wisconsin by Dr. John Greist

---

[1]Valerie Andrews, <u>The Psychic Power of Running</u>. (New York: Ballantine Books, 1979), p. 54.

[2]Gabe Mirkin and Marshall Hoffman, <u>The Sportsmedicine Book.</u> (Boston: Little, Brown and Company, 1978), p. 4.

[3]Jim Fixx, <u>Jim Fixx's Second Book of Running</u>. (New York: Random House, 1980), p. 101.

–2–

found jogging far superior to psychotherapy as a treatment for patients with clinical depression.[4] This coincides with a view widely accepted among psychologists and psychiatrists who see this exercise resulting in lowered levels of depression and anxiety.[5]

<u>Jogging aids in removing unwanted fat</u>. Whatever extra weight the runner is carrying makes running more difficult. Therefore, the incentive to lose weight increases. Losing weight often improves a person's physical appearance, but, more importantly, it can significantly improve one's health. Dr. Kenneth Cooper, a renowned authority on aerobics, states: ". . . obesity may be a more mysterious killer than many people expect." He estimates that over 50 million Americans are seriously obese, collectively carrying over one billion pounds of extra weight.[6] Anyone who is more than 20 percent heavier than his or her ideal weight is considered obese. Getting rid of that extra weight could add years to a person's life, and jogging can help you to accomplish this objective. A recent survey that appeared in Runners' World Magazine, showed that two-thirds of the runners who responded had lost between 10 and 20 pounds through jogging.[7]

The benefits of jogging are impressive. The fact that <u>it strengthens the heart</u>, lessening the risk of heart attack, stroke and heart disease, could prolong a person's life. <u>The emotional balance</u> it provides, helping to reduce one's anxiety and increasing ability to handle stress, could make a happier and more enriching life. And finally, the fact that it <u>aids in reducing unwanted fat</u> will improve a person's health. These are all good reasons for viewing jogging as the ideal exercise.

---

[4]Mirkin, p. 18.

[5]William P. Morgan, "The Mind of a Marathoner," <u>Psychology Today</u>, April 1978, p. 46.

[6]Kenneth H. Cooper, <u>The Aerobics Program for the Total Well-Being</u>. (New York: M. Evans and Company, Inc. 1982), p. 39.

[7]"Dietary Habits of Runners" in <u>The Complete Runner</u>, eds. of <u>Runners World Magazine</u>. (New York: Avon, 1978), p. 124.

Bibliography

Andrews, Valerie, The Psychic Power of Running. New York: Ballantine Books, 1979.

Cooper, Kenneth, The Aerobics Program for Total Well-Being. New York: M. Evans and Company, Inc., 1982.

"Dietary Habits of Runners," in The Complete Runner, eds. of Runners World Magazine. New York: Avon, 1978.

Fixx, Jim, Jim Fixx's Second Book of Running. New York: Random House, 1980.

Mirkin, Gabe and Marshall Hoffman, The Sportsmedicine Book. Boston: Little, Brown and Company, 1978.

Morgan, William P., "The Mind of a Marathoner," Psychology Today, April 1978, pp. 43–46.

ASSIGNMENTS

While 400–600 words is the typical length of a medium sized opinion essay, consult your instructor for specific directions.

1. Write an opinion essay in which you state an opinion you have formed about a certain place. List two or three good reasons for having formed it. A person writing an essay on his favorite restaurant, for example, might support it with these three points: (1) the food is exceptional, (2) the prices are reasonable, and (3) the service is prompt and efficient.

   ### Sample Theses

   1. The Milwaukee Zoo is fascinating.
   2. Our school library is inadequate.
   3. New York is my favorite city. The Big Apple is rotten to the core.
   4. I _____ this school.
   5. To me, home is _____.

2. Write an essay critiquing a book you have read. Defend your opinion with two or three supporting points. An essay on Stephen King's *The Stand,* for example, might deal with these main points: (1) the style of writing, (2) the suspense, and (3) the vivid character description.

   ### Sample Theses

   1. *The Godfather* is a thrilling book.
   2. *Emma* is a book you cannot put down.
   3. Alex Haley is a prolific writer.
   4. Don't bother reading *The Wiz.*

3. Write an essay in which you critique a musical performance you have attended or album you have listened to. A positive evaluation of a performance by the group, Van Halen, for example, might list these supporting points: (1) they perform mostly their own music, (2) they are visually exciting, and (3) they have innovative arrangements.

Sample Theses

1. Nobody can top *Matrix.*
2. I _____ Ozzie Osborne.
3. Opera is total entertainment.
4. Sweet Cheeks is my son's favorite rock group.
5. Gilbert and Sullivan is ageless.

2. Write an essay stating an opinion which you believe is opposite one held by the majority of your friends. Choose whether to document your view with outside sources, or reinforce it only from your own experience or reasoning. An unpopular view might be difficult to prove on your own. Therefore, it might be wise to cite outside sources as reinforcement. An essay on the undesirability of premarital sex might have as its supports: (1) it increases the risk of unwanted pregnancy, (2) it carries the risk of venereal disease, and (3) it often creates anxiety.

Sample Theses:

1. The drinking age should be raised to 21.
2. The Federal Government should reinstate the death penalty.
3. Prostitution should be legalized in the U.S.
4. The United States should not allow immigration.

5. Write an essay supporting your point of view about a particular activity. Give two or three reasons to support your opinion. Three supporting statements of the thesis: "Weightlifting is the perfect exercise," might include: (1) it builds muscles, (2) it improves health, and (3) it controls weight.

Sample Theses

1. Exercise can add years to your life.
2. Drinking endangers your health.
3. Cribbage is the perfect card game.
4. Golf is a dumb sport.

6. Write an essay which has as its thesis the solution to a problem. The problem should be stated clearly in an introductory paragraph which has the thesis statement as its concluding sentence. An essay indicating a solution for case-problem number

seven on page 298 might end with this thesis statement: Alice should tell Don that she won't marry him for these reasons: (1) marriage is based on communication, (2) marriage is based on mutual trust, and (3) the divorce rate in this country is approaching 40 percent.

Sample Theses

1. Halving the defense budget will end the recession.
2. Neighborhood watches deter crime.
3. Legalizing gambling nationwide will solve our economic woes.
4. Making it harder to get married will decrease divorce.

7. Write an essay supporting your opinion of a movie you have seen. Find two or three reasons for having formed your opinion. A favorable opinion essay on the movie *E.T.*, for example, might include three main points: (1) the special effects, (2) the characterization of E.T., and (3) the direction of Steven Spielberg.

Sample Theses

1. They don't make movies like they used to.
2. Movies are overly concerned with sex.
3. We need more humorous movies.
4. *Gandhi* was an unforgettable movie.

8. Write an opinion-essay on a TV show or series. List two or three reasons for having formed your opinion. For example, in critiquing *Hill Street Blues*, you might list these supporting statements: (1) it describes crime in a big city honestly, (2) it portrays police as having problems of their own, and (3) it honestly admits that sometimes the system fails.

Sample Theses

1. Newscasts give too much coverage to sports.
2. Educational television has superior programming.
3. Today's "sitcoms" are mostly poorly written.
4. _____ is a popular TV series.

9. Write an essay expressing a point of view about a particular hobby. Find two or three reasons to support your opinion. A thesis supporting the hobby of stamp collecting might employ these supporting ideas: (1) it is a painless way to learn geography, (2) it can be financially rewarding, and (3) it brings you into contact with all kinds of interesting people.

Sample Theses

1. I love model railroading.
2. People who raise pigeons are inconsiderate.
3. Clay modeling develops your imagination.
4. Collecting beer cans is a sign of immaturity.

CHAPTER 11

The
Business
Letter

OBJECTIVES

After studying this chapter you should be able to:
1. List the elements of a business letter.
2. Identify the content of each element.
3. Illustrate the two most often used forms of business letters.
4. Write a job application letter.
5. Write a thank-you letter.
6. Write a letter of complaint.
7. Write a letter of inquiry.

This chapter was written by **John D. Lewinski**.

The business letter may be a different form of letter writing from what you are used to. Up to now most of the letters you have written have been simply "newsy notes" to loved ones, communication to inform about things that have happened to you that you think will interest your reader. These letters are spontaneous rather than preplanned. You sit down, begin writing, and as thoughts occur to you, jot them down.

In writing the business letter, however, you are faced with a specific problem—how to evoke a desired response from your reader. For this reason your letter must be carefully planned and clearly and correctly written. If your letter creates a poor impression, your chances of getting that desired response are lessened. If your letter is unclear or lacks some necessary information, time and money may be wasted writing additional letters.

The first part of this chapter deals with business letter form. Although there are a number of forms for business letters, the two most common are the full block (page 233) and the semiblock (pages 223, 224). In the full-block form, the heading, inside address, salutation, body, complimentary close, and signature begin at the left margin. In the semiblock form, the inside address, salutation, and body (with each paragraph indented) are flush with the left margin, and the heading, complimentary close, and signature are on the righthand side. (This is the form referred to in the discussion below.) The second part of this chapter deals with the content of business letters by discussing examples of different types.

PARTS OF THE BUSINESS LETTER

A business letter should contain *six* distinct parts: the heading, the inside address, the salutation, the body, the complimentary close, and the signature.

The Heading

The heading is located in the upper right-hand corner and should include the writer's full mailing address and the date the letter was written. Both are important. The full address gives the reader a return address right on the letter, facilitating his reply. The date, which establishes the time the letter was written, can be referred to in future letters. Notice that the writer's name appears at the bottom of the letter, not in the heading.

> 507 Main Street
> Cudahy, Wisconsin 53110
> March 1, 1984

Many organizations have stationery designed for them with an engraved or printed letterhead. These letterheads often include the title of the organization, its full address, phone number, officers, and in some cases a brief description of what the organization does.

UWEX   UNIVERSITY OF WISCONSIN–EXTENSION

929 NORTH SIXTH STREET   MILWAUKEE, WISCONSIN 53203   (414) 224-1891

DEPARTMENT OF BUSINESS AND MANAGEMENT

Management Institutes ● Correspondence Study ● Special Classes

If letterhead stationery is used, the date should be typed in two spaces below the letterhead at either the center of the page or the right margin.

The Inside Address

The inside address is placed at the left margin and at least four spaces below the date. It contains the full name and address of the person or organization to whom you are writing. It is identical to the address on the envelope.

The inside address indicates exactly to whom the letter is sent. In many large organizations, the mail is originally opened by someone other than the addressee, perhaps a secretary or mail sorter. If the name of the person or department to whom you are writing is not on the letter, it may be misplaced or sent to the wrong person. The more complete the information is in the inside address, the greater the likelihood your letter will reach its proper destination. Include the full name and position of the intended reader, if known, and the department or division of the organization to which you are writing. Remember, your chances of getting a desired response are always better if your letter is addressed to a specific person. If, for instance, you are writing a letter applying for a job at a specific company, it would be in your best interest to call the company office and find out the name of the personnel director.

Mrs. Judy Miller
Personnel Director
Acme Welding Company
1472 North 35th Street
Chicago, Illinois 60684

The Salutation

Place the salutation two spaces below the inside address at the left margin. While the salutation is the greeting, it is a bit more formal than a simple "Hello." In a business letter the sex of the reader and the tone of the letter will determine the title to use. Here are some acceptable choices:

For Men	For Organizations	For Women
Dear Sir:	Gentlemen:	Dear Miss _____:
Dear Mr. _____:	Ladies:	Dear Mrs. _____:
		Dear Ms. _____:

Another function of the salutation is to set the tone of the letter. Consider the difference between a letter asking for a job interview and a letter complaining about a faulty product. You can set the tone of the letter by choosing the proper title and by adding or deleting the words "My" and "Dear". Here are some examples:

For a letter of stern tone:
Sir: or   Madam:

For a letter of neutral tone:
Dear Sir: Dear Madam:
Gentlemen: Ladies:

For a letter of friendly tone:

Men	**Women**
My Dear Mr. _____:	My Dear Mrs. (Miss, Ms.) _____:
Dear Mr. _____:	Dear Mrs. (Miss, Ms.) _____:
Dear *(First Name):*	Dear *(First Name):*

Although the salutation involves only a few words, it should be obvious that its proper use is an important aspect of the business letter.

The Body

The body of the business letter begins two spaces below the salutation. It is written in paragraphs that are single-spaced. A double space is used between paragraphs. The body, which contains the message you want to convey, is the heart of the letter. Since the purposes of different types of business letters are so varied, it is difficult to discuss the content of the body in any detail. However, some general rules apply:

1. Preplan the letter. Decide what and how much you want to say. Then write it out in a natural, to-the-point way. Be yourself.

Efforts to sound impressive usually result in an awkward, stilted style.

2. Make the letter "reader-centered." Write with the reader in mind, address yourself to his or her problems and needs. Try to anticipate what the reaction will be to your letter. Ask yourself, "Would I do what I suggest if I were the receiver of my letter?"

3. Organize your letter, keeping the main points together in neat paragraphs. Generally, you begin by stating your purpose in a simple, straightforward way. Then, clearly explain the details the reader will need to respond correctly to your letter. Your conclusion should indicate what you want to occur because of your letter. Your tone should not appear to dictate what it is you want done. Rather, it should lead the reader naturally to your desired response.

The Complimentary Closing

The complimentary closing is the writer's way of saying "goodbye" to the reader. It is located two spaces below the last paragraph of the body and slightly right of the center of the page. The way you close your letter is again determined by the tone and subject. Here are some suggestions:

For formal or stern letters:
Respectfully,   or   Respectfully yours,

For neutral letters:
Very sincerely yours,   or   Very truly yours,

For friendly letters:
Sincerely yours,   or   Cordially yours,

The Signature

The signature is important in making the letter a personal communication. Because it should be both legal and legible, it should appear in two forms: signed and typed. The typed signature assures legibility. Make sure your signature does not overlap either the complimentary closing or the typed signature.

Sincerely,

James Johnson

James Johnson

SOME DO'S AND DONT'S

1. *Do* type your letter. No matter how neat your handwriting, it is common practice to type the business letter.

2. *Do* preplan the letter. This will not only improve the content; it will help you space the elements properly on the page.

3. *Do* keep a copy of your letter. In the event of a question concerning your letter, you will be readily able to answer it.

4. *Do* try to keep your letters as brief as possible. Letters of no more than one page are best, whenever possible. If you do not attempt too many things with a single letter, chances are you will be successful.

5. *Do not* send your letter before carefully proofreading it. Errors in spelling, grammar, or typing reflect negatively on you, the writer. Further, they can cause misunderstandings or communication breakdowns.

EXERCISE

Rewrite the following letter in an accurate semiblock form:

George Krall
2730 Lake Dr.
Kenosha, Wis. 53140

Renata Smith, Mgr.
Church Supply Co.
4730 East Morgan St.
Chicago, Ill. 60607

Dear Mrs. Smith:

I wish to thank you for recommending me to Mr. Karl Stoll. I have just received word that I am to begin work June 7.

Mr. Stoll mentioned that you had given me an excellent recommendation which had much to do with my getting the job. I want to thank you for taking time out of your busy schedule to write a letter for me. I hope that I will live up to your faith in me.

Sincerely yours,

George Krall
George Krall
6/1/84

TYPES OF BUSINESS LETTERS

Because the purposes, forms, and lengths of business letters are so varied, representative samples of different types are included on the following pages.

Job Application

Perhaps the most important business letter you will ever write is a letter of application for a job. Because many jobs require interviews, the applicant must be able to write a formal letter requesting one.

Sally Johnson, a commercial arts major at a large Midwestern junior college saw this ad in her local newspaper.

> WANTED: Talented young artists to work for
> a national advertising company. Contact:
>
> Mr. Edward Brown
> Syndicated Talent, Inc.
> P.O. Box 1131
> Chicago, IL 60607

She wrote the following letter:

> 3535 East 3rd Street
> Milwaukee, Wisconsin 53202
> March 14, 1984

> Mr. Edward Brown
> Syndicated Talent, Inc.
> P.O. Box 1131
> Chicago, Illinois 60607

> Dear Mr. Brown:

> I read your ad for young artists that appeared in the March 13 Milwaukee News-Review. I would like to apply for one of those positions.

> I am a second year student majoring in commercial arts at Columbia College in Milwaukee. I am presently the Art Editor for our campus newspaper, The Columbian. For the past three years I have worked for a local advertising agency, Midwest Marketing Corporation, as an advertising artist.

> While my class schedule is rather restricting, I am available for an interview on Friday afternoons, and Saturdays. I

would appreciate an opportunity to call at your office for an interview. Please notify me if these times are convenient for you.

Sincerely yours,

Sally Johnson

(Miss) Sally Johnson

Notice how Sally indicated in her first paragraph how she heard of the position, and why she was writing. She then gave a few of her qualifications for the position. She concluded her letter by indicating her desire for an interview and requesting a response from the employer. These are wise practices for such a letter.

Compare Sally's letter with the following model of a good application letter.

MODEL FOR AN APPLICATION LETTER

Your street address (or P.O. Box)
City, State and Zip Code
Date

Name of person receiving letter
Title
Company Name
Full Address—Zip Code

Dear _____:

Indicate which job you are applying for. Tell where you heard of the opening or why you have selected this employer for an inquiry. If you are responding to a newspaper ad, give the date.

Try to arouse the employer's interest in reading your letter by mentioning briefly something you are preparing for or have accomplished which relates to the type of work for which you are applying. Describe your interest in the position, in the field of work, or in the organization. If you have work experience, be sure to mention pertinent data or accomplishments to show that you have specific qualifications in this field or for that particular type of work.

The closing paragraph should suggest your eagerness to arrange an interview. Include your telephone number and the hours when you are most likely to be there.

Sincerely yours,

Signature

Full name, typed
(Indicate title preferred, i.e.,
Mr., Miss, Mrs., Ms.)

If Sally was also sending a copy of her résumé with her letter, she might include a paragraph which would refer the reader to special sections or information contained in the résumé. She would then indicate that the résumé was enclosed by typing:

ENCLOSURE: Résumé

in the lower left corner of her letter. A copy of a résumé Sally might submit follows on page 226.

RESUME

I. *Personal Data*

Name:	Johnson, Sally M.
Address:	3535 East 3rd Street
	Milwaukee, Wisconsin 53203
Phone:	414-555-1324
Health:	Good
Date/Birth:	August 10, 1957
Place/Birth	Wauwatosa, Wisconsin
Marital Status:	Single
Height:	5'6"
Weight:	130 lbs.

II. *Education*

1975–1977 Columbia College, Milwaukee, Wisconsin
                Degree Sought—Associate of Arts
                Major—Commercial Art
                Minor—Advertising
                Grade Point—3.75
                Grade Point in Major—4.00
                Favorite Courses:
                      Commercial Art I—A
                      Commercial Art II—A
                      Display—A
                      Photographic Principles—A
                Extracurricular activities:
                      Art Editor—College Newspaper
                      Secretary—Student Government
                      Queens Court—1976 Homecoming

1971–1975 St. James Academy, Wauwatosa, Wisconsin
                Degree—High School Diploma
                Graduated 7th in a class of 147
                Studies included:
                      Art 101 and 102—A in both
                      Commercial Drawing—A
                      Business Math—A
                      Accounting for Business—B
                Extracurricular Activities:
                      Art Editor—School Newspaper
                      Assistant Artist—School Yearbook
                      Set Designer—Drama Club

III. *Experience*

    1974–1977 — Advertising Artist
                   Midwest Marketing Corporation
                   103 Downer Plaza
                   Milwaukee, Wisconsin 53204

    1972–1974 — Stock Person
                   Milwaukee Artist's Supply
                   1414 Penn Avenue
                   Wauwatosa, Wisconsin 53213

IV. *References*

Mr. Paul Scoggins, Manager
Midwest Marketing Corporation
103 Downer Plaza
Milwaukee, Wisconsin, 53204

Sister Mary Louisa,
Art Instructor
St. James Academy
4525 River Road
Wauwatosa, Wisconsin 53213

Professor Mary Bennett,
Commercial Art Department
Columbia College
613 North University Drive
Milwaukee, Wisconsin 53207

V. *Occupational Goal*

Someday, I would like to be managing art editor for a national magazine or company. In the interim, I wish to learn all I can about the world of commercial art.

Notice that Sally has five separate elements in her résumé. These are generally the minimum requirements in a résumé, but the order and content of each section will vary greatly. An examination of each element in Sally's résumé will help you to prepare your own.

Part I—Personal Data

Sally included a great deal of information in this section. Some people may say that she included too much. Many current texts suggest that information such as age, marital status, height and weight should not be included. However, it is also true that employers are often asked to provide reports to governmental and consumer groups on how many employees of certain types have been hired. Since employers are not allowed to ask for this information on application forms, the résumé may help them with those reports. As a résumé writer you should give the matter of how much detail to include serious consideration. Remember, the purpose of the résumé is to get you the interview.

Part II—Education

Sally also included a good deal of detail here about her formal education. Notice she included both classroom and extra curricular activities. However, she didn't include any other educational activities she may have participated in. For example, she may have taken some courses in C.P.R. through the Red Cross or perhaps she attended a weekend seminar on artists and media at the library. If you have had similar educational experiences, be sure to include them.

Part III—Employment

Sally apparently has held only two jobs in her life, or has she? She probably has done much more than that. She certainly helped her parents around the house. Maybe she babysat for a neighbor's child. Perhaps she worked at school, or at a playground during the summer. Maybe she worked as a volunteer for some service organization. Employers are often as interested in these types of work as they are in the more traditional ones. It shows them that you are an energetic, involved, willing-to-do-more person.

Part IV—References

Sally included three references in her résumé. A more common practice is to simply state . . . .

References: Furnished Upon Request.

This gives you the flexibility to match the references you use in each case to the particular job you are seeking. When you are asked to provide references, be prepared to give all the information Sally does. Also remember to get the permission of the person before you list that person as a reference.

Part V—Occupational Goal

This is a part often overlooked or misunderstood by the résumé writer. Notice that Sally includes both her long range and present goals. The purpose of this section is to show the employer that you have some ambition, some self-confidence, and some commitment to your career. It should indicate that, while you're looking for a starting job now, you have your mind set on being successful in your profession.

A final word about the résumé. It should do the absolute best job it can to sell you to the employer. It should be as unique as you are. It must not contain any errors of any kind. It must look good and be a complete, accurate presentation of your information.

It sometimes becomes necessary for a person with limited work experience to write a résumé. A résumé written by Sarah Beth Scott who was seeking employment after her husband had been killed follows on p. 229.

Career Goals

I have always been interested in the world of finance and banking. Several years ago I worked as a teller (see below) and now I would like to resume my career in the financial industry. Ultimately I would like to become an officer in a bank or savings and loan.

WORK EXPERIENCE

1972–Present—Domestic Engineer

> For the past several years I have been totally involved with the maintenance of my home and rearing of my children. As a single parent, this required 100% of my time. Now that the children are in school daily, I am eager to re-enter the career I was forced to leave when my husband died.

1969–1972   —Teller

> Delaware Street State Bank
> 2546 S. Delaware Street
> Phoenix, Arizona 05017
>
> My duties included handling normal daily banking activities for customers. I worked both lobby and drive-up windows. My last year I was promoted to assistant supervisor of tellers. Reason for leaving: My husband was killed in an auto accident.

1966–1969   —Checker

> August's Market
> 4644 East Cactus Drive
> Phoenix, Arizona 0515
>
> My duties included checking out customers, stocking shelves and some limited office work. Reason for leaving: To work in the bank.

Other Work Experiences:

1974–1976   —Chairperson

> Middle School PTA
> Phoenix Middle School—South
> 3535 South School Drive
> Phoenix, Arizona 05017

1976–1978   —Brownie Scout Leader
> Phoenix

EDUCATIONAL PREPARATION

1969–1972   —American Institute of Banking—Student

During the years I was employed by the bank, I took several courses through the A.I.B. educational system. Among those courses were:

Accounting I & II—Grades I–A
                                    II–A
                      Honor Student in Accounting I

Effective English—Grade A

Interpersonal Communication—Grade A

Principles of Banking—Grade B

1964–1968   —Phoenix South High School
                      Phoenix, Arizona 05017

Degree—High School Diploma
              Graduated in top 25% of class

Major Studies—Business
Minor Studies—Communication Arts

Favorite Courses: Interpersonal Communication—A
                                Management—A
                                Accounting—A
                                Business Machines—B

Other Activities: Member—Fund Raisers Club—
                                  1967–68
                                  Treasurer—Senior Class—
                                  1968
                                  Phoenix Jaycees—
                                  1966–68

PERSONAL INFORMATION:

Name: Sarah Beth Scott (Thomas)
Address: 4802 East Emmet Street
                  Phoenix, Arizona 05015

Phone: (602) 555-7271

REFERENCES:

Furnished upon request.

To return to Sally Johnson and her application for work in the ad agency, soon she received a response from Mr. Brown, indicating a date and time for an interview. She then wrote this letter to confirm the appointment.

3535 East 3rd Street
Milwaukee, Wisconsin 53202
April 2, 1984

Mr. Edward Brown
Syndicated Talent, Inc.
P.O. Box 1131
Chicago, Illinois 60607

Dear Mr. Brown:

Thank you very much for your letter of March 27 offering me an interview on Friday, April 6, 1984. I shall be most happy to talk with you at 2:00 P.M.

At this interview, I will bring some samples of my previous work, as you requested.

I am looking forward to meeting you and learning about your company.

Sincerely,

Sally Johnson

(Miss) Sally Johnson

Now, Sally began to prepare for her interview. First, she found out what she could about the company. She called the Better Business Bureau, and she discussed the company with her boss at Midwest Marketing and her college teachers. Next, she selected an appropriate outfit, nothing too dressy, but neat and clean. She realized that personal appearance is a big part of an interview. Finally, she considered how she would respond to some of the more common questions that interviews ask.

Why are you interested in this field?
Why are you interested in this company?
What are your occupational goals?

What hours would you be willing to work?
What salary would you require?
What special likes and dislikes do you have?
What special strengths and weaknesses do you have?

She also made a list of questions that she would like to have answered.

What are the job requirements?
What salary and fringe benefits are available?
What are the possibilities for advancement?
What are the hours, and when would she start the job?

During her interview, naturally Sally was nervous. But she kept her composure. She listened carefully to what Mr. Brown asked, and she responded honestly and briefly. She brought a copy of her résumé to refer to, as well as several samples of her previous work. When Mr. Brown asked if she had any questions, she asked several polite ones. After thanking him, she left the interview feeling that it had gone well.

Sally knew that she was not the only person being interviewed for the position. So, when she returned home, she sent the following letter to Mr. Brown:

3535 East 3rd Street
Milwaukee, Wisconsin 53202
April 12, 1984

Mr. Edward Brown
Syndicated Talent, Inc.
P.O. Box 1131
Chicago, Illinois 60607

Dear Mr. Brown:

I want to thank you for the opportunity to discuss the position of Art Consultant with your company. After our Friday interview, I felt I had learned a great deal about the real world of commercial art.

I especially want to thank you for your kind words about my pictorial display entitled, "Winter's Wonder." It is nice to know that someone in the business of commercial art appreciates my work.

I hope that you have heard from my references, and that I may hear from you soon.

Thank you again for taking the time to talk with me.

Sincerely,

Sally Johnson

(Miss) Sally Johnson

Notice how Sally refreshes the interviewer's mind about her interview and indicates her continued interest in the job, as well as thanking Mr. Brown.

We don't know whether Sally got the job or not. But we do know that she followed the proper letter-writing and job-application procedures. If you follow her example, your chances of finding that job will be enhanced.

Preparing for the Interview

1. Dress and grooming should be neat. You can overdress for an interview as well as underdress. Too much make-up or too much after-shave can be just as bad as no make-up or no shave. Be clean, well-groomed, and dress conservatively. Gaudy shirts or mini-skirts have their place, but the interview isn't one of them.

2. Come prepared to answer all questions. Normally an interview will involve filling out one of the company's job application forms. Therefore, you will need to know your social security number, the names, addresses, and phone numbers of your close relatives, and all the information contained in your résumé. It is a good idea to bring a copy of your résumé along for your own use in filling out the application. Accuracy and neatness might mean the difference between getting a job or not.

3. Do your homework. In order to answer some of the questions, you will have to know something about the company that is interviewing you. When were they founded? How big are they? What benefits do they offer? What place do unions play in the company? What is the pay scale? These and other questions should be answered before you enter the interview room. This will help you answer the interviewer's questions in a detailed way.

4. Participate fully in the interview. Good listening is essential. Listen to the exact question and give the best answer you can. Be courteous and pleasant, not flip or wise. Introduce yourself

as you enter. Use your full name, but drop the titles. Shake hands firmly, if the interviewer offers. Sit straight, but not rigid, as you are interviewed. Let the interviewer begin. Keep your answers brief, but complete. Use informal, but correct language and grammar. Maintain good eye contact. Don't interrupt the question. And, through all of this, try to remain alert, pleasant, and relaxed.

Other Business Letters

In this section, we will consider two additional types of business letters: the letter of adjustment or complaint and the letter of inquiry. As our society grows more complex and depersonalized, the need to seek redress or to obtain additional information increases. A clear and concise business letter is generally the most practical means to that end. Consider the following:

A. In September, James Wilson saw an advertisement on television for a collection of hit records from the 1960s. Since there were several songs on the album that he liked, he placed an order for the album with the Zapp Record Company in New York. To save the $2.25 C.O.D. charge, James sent a personal check for the full amount with his order. Then he waited. In October, his check cleared his bank, but still no record arrived. He waited all through November, but he never received the album. On December 5, he sent the following letter:

> 2765 Washington Avenue
> Los Angeles, California 90009
> December 5, 1984

Zapp Record Company, Inc.
1465 Park Avenue
New York, New York 10019

Gentlemen:

On September 14, 1984, I placed an order for one copy of your 2-record album, "Swinging Sixties." I enclosed a personal check for $10.95, which was the full amount of the advertised album, plus shipping and handling. That check was paid by my bank on October 8, 1984, and I have the cancelled check. However, I have not received my order.

Your advertisement says allow 6 to 8 weeks for delivery. I have now waited over 11 weeks. Is there some problem that would account for this delay?

I would appreciate it if you check on my order, and notify me of its situation at your earliest convenience. A response from you will prevent any further action on this matter.

Respectfully yours,

James Wilson

James Wilson

Notice that, while the letter is not angry or insulting, it is also not as friendly as the letters Miss Johnson wrote. The salutation and closing are much more formal in tone.

Also notice how James handles the message. In the first paragraph, he identifies the reason for the letter. He mentions names, dates, and amounts, so that the company can check its records. In the second paragraph, he reminds his reader that the company has not fulfilled its obligations, but he does this in a polite way. James concludes his letter by indicating what he expects from the company. While he suggests that he is prepared to follow this matter through, he doesn't directly threaten legal action or the like. If the company doesn't respond, he can then take more firm action.

Before he sent the letter, James did two more things, which are very good practices in this kind of situation.

1. He made a copy of the letter.
2. He sent the letter certified mail and attached his receipt to the copy of the letter.

While this procedure costs a little money, it is an inexpensive way of keeping a record of the whole transaction. We assume that the record company will explain the delay, and James will get his album. If he doesn't, he has a record of what he has done.

B. Often a person needs to obtain additional information about a product, an organization, or a situation. In this next example Betty Meyers, a student at a local junior college, is trying to decide what university she should attend to complete her education. While she has a good deal of information about the course of study she is interested in pursuing at Kennedy University, Betty still has some questions about the area, the housing situation, and job opportunities. She writes a letter of inquiry (see page 237).

Several things should be noted in Betty's letter. Notice how the tone is much more friendly than that of Mr. Wilson's letter of complaint. The first paragraph explains the purpose of the letter, and the next two ask the questions. Also, notice how Betty doesn't ask Mrs. Moore to answer the letter directly; she doesn't make a great demand on a person who is probably quite busy. Mrs. Moore may answer the questions herself, or she may refer Betty to the Director of Housing and the Director of Student Placement. In either case, Betty will probably get the answers she seeks.

Finally, notice that Betty has decided not to thank Mrs. Moore in advance. When she gets the response from Mrs. Moore, she may want to write a thank-you letter, similar to the one Miss Johnson wrote earlier.

12527 West Longwood
East London, Maryland 01212
April 8, 1984

Mrs. Margaret Moore
Director of Admissions
Kennedy University
Boston, Maryland 02109

Dear Mrs. Moore:

I am currently a sophomore at East London Junior College, planning to graduate this June with an Associate of Arts Degree in Computer Technology. I have applied for admission to your university, and am awaiting word on my application. In the meantime, several questions have arisen concerning my enrollment, and I feel it important to ask for your assistance.

First, I notice in your literature that you allow upper classmen to live in off-campus housing. Since I will be entering as a junior and will be 21 years old, I feel that I would prefer this arrangement to dormitory living. My problem is that I am unfamiliar with the area in which Kennedy is located, and have no idea about where to live and what to expect to pay. Could you possibly suggest someone I could contact?

Second, not being wealthy, I will probably need to find a part-time job in the area. I have had two years of experience as a key punch operator, and would like to find something in the general field of computer technology, if possible. Do you also know of any one I could contact to help me with this problem?

I am looking forward to several rewarding years at K.U.
I hope you will be able to give me some assistance in these
matters.

Sincerely yours,

Betty Meyers

(Ms.) Betty Meyers

Don't simply assume that "the establishment" won't respond to the
needs of the individual. A clear, concise, and purposeful business letter
can serve to remind the largest corporation or institution that its continued success is dependent on customer satisfaction.

EXERCISES

1. Find an ad in the help wanted section of your local newspaper
   for a job in your chosen field. Write a job application letter in response to the ad.
2. Write a letter to a former teacher or employer asking for permission to use his or her name as a reference on your résumé.
3. Write a letter thanking a prospective employer for a job interview.
4. Write a letter of complaint about a product or service you found
   unsatisfactory. Indicate exactly what you would like done to
   solve the problem.
5. Write a letter to one of your governmental representatives expressing your opinion on a current local, state, or national issue
   with which he or she is connected.

CHAPTER 12

Speech Content

After studying this chapter, you should be able to:

1. List the six steps to follow when preparing the content of your speech.
2. Discuss the procedure to follow when choosing a speech subject.
3. Explain the reasons for approaching speech as an audience-centered activity.
4. Write a clear and precise speech purpose statement.
5. Identify three broad sources of material to be used in your speech.
6. Demonstrate an ability to record material accurately.
7. Outline the three main parts of a speech.
8. Discuss three main characteristics of a communicative style.
9. Prepare an audience-centered communication.
10. Effectively use a speech preparation form.
11. Include effective attention factors in your communications.

If you are like most students, you probably face the thought of getting up to deliver a speech in front of a group of classmates with some apprehension. Perhaps you are not entirely clear as to how to develop an effective speech. You might be concerned with whether what you want to say will be interesting to your audience. You could be afraid that you will forget part of your speech, or say the wrong thing, or say it badly. You might even feel, "Why should I learn how to deliver a formal platform speech? I'll probably never have occasion to deliver one."

Although you may be called upon to make a formal public speech only a few times in your entire lifetime, the same skills are indispensable to effective face-to-face communication. People generally tend to equate ability to speak well with ability to think well. Therefore, the impression you make on others, even your own circle of friends, depends upon your ability to express yourself clearly and effectively in an easy, natural way.

Although there is no single formula that must be followed to be effective as a public speaker, two broad guidelines can help insure success: (1) say something worthwhile, and (2) say it in an easy, natural way.

SAYING SOMETHING WORTHWHILE

When you prepare a speech, you are concerned with two things: what you want to say, and how you want to say it. What you say is called the *content* of the speech, which includes the subject, the way you organize your material, the types of attention factors you choose, and your choice of words. While you should choose a subject from your own area of interest so that you know what you are talking about and have some enthusiasm for it, you must do so with your audience in mind. An audience will find your speech worthwhile if it is either interesting or useful to them. If the subject you choose has little to offer your audience in terms of usefulness and is not interesting of itself, your job is to make it interesting by handling your material in an imaginative and attention-getting way. It should be noted that although you are often free to choose any subject for a speech, the less interesting or useful the subject, the more difficult it will be to make the speech interesting. For example, unless you were in a class of music students, a speech on classical opera would require more imagination and effort than a speech on sky diving. The latter means daring, danger, thrills, and excitement to many; while opera might evoke similar responses in a few, it does not have nearly as broad an appeal.

Similarly, your classmates would be more inclined to see the usefulness of a speech on how to take a better snapshot than one on how to tune a guitar. Almost everyone takes snapshots, and most of us do not do so as effectively as we might. Consequently, a speech on how to improve this ability would be useful. On the other hand, probably the only person who would see the value of learning to tune a guitar would be someone who has just started learning how to play one. Anyone who knows how to play a guitar knows how to tune one, and the person who neither plays the guitar nor has a strong interest to play could care less.

SAYING IT IN AN EASY WAY

The way in which you say something is called *delivery*. Delivery includes such things as platform manner, voice, eye contact, and facial expression. Effective delivery should seem easy and natural. Other than an increase in volume for a larger audience, the *principal difference* between platform speaking and ordinary conversation should be in content. Since a platform speech is more carefully prepared than everyday conversation, your subject will, no doubt, be handled more imaginatively and your words chosen more carefully. Be sure to avoid using language with which you are unfamiliar. Use your own vocabulary, but eliminate words which might be inappropriate to the occasion.

An advantage to using your conversational style of delivery in front of an audience is that you will feel comfortable with it. If you try to change your way of speaking, your style will seem stilted and unnatural. The key to effective delivery is to be yourself. At first this might seem difficult—how do you get up in front of your classmates, many of whom you haven't met before, and be yourself? You will probably meet most of your fellow students during the semester on an individual basis anyway. Meeting others casually involves spontaneous, unplanned conversation. By delivering a carefully thought-out speech that deals with your own areas of interest, you show your classmates your best side. When listening to them, you get to know something about their interests. Both of you have, in effect, put your best foot forward, which should result in a clearer understanding of each other.

PREPARING SPEECH CONTENT

Specific instructions on how to prepare your speech for delivery will appear in the next chapter. Presented below are the six steps to follow when preparing the content of your speech.

1. Choose a subject.
2. Determine the purpose.

3. Analyze the audience.
4. Gather the supporting materials.
5. Organize the speech.

CHOOSE A SUBJECT

It may be that when you are given your speech assignment, you immediately think of a subject that you are interested in and that you feel will be interesting to your audience. If this happens, you can move right on to step two, analyzing your audience. However, if you find you don't know what to talk about, take out a piece of paper and jot down as many as you can of the things that you are interested in or have experience with. There is no better place to look for a subject than in your own back yard. Have you grown up on a farm? Did you go to school in a different part of the country? Were you in the armed forces? Do you have an unusual job? Are you turned on by a particular religion? Do you have special skills in music, photography, theater, auto mechanics, or fashion design? With a little imagination and some hard work, you can make these subjects interesting to your audience.

Examine Your Qualifications

It is important that you examine your qualifications for dealing with a particular subject. Are you qualified because of background or skill? Do you speak from personal experience? Can you offer your audience any credentials to show that what you have to say is reliable? A speech by a member of the school hockey team on buying the best ice skates for your money will probably be well received by his classmates. If you speak as a nonexpert, you will have to prove the reliability of your information. If you have special knowledge or experience, indicate this to your audience.

DETERMINE THE PURPOSE

After you have decided on your subject, you must develop a statement of specific purpose. Write your purpose as an infinitive phrase. Your statement should clearly identify your general purpose as being to inform, to entertain, to convince, to actuate, or to reinforce.

Formulate your purpose statement by considering exactly what you wish to accomplish. You must know your goal before you can plan the best way to achieve it. Most subjects can be developed in different ways in accord with various general purposes. For example, suppose that, because of both interest and knowledge, you choose pollution as your topic. You could develop a statement of specific intent for each of the following:

To inform: To explain to my audience the different types of pollution.

To entertain: To entertain my audience by playing and singing Tom Lehrer's song "Pollution."

To convince: To convince my audience that this nation must reorder its priorities to deal with pollution.

To actuate: To persuade my audience to begin collecting their cans and bottles for our local recycling project.

To reinforce: To make my audience more vividly aware of the spectre of a world killed by pollution.

Consider Audience Response

The succcess or failure of any communication must be measured in terms of audience response. The TV series that fails to entertain is soon cancelled, the unsuccessful salesman will be out of a job, the textbook that is difficult to understand is seldom reordered, and the uninspiring preacher speaks to an empty church. You will communicate more effectively if you plan your message with a specific, realistic audience response in mind.

Some responses are particularly difficult to achieve. A lack of time might prevent you from teaching your audience a complicated technique, such as giving a permanent or using the slide rule. Your audience might not have the background or experience that will enable you to teach them how to replace the bearings in an alternator or sew a collar on a dress. In addition, the attitude of your audience might be so opposed to your subject that they become impossible to approach; an example would be trying to promote George Wallace for President at a black student rally. In such cases the communicator must choose another, more realistic purpose.

ANALYZE THE AUDIENCE

The process of communication involves a sender, a message, a medium, a receiver, and a response. Whenever a breakdown in communication occurs, it is at one or more of these points. Breakdowns in speech communication often occur when the speaker fails to consider carefully both the receiver and his response. As a result, too many speeches end up with the speaker talking about matters of self-interest, with little regard for the needs or interests of his audience. An effective speech must be audience-directed.

Knowledge of your audience will help you plan a speech designed specifically for them. The more you know about an audience, the more likely you will be to establish a common ground of interest and information. Below is a list of questions to ask when analyzing your audience.

Who Is My Audience?

Before you begin to prepare your communication, consider who is included in your audience. In this course, you will probably be speaking primarily to your classmates, so you should learn all you can about them. Listen to them carefully, make note of their interests, consider their attitudes, wants, and needs, and then develop your message accordingly.

Will My Audience Find My Subject Interesting?

All too often communication fails because it has not been developed to interest the listener to whom it is directed. You know how hard it is to pay attention to a speech on a subject of no particular interest to you. The harder you have to work to pay attention, the less chance you have of getting something out of the material. Your job as a speaker is to develop your material so that your audience will find it interesting.

Will My Audience Find My Subject Useful?

People willingly pay attention to a communication when they have something to gain from doing so. When you can, show your audience how your information will be useful to them. Tell them why they *need* to listen.

What Does My Audience Already Know About My Subject?

Too technical an approach could leave your audience thoroughly confused; merely repeating what they already know will bore them. If you know that your audience has some knowledge in the subject area you have chosen, you must plan your communication accordingly. Perhaps you will deal in depth with a specific area of the subject, or you might select interesting details that are not generally known.

If your audience has little or no knowledge of your subject, you must explain unfamiliar concepts and terminology. When you are uncertain of the extent of their knowledge, treat your audience as intelligent listeners with the same information as the general public has of your subject.

WHAT CHARACTERISTICS OF THE AUDIENCE SHOULD I CONSIDER?

Education

The educational level of your audience should determine your word choice. The word "communication" comes from the Latin *communicare,* meaning to share what is common. When you communicate to others, you share ideas with them through a common vocabulary. You must write or speak to an audience in familiar words that they can understand.

Vocabulary

Consider the vocabulary of your listener when developing your material. Omit words or phrases which might be unfamiliar. If you have the choice of two words with the same meaning, choose the more common one. Your purpose is to communicate, not to impress.

No matter what the composition of your audience, stick to your own vocabulary. Do not inject idiomatic expressions that you would not ordinarily use into your speech to gain effect. Your audience might interpret this as condescension or insincerity, and react unfavorably.

Always treat your classmates as intelligent people with good vocabularies. Unless you are dealing with an unfamiliar subject, present information to them on the level you would want them to present it to you.

Age

Knowledge of the age of your audience can often help you in determining how to handle your subject. As a rule (although not exclusively), young people tend to be more liberal than older people, more willing to try change or to take a chance. They are also usually more physically active, inclined toward being participators rather than spectators. Your approach to selling people on the idea of investing in the stock market would take these factors into consideration. You would probably be wise to appeal to older people with a list of dependable blue chip stocks which offer little risk, while for a younger audience you might choose the more glamorous speculative stocks which could double or triple overnight.

Special Interests

Members of an audience frequently have a common interest. They might belong to the same organization or club, be in a similar business or profession, or have gathered together out of mutual concern for a particular problem. You should attempt to determine what these interests are and relate your ideas and supporting material to them.

Consider the common interests of your communications class. As college students, everyone in the class is probably interested in such social problems as poverty, pollution, drugs, and the arms race. In preparing your communication you must be sensitive to the attitudes and needs of your audience regarding these problems; you must want to communicate your ideas about finding solutions.

As a college student yourself, you are aware of other interests shared by your classmates. Perhaps the basketball team is enjoying a winning season, or an important social event is coming up. Keep these interests in mind as you prepare your communication.

IS THE ATTITUDE TOWARD MY SUBJECT FAVORABLE, INDIFFERENT, OR OPPOSED?

An Audience That Is Favorable

People tend to be less critical when they agree with the position of the communicator. Consequently, a favorable audience is likely to be more tolerant of weaknesses in your speech and be willing to accept your evidence. After all, you don't have to prove anything to someone who agrees with you.

This does not mean that speaking to a favorable audience does not offer challenge. The chief goal of communicating to a favorable audience is to reinforce their positive attitudes. If they enjoy guitar playing, the more effectively you entertain them with your guitar, the more successful you will be.

An Audience That Is Indifferent

If you believe that your audience is indifferent to your subject, your job is to stimulate their interest. You may do this either by getting and holding their attention with a fresh imaginative approach, or by demonstrating the importance of the subject to them, or by a combination of both. This action should be taken immediately, in your introduction. Use the various attention-getting devices; explain how your audience is affected by your subject, or if they have something to gain by paying attention to it. As you can see, attention is of prime concern with an indifferent audience.

An Audience That Is Opposed

In most cases, the hardest audience to deal with is one that disagrees with your point of view or dislikes your subject. Who hasn't spent hours arguing about politics or religion only to find herself even more convinced that she was right and the other wrong?

It is difficult to convince a person to change a point of view or an attitude that may have taken years to form. Studies indicate that there is little change in viewpoint among those who listen to or read things with which they strongly disagree. By the time a person reaches adulthood, many of his or her attitudes are pretty well fixed.

GATHER THE SUPPORTING MATERIAL

The key to finding effective supporting material is to begin early. Finding good ideas takes time. There are no shortcuts. Decide on your subject as soon as possible after you are given the assignment. This will greatly increase your chances of finding effective supporting materials. As we said earlier, the first place to look for materials is in your own back yard. What are your thoughts on the subject? Jot them down. Can you enliven your speech with a story from your own experience? By all means include it.

Another source of materials for speaking is mass communications, radio, or television. Talk shows, documentaries, news broadcasts, news analysis, and on-the-scene coverage of major events are just some of the kinds of programs that offer worthwhile material on a wide range of subjects.

Finally, the widest selection of speech materials can be found in the library. Every good library contains hundreds of sources. Newspapers, magazines, professional journals, pamphlets, yearbooks, textbooks, and reference books can often provide all the necessary supporting material for a successful communication. If you are not already, you should become familiar with the various guides to research that the library has available to you. For example, *The Readers' Guide to Periodical Literature* will help you locate articles written on thousands of subjects in magazines since the turn of the century. You can pick up the phone and call the ready reference section of your local library to get information ranging from who played free safety for the Green Bay Packers in 1964 to the present form of government in Greece.

Here is a final tip. Form the habit of recording the material you have gathered promptly and accurately. Some students prefer to keep the details of their readings in notebooks; for convenience of collecting, recording, and filing, however, the use of note cards is best.

When preparing note cards, observe the following rules:

1. Use a three-by-five or four-by-six inch file card.
2. Include only one idea per card.
3. Give each item a heading.
4. Follow the heading with the information. If the material is quoted exactly, use quotation marks. If you paraphrase, make sure you respect the author's meaning.
5. Indicate the exact source from which the information comes.

For new CIA Chief,
    a big rebuilding job.

As director of the Central Intelligence Agency, Adm. Stansfield Turner will face two stern challenges.

1. How to revive confidence in the CIA.

2. How to weigh accurately the strategic balance of power between the U.S. and the Soviet Union.

U.S. News and World Report, February 21, 1977

A Sample Note Card

ORGANIZE THE SPEECH

The function of organization is twofold. First, an audience can more easily understand and appreciate a message that is set in a clear framework. Second, an organizational pattern helps the speaker to eliminate wordiness, i.e., material that is unnecessary to the realization of his or her purpose. All speeches are divided into three parts—the introduction, the body, and the conclusion. The introduction should direct your audience's attention to the subject and make them want to listen. The body should communicate your ideas in a clear, meaningful way, and the conclusion should tie these ideas together in a neat package.

INTRODUCTION

The introduction to a speech has much to do with its success or failure. If a speaker fails to capture the attention of his audience in the introduction, he has little chance of regaining their interest. An introduction can have three purposes: (1) getting the audience's attention, (2) indicating the usefulness of the subject, and (3) indicating the purpose of the speech and its main idea. Although an introduction will often include all three of the above, at times one or two of them may be omitted.

Besides fulfilling these purposes, a good introduction has other characteristics. It must be appropriate to the purpose and main idea of the speech. A humorous introduction to a serious speech, for example, might cause the audience to feel that the speaker was not sufficiently concerned with his intentions. The introduction must lead naturally and easily into the body of the speech. Because the job is not only to get the attention of the audience but to hold it throughout the speech, a transition should be provided between the introduction and the body. Finally, an introduction should make an audience want to listen to the rest of your speech. The first impression you make is very important, so develop your introduction with your audience and subject in mind.

ATTENTION FACTORS

The attention factors listed below will help you develop an attention-getting introduction and can be used to make the body and conclusion of your speech more interesting.

The Startling

A minister once opened his sermon with the statement, "This is a goddamned miserable Sunday!" Needless to say, his audience snapped to attention. After a brief pause to allow them to recover, he explained that he had been just as shocked as they when he overheard the comment on his way to church that morning, and he followed with a blistering attack on profanity. Used sparingly, the startling can be an effective attention-getting device.

Humor

Humor can be an effective tool for the communicator. However, listeners will not be amused by hackneyed, clumsy, or "unfunny" attempts at humor, so you as a speaker should observe the following rules.

First, make sure your humor is relevant. Audiences are not impressed with stories which are dragged in by the heels. Your humor should be used to develop the theme of the composition. If you select the main points of your speech merely to permit the use of stock anecdotes or jokes, your humor is likely to appear irrelevant.

Second, make sure your humor is appropriate. There are some situations in which humor is in bad taste and therefore out of place. If the humor is too sarcastic or personal the audience will be offended instead of entertained; if it violates standards of good taste the audience may be embarrassed.

Finally, use humor that is brief and pointed. Humor should not take up more time than it is worth, its purpose being to provide relaxation, enjoyment, and entertainment.

Suspense

Everyone knows the value of suspense as an attention factor. We follow avidly the serial on TV or the comic strip of our local newspaper. We eagerly seek out the details of a local or national crime or scandal. We watch a football or baseball game, sweating it out with our favorite team.

When using suspense as an attention factor, remember not to tip your hand too soon. For instance, don't give away the outcome of the speech in your introduction. Beginning with the comment, "Let me tell you about the game we lost by inches," will reveal your conclusion at the outset. If you can excite the curiosity of your audience by developing your material in the form of a mystery or problem that they can solve with you, their attention will be aroused by their desire to find out the answer.

The Familiar

Use of the familiar is particularly effective in speaking situations. For years comedians have used the "local" joke, a reference to people, places, or events which are distinctly familiar to the audience. In New York, Johnny Carson used this technique in his opening monologue on the *Tonight Show*. He made jokes about Consolidated Edison (the New York electric power company), the Mayor, or the New York streetwalkers, and the audience roared.

You can add local color to your material by using names and places that the audience will recognize. For instance, in describing a night on the town, a reference to a popular hangout would be appropriate to a student audience. Refer to the interests and experiences of your audience whenever practical. It is also effective to refer to something said by a previous speaker.

The Vital

The vital can be the most forceful attention factor of all, especially when it relates to a strong motive inherent in the audience. People attend to what affects them directly—their health, their security, their survival. Slogans like "Fight Cancer with a Checkup and a Check" are directed at these motives.

The student speaker who began, "Within the next ten years three people in this audience will be dead from the effects of DDT in our environment," had his classmates eager to hear what followed.

The Real

Have you ever been caught up in a story in which the characters and plot were described with such vividness and clarity that you actually became part of the narrative? Speakers able to create this response use the attention-getting technique called the "real"—descriptive language to present a clear and definite picture of what is taking place. The person who describes a scene for an audience is, in effect, placing a mental picture before them. It is his or her job to select those details that the audience needs to know in order to get a clear picture of the situation.

Since using the "real" involves talking about actual people and places, it is wise to give names to the characters you describe, especially if they are important to the story. For example, it is easier to see you sitting next to "Marvin" or "Lolita" than next to your "friend." It is easier to picture "Miss Stonebreaker" than "the math teacher" you had.

The Novel

Most of us are attracted by the unusual. Some people spend hours looking through a hole in the fence of a construction site at workers erecting a building, while others spend hours in line waiting to see the latest innovation on stage or in the movies.

Unusual personal experiences arouse interest on the part of the audience. A deep-sea diver or parachutist would undoubtedly have a list of surefire experiences for holding the attention of an audience.

As a speaker you should constantly be on the lookout for new ways of saying things. Use your imagination; avoid the hackneyed and trite. Which of the following is a more interesting use of description: "The virgin forest," or "the unaxed woods"? While both say the same thing, the latter says it in a newer, more imaginative way.

Finally, consider combining the novel with the familiar. An old story with a new twist is a certain attention-getter. Obviously, not all the problems of communication are solved simply by getting and holding the reader or listener's attention.

A speaker might get attention and yet fail to obtain a desired response. However, you can be sure that the better you control the audience's attention, the better are your chances of accomplishing your purpose.

BODY

The body of a speech develops the speaker's ideas in detail. It should contain a statement of the main idea and supporting material that clarifies or reinforces the main idea. The first step in developing the body of the speech is to formulate a main idea statement. In order to do this, carefully consider the subject and purpose of your speech. What is your restricted subject? Your specific purpose statement? Next, write down exactly what you want to say in one sentence. When you have done this, ask yourself these questions: Does this say what I want to say in the best way possible? Will this statement be clear to my listeners? You may have to make several revisions before you come up with a statement with which you are satisfied. However, this step in your preparation is vital. Keep at it until your sentence states the main idea as well as it can be said.

Once your main idea statement is ready, you can begin arranging the supporting materials for your speech. In order to organize your ideas clearly and interestingly, you should have a plan. You might compare developing a speech to building a garage. Not many people would begin building a garage from a pile of lumber without a blueprint to guide them. The information you have collected is like a pile of lumber. Before you begin putting your material together, find a plan or pattern you can follow. Basic patterns of organization are discussed in Chapter 9. Once you discover the correct pattern for your speech, details will fall into place and you will acquire a sense of direction.

CONCLUSION

No matter how short your speech is, it must have a conclusion to round it off. Many experienced speakers feel that the conclusion is the most important part of the speech, since it leaves the listener with a final impression.

An effective conclusion should leave an audience with a sense of completeness. Usually involving a summary or restatement of the main idea, a conclusion should be brief, to the point, and developed in the same style as the rest of the speech. Both the language and mood of the introduction and body must be continued in the conclusion. (A humorous conclusion to a serious speech would reflect on the sincerity of the speaker.)

One final note. New material should never be introduced in the conclusion. Such an action will give your audience the impression that you have failed to plan your speech carefully and have added the new material as an afterthought. A number of methods for concluding a speech are listed below:

1. Summarize the important points.
2. End with an appropriate anecdote.
3. Present recommendations.
4. End with a quotation or poem.
5. End by restating the main idea.

AN EFFECTIVE STYLE

The manner in which a person expresses herself in language is called style. This book has stressed the use in speech of conversational style, with its frequent employment of the personal pronoun, which gives it an air of familiarity, as if the speaker were talking to close friends. To achieve a conversational style, make frequent use of the terms "us," "we," "our," and "you and I." Think of your speech as talking "with" your audience, not "to" them.

The level of usage in conversational style will vary according to the occasion. In general, the more formal the occasion, the more formal will be the language of the speech. However, regardless of the language used, a style, to be effective, must be communicative. A communicative style has three characteristics: clarity, interest, and appropriateness.

Clarity

Communication does not take place unless the listener understands the message. Too many speakers are concerned with what the audience will think of them rather than with whether they are communicating. By using multisyllabic words and flowery phrases, they try to project what they feel is the image of a successful orator. This is a mistake, because the effective speaker never tries to impress the audience with her vocabulary; she communicates, whenever possible, with a common vocabulary. If you want an effective speech style, choose terms that are appropriate and easily understood. If too much of what you have said is missed or misinterpreted, communication has failed.

For example, if a writer uses the word "exigency" in an essay, the reader unfamiliar with it can look it up; a listener has no such opportunity. Unless he knows the word or can determine its meaning from the context, he misses part of the message. This is avoided by the speaker who chooses a more familiar word, such as "urgency."

Unless you are delivering a formal speech, you should present your ideas in relatively short, uncomplicated sentences. Today's listeners may not spend the time or effort to search for your meaning. For example, a half century ago, when one-hour sermons were common, congregations were impressed with the verbal gymnastics of their clergy. Today the average sermon lasts about 15 minutes because the modern churchgoer demands directness and simplicity.

Interest

Clarity and interest are closely related to each other, since a listener is more inclined to pay attention to a message that he can easily understand. To insure clarity a speaker must explain abstract terms which are important to the understanding of the subject. While this can be accomplished through definition, a more interesting way is through illustration or comparison. Note how interestingly Martin Luther King clarifies the abstract concept of equal opportunity by comparing it to a paycheck:

In a sense we have come to our nation's capital to cash a check. When the architects of our republic wrote the magnificent words of the Constitution and the Declaration of Independence, they were signing a promissory note to which every American was to fall heir. This note was a promise that all men, yes, black men as well as white men, would be granted the unalienable rights of life, liberty, and the pursuit of happiness.

It is obvious today that America has defaulted on this promissory note insofar as her citizens of color are concerned. Instead of honoring this sacred obligation, America has given the Negro people a bad check, which has come back marked "insufficient funds."

But we refuse to believe that the bank of justice is bankrupt. We refuse to believe that there are insufficient funds in the great vaults of opportunity of this nation. So we have come to cash this check—a check that will give us upon demand the riches of freedom and the security of justice.

From "I Have a Dream," reprinted from *Rhetoric of Racial Revolt* (Denver, Colorado: Golden Bell Press, 1964), by permission of the publisher.

Another way of achieving clarity and interesting style is to choose the specific rather than the general. This is especially important in description. When the word "dog" is mentioned, what comes to mind? A collie? A poodle? A St. Bernard? Obviously, you can respond in various ways. With the more specific term "boxer" you get a clearer mental picture. This can be improved even more with added modification, e.g., "Cruncher, the boxer next door." If you want to be clear and interesting, be specific. Don't say, "a man came toward me," if he "staggered," "lurched," "ran," "stumbled," or "crawled."

Sometimes a word can appear to be specific and yet be difficult to visualize. Words that deal with statistics or measurements fall into this category. For example, it is estimated that last year 37 million people died of starvation, most of them children. Although it is specific, this figure is difficult to visualize. To say, "Ten thousand people die each day" is more vivid, since the number is easier to comprehend. An even more vivid and, therefore, more interesting image, is provided by saying, "As you listen to these words, seven people have died of starvation."

Appropriateness

You must use language appropriate to your audience. It would be obviously inappropriate to use medical terminology in presenting a speech on cancer research to a group of laymen. Not so obvious would be the use of technical terms (even though simple) in discussing carburetor adjustment to a general group of students. Since most people are unfamiliar with auto mechanics, you would probably be confusing some in your audience.

In most cases, it is best to avoid off-color stories or profanity. Although modern novels and movies tend to belie this, most listeners will consider the speaker who uses off-color material guilty of poor judgment. While you might draw the attention of your audience with the startling use of a four-letter word, any advantage you gain will be negated if some find the word offensive.

Finally, unless it is apparent that you are deviating for deliberate effect, observe the rules of good grammar. An audience will probably overlook or even miss an occasional grammatical slip, but if your speech is filled with errors, they will think less of you. Whether they are justified or not, an audience tends to judge a person's intelligence by his use or misuse of language.

The accompanying samples of the speech preparation form and speech preparation evaluation form are designed to help you become more aware of preparing speech content. When preparing your speech, fill out a copy of the speech preparation form. Have your listeners fill out a copy of the speech preparation evaluation form to give you feedback as to how successful you were in preparing the content of your speech.

SPEECH PREPARATION FORMS

Name_____ Date_____

Title of Speech _____

(Answer each question completely)

THE COMMUNICATOR

1. Why have I chosen this subject?

2. What qualifies me to deal with this subject?

THE MESSAGE

3. What is my specific purpose?

4. What response can I reasonably expect?

THE AUDIENCE

5. Who is my audience?

6. Will my audience find this subject interesting?

7. Will my audience find this subject useful?

8. What is the **audience**'s probable knowledge of my subject?

9. What characteristics of my audience should I consider in preparing my subject?

10. Is my audience's attitude toward this subject favorable, indifferent, or opposed?

SPEECH PREPARATION

Name_____

1. What was the communicator's subject?

2. How interesting was this subject to you?

low   high

3. How useful was this subject to you?

low   high

4. How effectively did the communicator get attention during introduction?

low   high

5. How much preparation was put into this communication?

low   high

6. What was the communicator's specific purpose? (One simple, declarative sentence)

7. How effective was the conclusion to the communication?

low   high

8. How well did the communicator accomplish his purpose?

low   high

COMMENTS:

CHAPTER 13

Speech Delivery

OBJECTIVES

After studying this chapter, you should be able to:
1. Name the four principal methods of delivery.
2. Explain why extemporaneous speech is the best method for most occasions.
3. List five techniques for controlling speech tension.
4. Identify the nonverbal aspects of platform manner.
5. Discuss the four reasons for maintaining eye contact.
6. List and explain the five different characteristics of voice.
7. Demonstrate your ability to use note cards effectively when delivering a speech.
8. Discuss at least five suggestions you have found helpful in practicing your speech for delivery.

You have finished the hardest part of your job when you have developed the content of your speech. However, the work you have done in analyzing your subject and organizing your material may be wasted if you fail to deliver your speech effectively. Good delivery demands preparation and practice. There are four principal methods of delivery: (1) manuscript, (2) memorized, (3) impromptu, and (4) extemporaneous.

While the way in which you present your speech will vary according to audience and occasion, the best method for most occasions is the extemporaneous speech, spoken with preparation but not written out or memorized. Let us consider each of these methods of delivery separately.

MANUSCRIPT

In formal situations, where the oral presentation must be very precise, you may find it best to read your manuscript verbatim. Be careful to avoid overusing the manuscript speech. While this method offers security to the speaker afraid that he will forget what he wants to say or say it badly, it has three disadvantages: (1) it is difficult to maintain eye contact with the audience while reading, (2) it takes skill and practice to read a speech in a spontaneous and convincing manner, and (3) it is almost impossible to change the language or content of a manuscript speech to fit the mood or reaction of an audience.

Although you may be tempted to accept these disadvantages in return for the security of a manuscript speech, the best advice is to read a speech only when its content demands exact word order, as would research papers and technical data. To deliver a manuscript speech effectively, consider the following suggestions:

1. Edit your speech by reading each sentence aloud. Avoid overly long or involved sentences. No matter how complex or technical your material, it must be communicated clearly.

2. Type the manuscript speech in capital letters, triple-spaced to allow easy reading. Type on only one side of the paper.

3. Become familiar with your material by practicing it aloud; this will help you to obtain maximum eye contact. Even though you are reading, you must read "to people."

4. Indicate pauses and places of emphasis.

5. Use gestures and bodily action to enliven your delivery.

MEMORIZED

While the memorized speech appears to offer ease of eye contact along with the advantages of a manuscript speech, it has two distinct weaknesses: (1) it takes a skillful actor to present memorized material in a natural, spontaneous way, and (2) the speaker who delivers a speech from memory runs the risk of forgetting. Unless you have complete confidence in your ability to deliver a speech naturally without losing your place, memorizing a speech is a risky method.

IMPROMPTU

An impromptu speech is one developed on the spur of the moment. Since it seldom allows opportunity for advance thought or preparation, it demands a great deal of the speaker. Unlike the writer of an impromptu theme, who can rephrase a clumsy sentence, the speaker finds it awkward to correct himself once he has said something. His audience receives his message the moment it is delivered. He has little time to analyze his subject, audience, or occasion, and must think on his feet as he chooses and organizes his material. While the impromptu method can often impart directness and spontaneity to the speaker's delivery, handling material that is not carefully thought out can often result in a rambling presentation. Experience in the planning, preparation, and delivery of extemporaneous speeches will provide guidelines for greater effectiveness in impromptu situations.

When you are called upon to deliver an impromptu speech, consider the following advice: (1) make sure that your central idea and specific purpose are absolutely clear to your audience, (2) keep your speech short and to the point, and (3) handle only one main point.

EXTEMPORANEOUS

Like the written or memorized speech, the extemporaneous speech is carefully planned and rehearsed with the difference that the speaker does not deliver the speech in a predetermined word order. He decides on his exact wording at the moment of delivery. Thus, the extemporaneous method offers the same directness and spontaneity as the impromptu method without the danger of the speaker's rambling off the point or repeating himself unnecessarily. You might compare extemporaneous speech delivery with the telling of a detailed funny story. Most people tell a funny story that they are familiar with extemporaneously. They know how the story is going to unfold, but they haven't memorized the word order. As long as they include those details necessary to make the humor clear, they can tailor the story to fit the occasion. The result is a relaxed, spontaneous style, which is the main advantage of extemporaneous delivery.

STAGE FRIGHT

You may be saying to yourself, "How can I say it in an easy, natural way when I'm scared to death up there?" If you feel this way, you have probably at one time or another experienced a case of stage fright. Stage fright is the fear that you will not do as well as you would like to in front of an audience. The symptoms may be any combination of the following: dry mouth, rapid pulse, quivering voice, uncontrollable trembling, loss of memory, sweaty palms, or queasy stomach. If a person is afflicted with stage fright what can he or she do about it? We suggest a two-way approach: (1) become familiar with the causes of stage fright, (2) use specific techniques to control tensions.

Causes of Stage Fright

When you deliver a speech in your communication course, you are communicating in a friendly situation. You are speaking to a classroom of students who are pulling for you and expect you to make mistakes, just as they will. In this kind of situation a speaker should feel relaxed and at ease—but many don't. Why? Many beginning speakers see the situation as threatening rather than friendly. They see their egos in jeopardy. They worry about others' seeing their weaknesses and imperfections, real or imaginary. Worrying too much about what other people will think of you is what causes stage fright.

A student has good reason to be fearful if she gets up to deliver a speech she has done little to prepare or practice. She not only has to worry about losing her place or forgetting what she was going to say; she has the added burden of having wasted the audience's time. Few of your classmates will react favorably to your presentation if they feel you are taking advantage of them. Sometimes a person may be well prepared but experience stage fright when speaking to what psychologists call "significant others." A student might find it easy to speak in a history or psychology class but freeze up in a communications course because the instructor is evaluating her performance. A Sunday school teacher may be relaxed and at ease when teaching class but be filled with fear when addressing the congregation.

Stage fright also occurs when risk is involved in the situation. Your instructor, for example, may become much less fluent when her supervisor drops in on the class to evaluate her performance. A young man might feel self-conscious and ill at ease when asking that special someone for a first date. You may, for example, have no difficulty communicating with your boss until it comes time to ask for that raise.

Finally, stage fright can occur because the speaker is in a depressed mood. Perhaps something tragic has recently happened to a friend or

A CASE OF STAGE FRIGHT?

Have you ever had a case of stage fright?

If you're an undergraduate theater student or a secondary school drama teacher, your stage experience has probably included at least one case of stage fright.

If so, you're just the person we're looking for.

The Durham Summer Theater's fourteenth season is only months away, and we're beginning our national search for talented, energetic students and teachers to study in our acting, management, and technical workshops and join our repertory company at the University of New Hampshire.

Of course, we can't promise a cure for stage fright. But the theoretical knowledge and practical training you'll receive will increase your confidence in your abilities, on stage and off.

Apprentices in the Undergraduate Theater Workshop undergo a rigorous eight-week schedule of classes in acting, voice and diction, scenic arts, lighting, costuming, and management. Secondary school teachers follow a similar program and also attend seminars on directing, production, and teaching theater techniques.

All workshop participants will have the opportunity to join the resident professionals on stage in the company's six major productions.

Workshops are held in the Paul Creative Arts Center's two air-conditioned theaters: Johnson Theater, a 721-seat proscenium theater, and Hennessy Theater, a 250-seat theater-in-the-round.

When you're not involved with workshops or performances, you'll find plenty of things to do close by. The University of New Hampshire is situated near some of New England's finest beaches; fresh-water lakes, the White Mountains, and Boston are all within easy driving distance.

Final plans for the 1977 Durham Summer Theater schedule are still being completed, but this season's productions are expected to include *South Pacific, Much Ado About Nothing, A View from the Bridge, Arms and the Man, Celebration,* and *The Real Inspector Hound.*

The Durham Summer Theater at the University of New Hampshire

Undergraduate Theater Workshop/June 26-August 19/ 8 credits (transferable)/some high school apprentices accepted

Undergraduate auditions/New York—Americana Hotel, April 14-16/Chicago—Loyola University, April 21-23/Los Angeles—by arrangement/University of New Hampshire—by arrangement, April 1-May 30

Theater Workshop for Teachers/Session I—June 26-July 22/Session II—July 25-August 19/teachers may enroll for one or both sessions/acceptance through application/enrollment limited

Information and applications/Linda L. Spohn, Managing Director, Durham Summer Theater, Paul Creative Arts Center, University of New Hampshire, Durham, NH 03824

Concept/Ken Silvia—Photo/Jack Adams, University of New Hampshire

loved one, or there might be a problem hanging over her head that seems unsolvable. It could be that a person is down without even knowing why. In any event, whatever affects the speaker's personality affects her speech.

How to Control Tensions

Since most speakers experience some nervousness when they appear before an audience, you probably will, too. Here are some suggestions on how to keep your nervousness at a minimum.

1. Develop an attention-getting introduction. It is important to get off to a good start with your audience. A novel or humorous introduction will put your audience in the right frame of mind and help you relax as well. Suggestions on how to develop attention-getting introductions are found in Chapter 12.

2. Instead of worrying about your own speech, listen carefully to the speaker you are going to follow. Perhaps there is something in his speech that you can refer to in your introduction. This will take your mind off of your own plight and start you on the right foot. Your audience will be impressed with your imagination.

3. Make sure that you carefully develop a speech that is audience-centered. If you feel that you have something worthwhile for your audience, chances are your concern will shift from yourself to the ideas you are trying to communicate. Suggestions for developing an audience-centered speech are found in Chapter 12.

4. Practice your speech from three to five times. The idea is to practice enough so that your ideas can be recalled quickly and easily but not so much that you unconsciously memorize it. When you are well prepared, speaking is fun.

5. Develop a positive mental attitude about speaking. It is natural to be nervous when standing before an audience. As you get more and more practice in speech making, you will find that this nervous energy can be transferred into making your speech more vibrant and enthusiastic.

PLATFORM MANNER

In a broad sense, platform manner can include all of the speaker's non-verbal communication—the way the speaker walks up to and away from the platform, his or her facial expression, posture, gestures, and attire. The speaker who approaches an audience in a positive way says to the listener, "I have something to offer that I think you will find rewarding." An audience begins evaluating a speaker as soon as he or she comes into their line of vision. If you want to create the right impression, walk to the speaker's platform in a firm, energetic way. Good posture projects alertness and self-confidence. After you have reached the lectern, pause briefly and look out at those in your audience in a friendly, interested manner. If a smile is in order, by all means smile. The important thing is that your facial expression should be appropriate to your subject matter; it should set the mood for your speech.

It is usually a good idea to maintain good posture when addressing an audience. Speakers who slouch over the lectern or affect too casual a pose tend to receive an indifferent response.

There will be times when it will be necessary for you to move around in front of your audience, to walk to a chalkboard or map, to demonstrate a way of doing something, or simply to move closer to them to develop a more intimate mood. There is one simple rule to follow when you are in front of an audience. Anything you do, whether it is sitting on your desk or walking to the window, is acceptable as long as it does not call attention to itself. A movement is unacceptable when the audience thinks, "I wonder why he's doing that?"

Gesture is another characteristic of platform manner. In casual, relaxed conversation we habitually employ a wide range of gestures. We nod our heads, shrug our shoulders, wrinkle our brows, or wave our hands to emphasize what we have to say or to describe something.

If, when presenting your speeches, you find it difficult to use gestures successfully, wait until you feel the urge to use them. To be effective, gestures must come naturally and instinctively. A beginning speaker is often overly conscious of his or her audience. It is better to wait with your gestures until you are more relaxed in the speaking situation, since an awkward gesture is worse than no gesture at all.

The clothes worn by a speaker should suit the occasion. For a classroom speech, wear what you would normally wear to class; for a more formal occasion, dress accordingly. In both cases your clothes should be cleaned, pressed, and in good repair. Clothing which does not call attention to itself is always the best choice.

The conclusion of your speech should be carefully planned so that you can finish with your eyes fixed on the audience. After a brief pause, leave the speaker's platform with the same air of confidence with which you approached it. Don't indicate by your facial expression or gesture that you were at all dissatisfied with your performance. Let your audience evaluate you.

EYE CONTACT

Good eye contact is an aid in holding attention, and necessary for feed-back from the audience. In general, your eye contact will be effective if you look slowly from one individual to another; if your eyes dart rapidly from person to person, the effect will be shifty or unnatural. Although it isn't necessary to look at each individual in your audience, be careful to include persons from all parts of the group. Do not develop the habit of looking mostly to one side of the room or at just those nearest you.

Eye contact is an aid to holding your audience's attention for a num-ber of reasons. First, we indicate our interest in others by looking them in the eye. One of the most important things a speaker can do is to con-vince each listener that he or she is being addressed as an individual. An audience will tend to respond to a speaker who demonstrates that interest.

Second, eye contact is thought of as an indication of straightfor-wardness and honesty. We look people right in the eye when we are open and aboveboard, and avoid someone's eyes when we are saying something dishonest or embarrassing. Looking your audience right in the eye will convince them of your honesty and sincerity.

Third, we speak to our audience nonverbally as well as verbally. We say a great deal to them with our facial expression, especially the eyes. Facial expression can aid greatly in making meanings clear, giving em-phasis, and expressing moods. Obviously, an audience will have difficulty seeing your facial expression if you are staring out the window or at your notes.

The final reason for establishing eye contact is to obtain feedback from the audience. We look at people while communicating to them be-cause we are interested in their reaction to what we are saying. They in-dicate this through changes in facial expression, posture, and gestures. This feedback tells us how well we are communicating, whether our lis-teners are interested or bored, clear or confused, friendly or hostile, thus giving us the opportunity to respond appropriately.

VOICE

The very least a listener can expect of a speaker is that he or she speak in a voice loud and clear enough to be heard and understood. It takes too much effort to listen to a speaker who mutters or speaks too softly. How-ever, if you want to be an effective speaker, you must do more than the bare minimum. Your voice must be an asset to you; it must help to make what you say more interesting and meaningful. The different characteristics which express meaning and add variety to your voice are: volume, rate, articulation, quality, and pitch.

Volume

Volume refers to the loudness or softness of your voice. Obviously, you must increase your volume to be heard in a large room or in a situation with a high degree of surrounding noise. Don't be misled by the fact that you can hear yourself adequately. If it takes effort on the part of the listener to hear you, you are probably not communicating effectively.

Rate

Rate, the speed at which a person speaks, is dependent upon two elements—duration and pause. Duration is the length of time a word is prolonged. It is an effective way to emphasize, and is often used in conversation, particularly to accentuate modifiers, e.g., "He has a *fabulous* record collection—we had a *fantastic* time." Pause, together with duration, determines the rate at which a person speaks. If a person cuts words off short and allows little pause, the rate will be rapid. Most beginning speakers tend to speak faster than they should, because a person tends to increase the rate when either nervous or excited. In addition, many people tend to associate pause with nonfluency, with the idea that a person pauses because he or she does not know what to say. Ironically, this attitude toward pause as an indicator of nonfluency is often formed while a child is being taught to read in the primary grades. The child who reads slowly and haltingly, pausing before unfamiliar words, is thought of as a slow learner. The child who reads at a fairly rapid rate with few pauses is considered bright and given praise. The result is that the student is taught to avoid pause.

Articulation

We learn to speak by imitating the speech of those close to us. Consequently, our habits of speech often resemble the speech habits of those we have imitated. If we are lucky, and those we learn from speak distinctly, we tend to speak distinctly. However, if those we learn from tend toward indistinct speech, the chances are that our speech will also be indistinct. Unless the problem is physical, indistinct speech is caused by poor articulation, which is the process of forming the consonant and vowel sounds of words. It is a necessity for successful communication, since if you fail to articulate your words clearly, you will be difficult to understand.

The two common errors of articulation are substituting one sound for another and leaving off the endings of words. For example, "this" becomes "dis," "student" becomes "stoont," and "asked" becomes "ast." An audience forms an unfavorable impression of a speaker who says things in a careless way. If the impression you give to others is important to you, make sure your articulation is precise.

Improving your articulation may not be easy if bad habits are ingrained in your speech. The first thing you must do is become aware of your weaknesses. What are your specific problems—running words together? Leaving off word endings? Substituting sounds? Although you can become aware of your problems by listening carefully to yourself as you speak, it is preferable, if you have the opportunity, to record your voice with a tape recorder or video tape. Tape yourself not only while practicing your speech but during ordinary conversation as well. Once you have determined your problems, make a list and study them.

Quality

A pleasant voice is free from undue harshness, huskiness, hoarseness, breathiness, and nasality. Unless a person has some problem caused by a disease or physical defect, he or she should be able to speak in a voice which is pleasant to listen to. Serious speech problems should be handled by a trained speech therapist. For those with minor difficulties, Jeffrey and Peterson make the following suggestions:

1. The speaker should learn to hear his voice as others hear it. An almost universal reaction of persons upon hearing a recording of their voice for the first time is, "That's not me. There must be something wrong with the recorder." But, of course, there is nothing wrong with the recorder and the recording, as classmates or friends will verify, is a faithful reproduction of the individual's speech. The speaker's initial reaction reveals that most people do not hear themselves as others hear them. This is in part because some of the sound is carried from the voice box to his ears through the cheek and neck bones. But it is also in part because most people have become so accustomed to hearing their own voice that they really do not listen to themselves carefully or analytically.

   Quite clearly, the first step in learning to hear one's voice as others hear it is for the speaker to record and listen to his speech frequently. The second step is to develop an awareness at all times of how it sounds.
2. To avoid strain, one should speak at a comfortable pitch level.
3. The speaker should maintain adequate breath support.
4. He should remain relaxed while speaking.
5. If strain or hoarseness occurs regularly, the speaker should consult a speech correctionist.

Robert C. Jeffrey and Owen Peterson, Speech: *A Text with Adapted Readings* (New York: Harper & Row, Publishers, 1971), pp. 385–86.

Pitch

Pitch refers to the highness or lowness of a speaker's voice. Everyone has a natural pitch level at which he can speak most comfortably. Problems in pitch can occur when a person tries to speak at a pitch which is higher or lower than his natural level. Suppose, for example, that a young man with a natural tenor voice feels that a bass voice is more masculine. His attempts to speak in a lower voice result in a husky and rasping sound. Instead of his natural, resonant voice, he produces a voice with an unpleasant quality, lack of adequate volume, and monotony in pitch. The size and length of your vocal chords determine the tone of your voice. If you want to avoid problems with your voice, speak at your most comfortable pitch level.

A natural conversational style is characterized by a variety of pitches. In normal conversation, these inflections come spontaneously. The best way to insure that your inflection will be interesting and meaningful is to choose a subject which you desire to communicate to your listeners. When you are concerned with expressing your true feelings, your inflection will come naturally.

PREPARING THE SPEECH FOR DELIVERY

An extemporaneous speaker delivers his speech from notes which include his main ideas and supporting materials. Many experienced speakers put their individual ideas on separate cards rather than together on the same page. An individual note card isolates an idea so that it can be seen at a glance; after the speaker has dealt with the idea, she can move on to the next card. Although your audience expects you to use notes in an extemporaneous speech, you should do so unobtrusively. Remember, anything that calls attention to itself can distract from what you are saying. Note cards are much easier to handle if you must deliver the speech without a lectern. You can hold them in one hand and still be able to gesture freely. However, in most platform situations a lectern will be available to you. Once you have reached the lectern, put your notes down and leave them there; notes are to remind you of what to say, not to read verbatim. When you finish with a note card, move it to one side as unobtrusively as possible.

There is one instance when you should call attention to your notes. When reading a direct quotation, hold your notes up so that your audience can see that you are taking special care to be accurate.

Be sure that you can read your notes easily. Notes are easy to read when they are typed in capital letters, and double- or triple-spaced. Use only one side of the paper, since turning over your notes is both awkward and time-consuming. Each note card or page should be clearly numbered to prevent you from losing your place.

Avoid writing your notes in too much detail. Coming to the speaker's platform with an overly detailed guide may tempt you to read your speech, thereby defeating the whole purpose of the extemporaneous method.

Finally, don't let the fact that you are using a guide inhibit your gestures or facial expression. Spontaneous, convincing delivery requires bodily action and expressiveness.

Following are two types of note cards prepared for a student speech on diabetes. Create similar copy of your own to see which type is most effective for you.

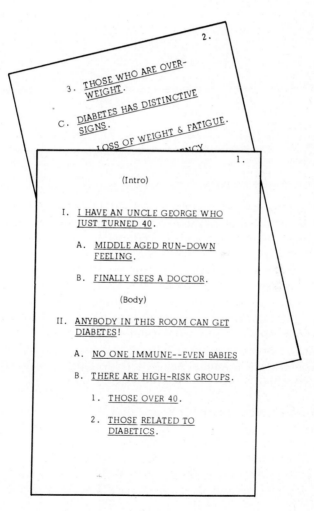

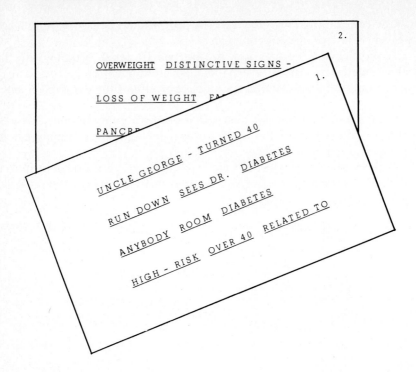

Practicing the Speech

The key to effective delivery is practice. Few experienced speakers would deliver an extemporaneous speech without practicing at least two or three times. Practice offers an additional benefit to you as a beginning speaker. While practicing in a relaxed atmosphere to improve a specific speech, you can take stock of your strengths and weaknesses as a speaker.

After you have practiced your speech a few times, deliver it as if you were in front of an audience. Doing your best in practice will give you a good idea of the quality of your ultimate performance. If possible, deliver your speech to someone who can evaluate it objectively. If it is possible to tape record or videotape yourself, by all means do so. Self-evaluation is a prerequisite to improvement. Below are specific suggestions for practicing your speeches.

Suggestions for Practicing Your Speech

1. Practice delivering your speech from three to five times. The idea is to practice enough so that you will feel confident and relaxed when it comes time to deliver your speech, but not so much that you unconsciously memorize it. In other words,

practice enough to develop fluency in the way you express your ideas, but not so much that you lose spontaneity.

2. Don't try to deliver your speech the same way twice. Become reconciled to the fact that you might forget something during practice. The important thing to remember is that if you practice your speech carefully, you will have no difficulty in remembering the main ideas when you deliver it. After all, if you forget a statistic or example during the speech, who is going to know besides you?

3. Go through the entire speech during each practice. Inexperienced speakers often stop and go back to the beginning after they have made a few mistakes. This is unwise. Accept the fact that some hesitation or groping for words is inevitable and continue through to the end. If the rough spots don't work out by themselves, you can work on them before you practice the speech the next time.

4. Practice as if you were actually delivering your speech to an audience. If at all possible, try to practice with the same volume and animation you will use when it comes time to deliver your speech. There is a certain amount of acting involved in giving a speech. Develop this "performance" attitude in practice, and you will do a much better job when it comes to the real thing.

5. Practice with the same note cards or manuscript you plan to use when delivering your speech. If you are planning an extemporaneous delivery, don't practice from a manuscript or outline and then walk up to the speaker's platform with a set of notes you have never used before. Also, don't practice from notes you have scribbled changes and comments on and then type up a brand new set to use in class and expect to do a good job with them. Make sure that the notes you bring on the day of delivery are the same ones you used in your last practice.

6. Don't practice individual gestures. It's fine to gesture naturally while practicing, but don't decide that at a certain place in your speech you will pound your fist on the lectern or point your finger at the audience. To be effective, gestures must be spontaneous.

7. Practice with the aids you will use in your speech. One guaranteed way to cause butterflies in the stomach is to stand in front of an audience with a visual aid that doesn't work. Furthermore, it might take you longer to demonstrate something with an aid than you thought it would. Finding this out in practice could prevent an embarrassing situation.

8. Time your speech in practice. Develop your speeches so that they fall within the time limit of the assignment. Mark Twain told the story of going to listen to a minister he had heard was one of the finest in the area. After listening to him for the first

15 minutes he was so impressed he decided to leave $20 in the collection plate. Another 30 minutes passed, and he lowered it to $10. Finally, one hour later when the sermon was over and they passed the plate around, he took out $5 and stalked out.

9. Whenever possible, practice in front of a live audience. Even if you have to bring your little brother and his friend into the room, it helps to practice delivering your speech to a listener. If you can find a listener who will give you some constructive evaluation, all the better.

10. Tape record or videotape your practice when possible. If you have access to recorders at home or in school, by all means make use of them. They are excellent aids to self-evaluation.

The accompanying speech evaluation form is designed for both student and instructor evaluation. It lists those characteristics of delivery and content which should be considered when evaluating a speaker.

Name_____ Topic_____ Date_____

SPEECH EVALUATION SHEET

Grade_____

Poor –	1	2	3	4	– Excellent	COMMENTS
A. DELIVERY						
1. Platform Manner						
2. Eye Contact						
3. Fluency						
B. VOICE						
1. Volume						
2. Clarity						
3. Variety						
C. CONTENT						
1. Interestingness						
2. Organization						
3. Audience Analysis						
4. Purpose						
D. LANGUAGE						
1. Clear						
2. Appropriate						

```
                            SELF-EVALUATION FORM


        NAME_____ DATE_____ GRADE_____
        SPECIFIC PURPOSE_____
        _____


        STRENGTHS
        _____


        WEAKNESSES
        _____


        AUDIENCE RESPONSE
        _____


        WAYS TO IMPROVE
        _____


        COMPARE YOUR EVALUATION
        WITH EVALUATION OF THE
        INSTRUCTOR AND OTHERS
        _____

        DID YOU FULFILL
        YOUR PURPOSE?
        _____
```

It is important that a speaker be able to evaluate his or her performance objectively. Fill out a self-evaluation form after each speech you deliver. This will help you to clarify your strengths and weaknesses as a speaker.

EXERCISES: SPEAKING ASSIGNMENTS

Following the suggestions given on the preceding pages, prepare and deliver whichever of these assignments your instructor chooses.

INTRODUCING A CLASSMATE

Interview a classmate, questioning him about his or her hobbies, likes and dislikes, goals, attitudes, or anything you feel will be of interest to the class. Take careful notes. Then, have your classmate interview

you. After class, review your notes selecting the information you believe is most interesting. Arrange this information in an order which will be easy for you and your audience to remember. Deliver this speech to class as your instructor directs.

Suggestions

1. Make sure you pronounce your classmate's name *distinctly* and *correctly.*
2. Be accurate. Don't try to make your classmate out to be someone he or she is not.
3. Be as friendly and interesting as you can.
4. Be familiar with your material. If you need a note card, use only one.

READING A COMMERCIAL

Read a one–two minute radio or TV commercial that you have written yourself or picked up from a local broadcaster. Study it carefully to decide how best to indicate meaning and emphasis. Practice it so that you can deliver it easily and naturally.

Delivery: It is important that you communicate sincerity to your audience. You can do this best by using a conversational style. Be yourself. Try to inject color and feelings into your words and phrases by being enthusiastic about the product. Smile when you speak.

Model

MISTER DONUT

(Establish and fade background for announcer.)

ANNCR: Before he opens his own shop, each MISTER DONUT owner goes through a rigorous five-week training course on how to make the finest and freshest donuts a person can buy. That's why they're able to make over 100 varieties of fresh donuts . . . honey dips, chocolate, bavarian cream, toasted coconut . . . even fancy pastries like eclairs and bismarks and blueberry bursts. Why, these fellows have such good-looking fancy donuts, some of them look as good as miniature wedding cakes. Come on in to Mister Donut and buy a dozen . . . for the kids, or your guests or the gals at the office.

Visit the Mister Donut Shop, at 3151 South 92nd Street . . . or . . . the Mister Donut Shop, at 9230 West Capital Drive . . . in Milwaukee.

(Music to fill)

Used with the permission of Mister Donut of America, Inc. and The Sycamore Corporation.

A LETTER TO THE EDITOR (An expression of viewpoint; two–three minutes)

Write to the "Letters to the Editor" column of one of your local newspapers expressing a point of view. It will be helpful if you familiarize yourself with these columns in order to be aware of the rules and format to follow. A reader will judge you on your style and grammatical correctness. A simple, to-the-point style must still be interesting.

Delivery: This speech will be delivered in the manuscript method of presentation. Remember, the successful speaker reads as though she were speaking extemporaneously. Practice to deliver this speech in a spontaneous, convincing manner.

Suggestions

1. If you are writing in response to a published letter, read it so that your audience is clear as to what you're disagreeing with.
2. Write as if you were speaking—in an informal, direct way.
3. Read the letter aloud to a friend or two.
4. Become familiar enough with the letter to develop good eye contact.
5. Proofread your letter to eliminate weaknesses in style and grammatical errors.

THE IMPROMPTU SPEECH

Deliver a two–four minute impromptu speech. Your purpose may be to inform, persuade, or entertain. You will either be given a subject or allowed to choose one from a list made available to you shortly before you begin speaking.

Delivery: Use the limited time available to you to decide on your purpose and specific intent. Make sure that both are absolutely clear to your audience. Keep your speech short and to the point. Handle only one main point in the body and restate your central idea at the conclusion.

Sample Topics

1. Honesty as the best policy
2. My views on socialism
3. The ideal wife (husband)
4. The most useful profession
5. If I had it to do over again

6. What I consider a good movie
7. City versus country living
8. The most useless profession
9. A day I would like to forget
10. Thirteen, my lucky number

READING PROSE OR POETRY

Choose a selection of prose or poetry. Study it carefully in regard to meaning and mood. Practice it until you can deliver it effectively. In order to read well, a person must understand the meaning and mood of the material, and be able to convey that meaning and mood to his audience.

Suggestions

1. *Choose your reading carefully.* Pick something interesting that you can handle intelligently.
2. *Time your reading.* Your selection must fall within a two–three minute time limit.
3. *Insure understanding.* Preface your reading with any information that will contribute to your listener's understanding.
4. *Use effective speaking techniques.* Speak clearly and distinctly, using variations in rate, pitch, and volume to convey the author's meaning and to make the reading more interesting. Know your selection well enough so that you can maintain adequate eye contact with your audience. It might be a good idea to copy your selection double-spaced on note cards or half sheets of paper.

Model

The reader's job here is to communicate the attitudes of the two speakers in the poem.

SLOW DOWN?

Slow down, black man, you tell me.
You're moving much too fast
At the rate you're going
You surely cannot last.
You're entitled to your rights,
You're going to get them, too.
But, you're rushing things too fast
And, that ain't good for you.
Sure you're demonstrating,
You're picketing and such
I know you want your rights.
But, you're crowding things too much.
Slow down, black man, Slow down.
Heed the words I say

You're injuring your cause
This is not the way
Things will be all right.
You haven't got to worry.

But, slow down, black man. Slow down.
Don't be in such a hurry.
I get the Message white man.
It's coming in loud and clear.
But, you ain't saying nothing.
It's like, Mister, I can't hear.
How long you been a black man?
How long you been a "boy"?
What rights does the nation have
That you cannot enjoy?
It's easy for you to say,
"Black man, take it slow."
But, do you know segregation?
Have you ever met "The Crow"?
You don't fool me, Mr. White Man.
You ain't dealing from the top.
You don't mean "slow down."
You mean, damn it, "NIGGER, STOP!"

Slow down, black man, you
tell me.
Man you got your gall.
You've never cried for justice
You don't understand at all.
Have you ever lost a brother
To the fury of a mob?
Has the color of your skin
Stopped you from getting a
job?
Slow down, black man, you
tell me.

Well, mister, that's all right.
It's easy for you to say.
Who've never known a
slight.
I have been going slow
For more than five score
years
And yet and still I know
The same old hate and
fears.

Have your brethren been
lynched?
For the crime of being white?
Have you seen your mother
tremble
When the klansmen rode at
night?
I've been patient, Mr. White
Man.
The Lord knows I have been
But, I ain't as good as Job
My patience has an end.
You bomb my house of
worship.
You kill my babies, too.
Slow down, black man, you
tell me.
Well, man, that's up to you.
I'll slow down, Mr. White
Man.
I promise you I will,
When jimcrow is interred—
And we stand on freedom
hill.

With permission of the author, Ben Anderson, Mt. Vernon, New York.

A SPEECH OF CRITICISM

**Deliver a two–four minute speech or write a 250–500 word essay in
which you criticize a person, policy, or organization. Pick a subject
that really annoys you. Express your views in a direct, to-the-point
manner, emphasizing your annoyance with the language you use. If
you deliver this as a speech, underline your irritation with facial
expression, gestures, and tone.**

Delivery: **This speech should be delivered extemporaneously. The more spontaneous and direct you are in your presentation, the more clearly you will communicate your conviction and sincerity to the audience. This is an expression of** *your* **viewpoint. Indicate your attitude with emphasis, intensity, and force.**

Suggested Topics

1. Let's end our hypocritical attitude toward (censorship, segregation, communism, religion, etc.).
2. Welfare is another word for stealing.
3. People who brand all long-haired teenagers as hippies are ignorant.
4. Let's get the bigots out of our judicial system.
5. When are we going to stop kidding ourselves about America being a free country?
6. Allowing students to protest is undermining the principles upon which our colleges and universities were founded.

RELATING A PERSONAL EXPERIENCE (To entertain)

Deliver a two–five minute speech or write a short narrative of 300–500 words in which you relate a personal experience. Describe the situation in enough detail to create a mental picture for the reader or listener. Develop your material informally, with emphasis on details of action.

Delivery: **This speech should be delivered extemporaneously. An audience will expect you to have almost total eye contact when talking about your own experiences. The more spontaneous and relaxed you are, the more your audience will enjoy your presentation.**

Suggested Topics

1. My last day on the job
2. A visit to the Internal Revenue Service
3. My uncle George
4. A brush with death
5. A day in Vietnam
6. My first date
7. My most embarrassing experience

SPEECH TO ENTERTAIN

Either describe a stimulating experience of yours (i.e., an exciting event, a memorable trip, an unforgettable performance) which you feel would be interesting to the class, or deliver a speech in which you use humor to entertain your audience. You may, for example, treat a serious subject lightly or a light subject seriously. Contact is very important; speak directly to your audience. The more clearly the audience can visualize what you describe, the more effective will be your speech.

Choose a subject whose effectiveness will be increased by use of a visual aid. Studies indicate that a person learns more readily when he is given the opportunity to see as well as hear what is being explained. Visual aids may consist of charts, diagrams, maps, pictures, photographs, models, film strips, projectors, records, physical gestures—in short, whatever provides an extra audio or visual dimension to the words the audience hears.

Suggestions

1. Use vivid, colorful language to stimulate the senses of the audience.
2. Organize your material clearly.
3. Be friendly and relaxed. Avoid being overresponsive to your own humor.
4. Read such authors as Art Buchwald, Dick Gregory, Al Capp, and Dorothy Parker to get an idea of effective satirical style.

Sample Topics

1. How to wash a bull elephant
2. How to get a fair share of the government "giveaway"
3. A moment I'll always remember
4. Camping can be fun, for bears
5. My first and last day on the job

A DEMONSTRATION SPEECH

Deliver a two–five minute speech in which you demonstrate a technique or procedure. Accompany your delivery with an appropriate visual aid. Pick something that you enjoy doing and do well. Consider whether the audience will see the usefulness of your information. Topics which offer little utility to the audience must be made interesting in order to hold attention.

Delivery: **This speech should be delivered extemporaneously. Demonstrating something requires freedom of movement. You might have to use your hands, arms, legs, or body to explain something to your listeners. Therefore, the less dependent on notes you are, the better.**

Sample Topics

1. How to take an effective snapshot
2. How to fillet a fish
3. How to set a broken leg
4. How to mix a strawberry daiquiri
5. How to dance the "Big Apple"

SPEECH TO INFORM

Choose a subject in which your main job as a speaker is to present information. Present your material in such a way as to hold and maintain audience attention so that they can readily understand and remember.

Delivery: **This speech can be delivered either with manuscript or extemporaneously. Keep the pattern of development simple so that you move from one idea to another smoothly.**

Suggestions

1. Decide whether your audience is listening to the information out of curiosity or need.
2. Present material that is unknown by relating it to what is known.
3. You may need to summarize from time to time to make your points absolutely clear.

Sample Topics

1. The Koala bear
2. Today's average student
4. The real story of Howard Hughes
4. Planting a garden
5. The native American

SPEECH TO INFORM USING A VISUAL AID

Choose a subject whose effectiveness will be increased by use of a visual aid. Studies indicate that a person learns more readily when she is given the opportunity to see as well as hear what is being explained. Visual aids may consist of charts, diagrams, maps, pictures, photographs, models, film strips, projectors, records, physical gestures—in short, whatever provides an extra audio or visual dimension to the words the audience hears.

Delivery: This speech should be delivered extemporaneously. The speaker must be free to move to her map, chart, or diagram, or to use both hands in demonstrating a technique.

Suggestions

1. *Keep visual aids out of sight when not in use.* Don't display your aid until you are ready to use it, and remove it as soon as you are through with it.

2. *Visual aids should be easily seen.* Be sure that the aid is large enough to be seen by all. Stand to the side of an aid so that you can speak directly to the audience.

3. *Visual aids should be clear and relevant.* Unless an aid is easy to understand and related to the subject, it can confuse rather than clarify. Don't use a visual aid just for the sake of appearances.

4. *Practice using your visual aid.* When you practice your speech, have your visual aids ready and use them. If possible, practice using your aid in the room in which you will be speaking. Make sure that the necessary equipment is available. Stand at the back of the room to insure that your aid can be clearly seen or heard.

Sample Topics

1. Mark Twain, America's great wit
2. The laser beam
3. The art of tree dwarfing
4. How to beat the stock market
5. Automobile lubrication

RELATING A PERSONAL EXPERIENCE (To persuade)

Deliver a two–four minute speech or write a short narrative of 300–500 words in which you relate a personal experience to persuade. Describe the material in enough detail to create a mental picture for the reader or listener. Develop your material informally, with emphasis on details of action. A personal story is an excellent means of reinforcing or clarifying your ideas.

Delivery: This speech should be delivered extemporaneously. An audience will expect you to have almost total eye contact when talking about your own experience. The more spontaneous and relaxed you are, the more your audience will enjoy your presentation.

Sample Topics

1. Getting involved can pay off
2. Don't depend on the other driver
3. The grass is always greener on the other side
4. Sometimes it pays to be ignorant
5. A first-aid course could save a life

CHAPTER **14**

Group
Communication

After studying this chapter, you should be able to:
1. Define the duties of a participant in group discussion.
2. Recognize the duties of the moderator in group discussion.
3. Write a discussion problem-question.
4. Explain the characteristics of the eight types of discussion.
5. Discuss the two basic functions of discussion.
6. Identify the steps to follow in problem-solving discussion.
7. Describe the case-problem approach to discussion.

Hardly a day goes by without your participating in a number of small group discussions. Most of them are informal talks with others about matters of mutual interest. Others occur more formally in organized committees and action groups.

Discussions have also been a vital part of your formal education. Most of us got our first taste of class discussion in kindergarten or first grade. Probably a majority of the courses you are now taking are lecture-discussion. Yet, in spite of your considerable experience with group communication, many of the discussions that you engage in fail to produce fruitful results.

There are a number of reasons why discussions fail. Sometimes the participants do not have the necessary information and the discussion becomes a "pooling of ignorance." At other times the discussion lacks a spirit of cooperation and ends in aimless argument. Lack of communication, lack of understanding, and a tendency to stray from the subject may also lessen the possibility of agreement or understanding. How many discussions between parents and children have ended with the participants stalking off because of any or all of the above obstacles?

The advantages of becoming a more effective discussion member are obvious. A study of the forms and principles of group discussion, together with guided practice, will help you to become more effective in both formal and informal discussion situations.

PARTICIPATING IN DISCUSSION

There are those who take part in discussion but contribute little or nothing to the outcome. Some think they have all the answers and reject any view contrary to their own. Others are so poorly prepared that they have nothing to offer in solving the problem. Still others lack an understanding of the nature of discussion. They would be glad to participate, but just don't know the rules of the game. The quality of participation may mean the difference between success and failure of the discussion. The duties of the discussant may be characterized as follows.

Be Prepared

There is a tendency among participants to let someone else do it when preparing for a group discussion. If the topic for discussion can be investigated ahead of time, do so. When you locate evidence important to the discussion, put it down on note cards, being sure to document it carefully. In a symposium, have your speech well enough prepared for an effective extemporaneous delivery with good eye contact.

Be Cooperative

Effective group thinking can only take place when members of the discussion put the common good of the group above personal interests. The purpose of the problem-solving discussion is to arrive at a solution acceptable to the entire group. This means that the members must be willing to compromise their viewpoints in order to resolve the conflict.

Be Friendly

Effective discussion is only possible when an attitude of goodwill prevails. When you find yourself disagreeing with others in the group, be sure to do so in a pleasant, friendly way. Remember, group thinking depends on teamwork. Personality clashes or any form of hostility in discussion inhibits participation. The free expression of ideas occurs only in an open, friendly atmosphere. To promote friendliness, discussion members should be encouraged to call each other by their first names.

Keep An Open Mind

To be an effective participant in a discussion, you should learn to appreciate the views of others. When you listen to another's opinion, try to put yourself in his or her place, remembering that no two people see things alike. That doesn't mean that you should accept everything the other says, but rather that your mind should be open to new avenues of thought. While it is important to value your own opinion, you must be willing to admit that other opinions may also be reasonable. Be aware that your opinion might be wrong and be willing to alter it. Only a fool never changes his mind.

Share the Spotlight

While you should take a full and active part in attempting to solve the problem, don't monopolize the discussion to the extent that others cannot be heard. In fact, when you notice that one of the discussants is not contributing, try to draw him or her out; find out how that person is reacting to the ideas being presented. Group thinking is, necessarily, thinking out loud. Unless every person in the group makes his or her thoughts known to others, the full value of their knowledge and experience will not be brought to bear upon the problem.

Listen Carefully

Listening critically is indispensable to effective group thinking. Pay careful attention in an attempt to understand fully what the other person means. Too many discussion members comment on what they "thought" someone meant without first making sure their understanding was correct. If you are in doubt, ask. Furthermore, it is each member's responsibility to test the thinking of others as it is expressed in the discussion. If you think someone is unclear in his or her thinking or on the wrong track, say so before the discussion continues.

Participate Freely and Enthusiastically

Each member of the group has a responsibility to participate. If you have a comment that you think is appropriate, make it. Avoid long speeches. Submit your contribution in one or two short sentences, or perhaps in the form of a question. The right question may prove to be just what the group needs to move forward in settling a problem. Furthermore, a question has a tendency to promote cooperation, whereas a critical comment might evoke hostility. Use your own background and experience to appraise and evaluate the contributions of others.

Stick to the Point

If you are like most discussion members, you probably have opinions or ideas that you would like to present to the group at the outset. You will greatly aid the progress of the discussion if you withhold these remarks until they are pertinent. When you speak, speak to the point. This is especially important while evaluating and analyzing the problem. Follow the suggested pattern of the discussion and deal with the issues at hand. If you can deal with each aspect of the problem completely, you will avoid delay caused by backtracking to an issue that should already have been resolved.

MODERATING THE DISCUSSION

Although each member of the group must share the responsibilities of leadership, it is often wise to choose a moderator to guide the discussion. The specific duties of the moderator are to:

1. Open by briefly introducing the topic and the group members to the audience.
2. Guide the discussion, using a flexible outline.
3. Resolve tension by using tact and humor.
4. Stimulate all members to participate.
5. Provide transitions and summaries to help members see what has been accomplished and what remains to be done.
6. Be aware of the time to insure that all points are discussed.

TYPE OF PROBLEM	HOW TO HANDLE IT

WON'T TALK

SUGGESTION: YOU HAVE TO FIND SOME WAY OF DRAWING HIM OUT WITHOUT EMBARASSING HIM.

SAY — " _____ , how do you feel about . . . ?"

"May we hear from anyone else?"

"Has everyone had a chance to have their say?"

TALKS TOO MUCH

SUGGESTION: BE DIPLOMATIC. HE MAY JUST BE EAGER TO HAVE A SUCCESSFUL DISCUSSION.

SAY — " _____ , could you summarize your remarks, so we can get to some other opinions?"

"Good point _____ ! Can we hear what some others think?"

UNCLEAR

SUGGESTION: TRY TO FIND HIS MAIN POINT AND THEN RESTATE IT SO THAT IT MAKES SENSE.

SAY — "If I understand you correctly, you feel . . . ."

"Now let's see if I've gotten this straight. You . . ."

ARGUMENTATIVE

SUGGESTION: KEEP YOUR COOL. A FRIENDLY RESPONSE WILL HELP TO CHECK HIS ANGER. FIND SOMETHING YOU CAN AGREE WITH.

SAY — "I see your point _____ ! Now let's look at a different side."

"That's one way of looking at it. How about anyone else?"

INATTENTIVE

SUGGESTION: BE FRIENDLY. THE PERSON MIGHT HAVE A PERSONAL PROBLEM THAT IS DISTRACTING HIM.

SAY — " _____ , we've kind of left you out of the discussion. What do you think?"

"Sally seems to feel . . . . What is your opinion _____ ?"

7. Encourage informal, spontaneous participation.

8. Summarize the progress made at the close of the discussion and indicate the differences that remain unresolved.

9. Take charge of the forum period.

As indicated above, some specific duties of the moderator are to keep the discussion moving, to resolve tension, and to stimulate participation. Five problem situations that can block effective discussion are shown in the accompanying table, together with suggestions as to how they might be handled.

WORDING THE DISCUSSION PROBLEM

It is important that the discussion topic be carefully worded. A well-written problem will increase the likelihood that the group will come to a satisfactory conclusion within the time limit. When phrasing a discussion problem, keep in mind the following suggestions:

1. The problem should be worded as a question. Discussion is a process of inquiry. The members of the group are searching for an answer.

2. State the problem clearly. The group will save considerable time if the discussion question is phrased as clearly as possible. Discussion problems are usually unclear for one of two reasons: They are too complex, or they are too general. Use familiar words that can easily be understood. Be as specific as possible.

3. Phrase the problem-question objectively. Avoid writing a question that suggests a bias for a particular point of view. The question, "Should the alarming violence on television be regulated?" suggests a fixed attitude before the discussion even begins.

4. Make the problem-question multisided. A multisided problem is one that allows for more than one or two answers. The question, "Should marijuana be legalized?" can be answered either yes or no. This could be done by simply polling the group. Why have a discussion? The question would be made more multisided if it read: "What changes should be made in the marijuana laws?"

5. The problem-question should be open-ended. A discussion question must consider all possible answers. In our example, "What changes should be made in the marijuana laws?" we are ignoring the question, "Should the laws be changed at all?" To

make the discussion problem open-ended, add the phrase "if any." Thus your open-ended question would read, "What changes, if any, should be made in the marijuana laws?"

TYPES OF DISCUSSION

The eight basic types of discussion are the panel, the symposium, the round table, the lecture-forum, the film-forum, the dialogue, the interview, and role-playing.

The Panel

A panel discussion usually involves from three to eight members, including a moderator. They sit in front of an audience in a circle or semicircle so that they can see and react to each other. Ideally, the members of a panel have varied backgrounds and viewpoints which make for an active exchange of ideas and experiences. The language of panel discussion is usually informal, with each member expressing an opinion in a normal, conversational way.

Many panels are followed by an open forum, an audience participation period. After the moderator has summarized the discussion, he or she invites the audience to ask questions of or make statements to individual members or the panel as a whole. It is the moderator's job to field the questions, repeating or rephrasing them when necessary.

The Symposium

While the panel discussion is essentially informal, give-and-take conversation, the symposium consists of a series of prepared speeches. The subject or problem is divided into parts, and each speaker develops the part assigned to him. The available speaking time is divided equally among the speakers, who talk directly to the audience rather than to each other. A moderator opens the discussion and introduces each speaker and his topic. After each speaker has come to the lectern and addressed the audience, either the moderator or the speakers themselves summarize the discussion. Following the summary, the moderator may turn the symposium into a panel or move to a forum period.

The Round Table

As its name implies, this form of discussion generally takes place around a round table or in a circle. The reason for the round table is to provide those involved members with a feeling of equality. The circle has traditionally been a symbol of unity; when seated in a circle, everyone is in a position equal to that of his or her neighbor. Like the panel, the round table discussion is a kind of magnified conversation, since the participants look at each other. The difference is that in this form of discussion everyone is involved; there is no audience. Committee meetings and conferences are usually conducted as round table discussions. This form is especially appropriate for classroom discussion, where a stimulating topic handled well can result in a lively give-and-take among all members of the class.

The Lecture-Forum

In the lecture-forum, a single speaker delivers a prepared speech on a subject. After she has covered the topic thoroughly (lecture), she answers questions from the audience (forum). Variations of the lecture-discussion technique are frequently used by classroom instructors and political candidates. A challenging speaker can stimulate an enthusiastic reaction from the audience. The lecture-forum can be an effective discussion form in the classroom if the student speaker has the necessary expertise to give a subject the extended treatment necessary.

The Film-Forum

Sometimes students show a lack of enthusiasm for an issue because they know little about it. One discussion technique designed to deal with this type of situation is the film-forum. The success of this form of discussion is dependent to a great extent on the quality of the film used. Since the purpose of the film is to give information rather than to persuade, the film-forum is most effective when the film being used is objective rather than slanted. When used in the classroom, films should not exceed 15 minutes in length to allow time for adequate discussion.

The Dialogue

Perhaps you have taken a college-credit course on television that used the dialogue approach. The dialogue is a form of discussion involving two persons. It is highly effective when the participants know their subject well and engage in an articulate and meaningful exchange of ideas. Dialogue is a useful form of discussion in the classroom, since it provides the students with the opportunity to do team research. Students choose their own partner, because rapport between dialogue participants is vital.

The Interview

In the dialogue, both participants share responsibility for the presentation of material. In the interview, the person being interviewed is the source of information. The interviewer's job is to keep the discussion moving and on the right track. A good interviewer can get a wealth of information from a knowledgeable guest.

The interview is an excellent means of revealing information. For the best results, an interview should be carefully planned. A line of questioning should be blocked out in advance so that both participants know where the discussion is heading.

Role-Playing

An excellent way to introduce a discussion problem is through the technique of role-playing. In role-playing the players take part in a brief drama built on a "real-life" problem. The actors in the drama each take the part of a specific character in the problem. They then act out the situation, expressing the views they feel the character they are playing would have. The drama is unrehearsed, and the problem is usually given to the participants on the day the role-playing is to take place.

Role-playing can be an effective way of pretesting a situation. Skill in handling oneself in an interview could make the difference between a student's getting a job or missing it. A series of mock interviews with students playing the roles of personnel director and interviewee provides excellent practice. Students will derive a greater feeling of confidence toward the interview situation and an increased understanding of management's position as well.

Role-playing is particularly useful in clarifying a situation. Often, after seeing the roles played, a group can more fully understand the problem. Role-playing, for example, can be used to facilitate the case-problem approach to discussion. In discussing case-problem 20 on page 300, a group may decide that to solve the problem the friend should tell Glenda that her mother is shoplifting. At this point, the instructor might step in and say, "All right, class, let's see how well that solution will work. Joan would you play the role of Glenda? And Fred, how about you being the friend who is going to tell her that her mother is shoplifting?"

Selecting a Role-Playing Problem   The problems below, which we have used for our classes, have been prepared with today's college student in mind. Additional problems may be developed by members of a group in a discussion situation, or by individual students as part of a class assignment.

One final note. After engaging in role-playing these problems, allow time for those in the audience to give their views and reactions to the drama.

1. A student who is of legal age is asked by his friends to buy the liquor for a weekend beach party. He knows he can get charged with contributing to the delinquency of minors if he is caught. He also wants to keep the status he has among his friends. What should the student do?

2. A new employee in a plant has a mother who must have open-heart surgery. She lives in another state, and the employee would like to take a four-day leave of absence to be with her. The plant is behind in filling orders and everyone is working a seven-day week. How should the employee handle the situation?

3. The students in an English class feel that the instructor assigns an excessive amount of homework each day. The instructor is teaching the course for the first time. How should the students handle the situation?

4. A student who will graduate in three weeks is offered a job that will start on the morning of her last exam. Her instructor has indicated that she will give no early or make-up exams. What should the student do?

5. A secretary has recently begun a new job for an insurance company. The fringe benefits are excellent, the pay is good, but she runs into a problem. Her immediate supervisor is constantly making advances toward her that she resents. How should she handle the situation?

6. A first-year bank employee has been late for work an average of two or three times a week for the last month. His wife, who is in the hospital, will remain there for at least another week. The reason he has been late is that he has to feed, dress, and drive his three school-age children to school each day. His supervisor has called him in to talk about his tardiness. How should the bank employee handle the situation?

Additional Suggestions for Role-Playing

1. You have just graduated and are being interviewed for your first job.
2. A persistent salesman refuses to leave when you tell him to.
3. A policeman is about to ticket your car as you arrive on the scene.
4. A clerk who waited on you 15 minutes ago now refuses to accept a return because you misplaced the receipt.
5. A teacher wrongfully accuses you of cheating.
6. A friend denies that he owes you $20.

THE FUNCTIONS OF DISCUSSION

In general, discussion has two functions: educative (information-seeking) and problem-solving.

Educative Discussion

Many of the discussions in which you participate do not seek agreement or action. Some are strictly social gatherings whose purpose is recreation or enjoyment. And yet, many times you get more than enjoyment from these discussions. They benefit you by adding to your background and experience. Their function is to make you better informed about the topic discussed. You often talk with others about dating, drugs, politics, or any matter of genuine interest in an attempt to increase your understanding. If you are lucky, and the information you get is accurate, you might become better equipped to make up your own mind on the question. Discussions of this type are called informative or educative discussions. Perhaps the most familiar example is classroom discussion, one of the important purposes of which is to stimulate thinking. This makes it especially appropriate for a course in communication skills. A lively classroom discussion of a controversial speech or essay can stimulate a speaker's or writer's thinking and motivate him or her to communicate to what has now become a more "real" audience. The informal exchange of ideas about a book or movie can often provide feedback as to the views of other members of the class. An all-class discussion during the first few weeks of the course can clear up many students' misconceptions about a communications course and indicate which attitudes need to be developed during the coming semester.

PATTERNS FOR EDUCATIVE DISCUSSION

Your discussion will proceed more efficiently if it follows a specific organization. The basic organizational patterns below, which are discussed on pages 183–89 can provide an effective plan for guiding educative discussion.

General-to-Specific

The symposium is particularly well suited to general-to-specific organization. In the symposium, the subject is divided equally among the speakers who each deal with a specific part of the whole.

Chronological

A group studying the laser beam might organize their discussions in this way:

1. How and when was the laser beam developed?
2. What are the present uses of the laser beam?
3. How will the beam be used in the future?

Spatial

A travel/interest group setting up a film forum series on a visit to the Scandinavian countries might organize their series this way:

1. Norway today
2. A visit to Sweden
3. Beautiful Denmark

Order-of-Importance

In many cases discussions which are restricted by a time limit will follow an order-of-importance organization. An informational congregational meeting at a temple or church, for example, would usually list the most important items first on the agenda to assure that they would be discussed in the allotted time.

Other patterns that could be used for educative discussion are pro-con, question-to-answer, and effect-to-cause.

Problem-Solving Discussion

Life is a succession of problems and decisions. Questions arise which require answers. Should I experiment with drugs? What kind of car should I buy? What should I major in? How far should I go with sex? Although these problems can be solved by the individual involved, chances are that a group solution will be more soundly conceived. Properly guided, group thinking offers a number of advantages over independent problem-solving.

First, the more people working on a problem, the more information is available to solve it. One individual's background and experience can seldom match those of a group. In order to be effective, there should be enough members in the discussion to provide for adequate contributions. Too few members limit the flow of ideas; too many create confusion. The preferred number of participants in a problem-solving discussion should range from three to eight, although a good classroom discussion of a provocative problem can be held with as many as 25.

Second, group thinking provides greater opportunities for problem-solving. The more people you have looking at a problem, the more likely you are to solve it correctly. In a group, an error by one individual is likely to be spotted by someone else.

A Pattern for Problem-Solving Discussion

The process of group thinking can be organized into a series of steps roughly paralleling John Dewey's steps to reflective thinking. The sequence of steps can be used as an outline or pattern for discussion. The discussion usually begins with identification of the problem and proceeds step by step to implementation of the solution. The steps in the process are as follows.

Identifying the Problem   Many discussions fail to get off the ground because the problem is not clearly understood by the participants. The first step in discussion, therefore, is to have the members pinpoint the discussion problem. Good teamwork in thinking can only begin when each member has a clear understanding of the problem at hand. Problems for discussion should always be stated as questions.

If the group is careful in phrasing the question as clearly as possible, they will avoid confusion later. For example, the question, "How can we halt pollution?" is unclear. Whom do we mean by "we"? Do we mean the group, the government, the people of the world? What type of pollution are we talking about? Do we mean air pollution, water pollution, noise pollution, or every type of pollution there is? The question, "What steps should the U.S. government take to curb industrial pollution of air and water?" avoids needless quibbling over definition of terms.

Analyzing the Problem   Once the members have demonstrated a common understanding and agreement as to the issues, the causes and nature of the problem should be explored. There are times when a solution becomes obvious after the causes of a difficulty are identified. Once the causes are listed and agreed upon, an exploration of the problem can begin. The group should consider such questions as these: "Who is affected by the problem?" "How serious is it?" "Under what conditions must it be solved?"

A thorough investigation of the present situation will give members of the discussion a clear picture of the conditions that need correcting.

Finding the Best Solution   This step involves proposing possible solutions and then measuring them by the guidelines established above. It is usually a good idea to list all of the solutions before evaluating them. Such questions as these are asked: "How long will it take to carry out the solution?" "How much will it cost?" "Is the solution practical?" An important part of this step is for the group to determine that the solution will not cause some new problem.

Actuating the Solution   Whenever you deal with people, it is wise to consider just how a solution is going to be fulfilled. It might be useful to have members of the group role-play the parts of those people involved in carrying out the solution. When considering how people may react to a course of action, the group may discover that they cannot put their solution into operation.

USING CASE PROBLEMS

Ability in group discussion is best developed through guided practice. The writers have found that the use of case problems as discussion questions is an effective way of stimulating this practice. Students respond to the challenge of coping with real issues geared to their level of interest and understanding.

Another advantage to dealing with problems in human relations is that they aid in developing those characteristics which contribute to the development of effective citizens—an understanding of and flexible attitude toward the beliefs and opinions of others, the recognition of a variety of points of view, a realization of the effectiveness of group problem-solving, and a greater belief in the worth of one's own opinion.

These case problems are brief scenes from everyday life and show only the incident, not its outcome. They are the kinds of situations that the student has encountered or is likely to encounter at home, at work, or at school. They are designed to encourage the student to think carefully, analytically, and understandingly about the situations they describe.

There is no "right" or "wrong" answers to these case problems. The solution chosen will be a reflection of the attitudes and sentiments of the group. The group members should make every effort to reach agreement on a solution for each problem. If they cannot come to unanimous agreement, the solution should be chosen by majority opinion. A suggested format is the following:

1. Moderator introduces panelists.
2. Moderator identifies the problem.

3. Panelists, under the moderator's direction, analyze the problem, suggesting possible solutions.

4. Moderator opens the discussion to the entire group. Questions and comments may be addressed to the group or to individual panelists.

5. Moderator summarizes the conclusion of the panel.

CASE PROBLEMS

1. Fred and John, close personal friends, work together part-time stocking shelves at a local supermarket. Fred has been working to buy himself a new car while John has taken the second job to help support his widowed mother and nine brothers and sisters. One night after closing time, Fred notices John carrying a case of powdered milk out to his car.
What should Fred do?

2. You have two close friends, Bob and Jim. Jim has just been arrested for possession of heroin. The police found the heroin in Jim's car but Jim claims that he doesn't know how it got there. You know that Bob hid it there for safekeeping. Bob refused to reveal this.
What should you do?

3. John, a white student at a small out-of-state technical college, has fallen in love with Cindy, a black student at the same school. He plans to take her home for Christmas, but he doesn't plan to tell his parents beforehand that she is black. He argues that his parents have always insisted that they are unprejudiced, and now he will be able to judge by their reaction if they are honest. Cindy does not agree.
How should the situation be handled?

4. Joan and Donna have been friends since childhood. Both are eighteen. Lately, Donna has been seeing a lot of an older married man. Joan advises Donna to break this off, but Donna is convinced that the man plans to get a divorce and marry her. Donna has told her parents that she will be visiting Joan for the weekend so that she and the man can go off together.
What should Joan do?

5. Upon your college roommate's return from summer vacation, she tells you that she is engaged. When she shows you her fiance's picture, you recognize him as a former classmate who has a reputation for being promiscuous. You like your roommate very much.
What should you do?

6. Paul found what he believed were LSD tablets in his sister's room. When he questioned her about it, she insisted they were antibiotics for a cold. He has noticed that she has seemed unusually withdrawn lately. He has revealed all this to his parents who have told him not to

let his imagination run away with him. They have always overly indulged the sister.
What should he do?

7. Don and Alice are required by law to take a blood test before marriage. During the examination it is discovered that Don has had a venereal disease. When Alice questions him about it, he does not answer her.
What should Alice do?

8. When visiting his friend Ralph for the weekend, Carl sees him take $10 from his mother's purse. On the following day Carl is present as the mother accuses Ralph's brother Tim of stealing the money. She punishes Tim by taking away his use of the car for one month.
What should Carl do?

9. While you are riding home with Ed, a good friend, he backs into a parked car, causing considerable damage. Although he has liability insurance, he refuses to leave his name, explaining that he has already had two accidents this year, and that another will result in his insurance policy's being canceled. Ed drives you to and from work every day.
What should you do?

10. Harry and Tom are hometown neighbors and dormitory roommates in college. Tom is concerned because Harry has been experimenting with hard drugs which have seriously affected his school work and his personality. Tom feels that something must be done before Harry becomes hopelessly addicted.
What should Tom do?

11. Julia is engaged to be married to Fred. The wedding is less than two months away and Fred suggests that they begin their sexual relationship so that they will be sure that there are no physical or psychological barriers to a happy marriage. Julia believes very strongly that she should remain chaste before the marriage. Fred insists.
What should Julia do?

12. In 1950 John Graff was sentenced to life imprisonment for the murder of his business partner, Harry Fosdick. During his trial and imprisonment, John had protested his innocence. After being released in April, 1970, having served the full twenty years at Joliet Prison in Illinois, he returned to Chicago, his hometown. Two days later he ran across Harry Fosdick, the man he had been convicted of murdering. At this meeting, Fosdick, in the presence of witnesses, admitted that he had intentionally framed Graff. The following day Fosdick was found murdered. When arrested for the murder, Graff admitted his guilt but claimed that he was temporarily insane at the time.
What punishment, if any, should Graff get?

13. Betty and Ralph have been married for nine months. They live in a small apartment decorated and furnished with second-hand items.

Lately, Betty's parents have been buying her expensive clothes. They have also insisted that she go shopping with them to pick out some new furniture that they will pay for. Ralph resents this.
How should this situation be handled?

14. Henry, a rookie police officer, has been assigned to the vice squad temporarily to do undercover work. His job, for which he has grown a full beard, is to uncover prostitution. During his first night on the job, he is propositioned by a woman he recognizes as the wife of a fellow police officer. Because of the beard, she does not recognize him.
What should he do?

15. Penny Smith, a white coed, worked as a volunteer staff person for the political campaign of Wanda Jones, a young, idealistic black woman. Wanda ran against George Alport, a member of the American Nazi Party. Wanda won a narrow victory which Penny, through involvement in the election, can prove was the result of voter fraud.
What should Penny do?

16. Your wife's twin brother owns an apartment building in a depressed area of town. He complains to you that he has been having difficulty with his tenants who are often months behind in their rent and who have been damaging his property. He jokingly tells you that a good fire would solve all of his problems. A week later the apartment building burns down. No one was injured in the fire which is being investigated.
What should you do?

17. Fred's 15-year-old daughter, Sue, has recently begun a part-time job as babysitter for his employer's young children. After her second night on the job, she informs Fred that the children have confided to her that they are often beaten by their father. She says she has seen the marks of this abuse. She feels the authorities should be notified. Fred is concerned about his job.
What should he do?

18. Sue and Bess have been best friends since childhood. Recently Bess has started a new job working in an office with Sue's husband Sam. She soon learns that Sam is a ladies' man. It is common knowledge that he is having an affair with one of the secretaries. Bess believes that if Sue finds out it will destroy her marriage.
What should Bess do?

19. Your wife's brother is a student at a local technical college. He confides to you that he is a member of a group that plans to protest the construction of a nuclear power plant in the area. Two weeks later you learn that vandals have done over one million dollars of damage to the plant. When you try to contact your brother-in-law, he seems to have disappeared.
What should you do?

20. While you are shopping with your good friend, Glenda, and her mother, you see the mother slip several expensive items into her purse. Glenda, who you have always known to be scrupulously honest, does not appear to have noticed this.
What should you do?

DISCUSSION RATING FORM

The accompanying discussion rating form is designed for both student and instructor evaluation. It lists the characteristics to be considered when evaluating a discussion.

DISCUSSION RATING FORM Scale 1 superior 2 above ave. 3 average 4 poor	Names	(John M.)	(Mary S.)	(Robert R.)	(George S.)
PARTICIPATION—Listened carefully; was prepared; was spontaneous; used pertinent information; tested the thinking of others.					
ATTITUDE—Was friendly; tactful; cooperative; flexible; objective.					
THOUGHT PROGRESSION—Spoke to the point; stayed on the subject; used time wisely.					
COMMUNICATIVE SKILLS—Used adequate volume; was clear, was conversational; observed the rules of grammar.					

OVERALL RATING FOR GROUP _____

COMMENTS:

EXERCISES

1. Prepare a list of topics suitable for class discussion.

2. Write an original case problem that would be suitable for class discussion.

3. a. The instructor will divide the class into groups of four to six each. Each group will have a planning meeting to elect a chairman and choose a discussion topic.

   b. The group should decide upon an outline listing points in the order in which they will be discussed. A time limit should be established for the discussion.

   c. After the planning session, each member should research the topic in order to support his or her opinion with factual evidence and testimony.

CHAPTER **15**

Handbook

HANDBOOK

This handbook can be used in two ways: (1) as a brief review of the basic structure of speech for effective oral and written communication, or (2) as a quick reference to check your usage against what constitutes correct writing and speaking practices.

Section I reviews the rules and presents models for the eight parts of speech: nouns, pronouns, verbs, adjectives, adverbs, prepositions, conjunctions, and interjections.

Section II reviews clauses and phrases which often serve as one or another of the parts of speech.

Section III deals with the accepted rules for clear punctuation.

PARTS OF SPEECH

The term *parts of speech* refers to the way words are classified according to their forms and their uses in sentences. Every word in the English language falls into one or another of these eight classes: verbs, nouns, pronouns, adjectives, adverbs, prepositions, conjunctions, and interjections.

Some words are more versatile than others and, depending upon their use in a sentence, can serve as more than one part of speech. The word *down,* for example, serves as five different parts of speech in the sentences below:

1. Douglas *downed* the football on the three-yard line. (Down is a verb because it tells what happened.)
2. A sleeping bag filled with *down* is expensive. (Down is a noun because it is a name.)
3. Ellen made the *down* payment. (Down is an adjective because it describes a name.)
4. The house burned *down.* (Down is an adverb because it modifies a verb.)
5. The ball rolled *down* the hill. (Down is a preposition because it shows relationship or direction.)

Note: The way a word is used in a sentence is the only valid reason for classifying it as a part of speech.

This section provides a review of the parts of speech. Knowing the characteristics of the various classes will help you to analyze and improve the sentences you write. Parts of speech function in a sentence in the following ways:

Verbs assert
Nouns and pronouns name
Adjectives and adverbs describe or modify
Prepositions show relationships or direction
Conjunctions join or link
Interjections exclaim

Verbs—

A verb is a word or group of words that describes a physical or invisible action or affirms a condition. A verb says something about what is happening to sor.eone or something.

The punter *kicked* the ball. (physical action)
Sally *believes* in herself. (invisible action)

He *has* a cold. (condition)
It *was* raining. (condition)

Note: The two most important conditional verbs are *to be* and *to have.*

Verbs change form more frequently and more extensively than any other part of speech. Grammatically, they show tense, person, number, voice, and mood.

Tense   Tense is the grammatical term for the change in verb form to indicate time. Verb tense tells us when the action takes place.

The six principal tenses in English are present, past, future, present perfect, past perfect and future perfect.

Verb Tenses

Present	Arnold is handsome.
Past	Sadie passed the exam.
Future	I will be a senior next year.
Present Perfect	He has finished his paper and is having it typed.
Past Perfect	She had already left before I arrived.
Future Perfect	He will have finished a case of beer before he is through.

Present   The simple present tense is used to indicate action occurring in the present with no reference to time.

I like your dress.
This is my third piece of cake.

The present tense can also be used to indicate ongoing or habitual action:

He is forever misspelling words.
Water freezes at 32°F.

Past   The simple past tense indicates that an action occurred entirely in the past:

Henry walked to school.
He was really angry.
She chose a partner for the dance.

Future   The simple future tense indicates that an action will occur after the present and is often found by using the words shall or will together with the main verb:

I shall be leaving in an hour.
I will be there by tomorrow.

The future tense can also be formed in other ways:

1. By combining an infinitive with *be* or *go.*
    Alice is going to be a doctor.
    Joyce is to go next week.
2. By combining the present tense form with an adverb of time.
    The baseball season begins this Tuesday.
    He is arriving this week.

Present Perfect   The present perfect tense takes place in the past and extends to the present. It is formed by combining the past participle of the main verb with a form of the helping verb *have:*

She has finished typing her term paper and is now proofreading it.
I have loved her since I first laid eyes on her.

Past Perfect   The past perfect tense is used to show that one past event preceded another. The helping verb *had* is combined with the past participle:

She had left before I arrived.

Future Perfect   The future perfect tense is used to indicate the earlier of two actions to be completed at a future time. It is formed by linking the helping verbs *will have* to the past participle:

By the time Chris gets here, we will have eaten.

Regular and Irregular Verbs

Regular verbs form the past tense and past participle by adding *–d* or *–ed* to the present tense:

talk + ed = talked
walk + ed = walked
complete + d = completed
use + d = used

A verb that does not add *–d* or *–ed* to the past tense is called an irregular verb. The principal parts of many of the most commonly used irregular verbs are listed below. Your dictionary lists the principal parts of all irregular verbs, that is, the present tense (arise), the past tense (arose) and the past participle (arisen). If only the present form is listed, the verb is regular.

Present Tense	Past Tense	Past Participle
am, is, are	was, were	been
begin	began	begun
bet	bet	bet
bite	bit	bitten
break	broke	broken
bring	brought	brought
buy	bought	bought
catch	caught	caught
choose	chose	chosen
come	came	come
cut	cut	cut
dive	dived, dove	dived
do	did	done
drink	drank	drunk
drive	drove	driven
eat	ate	eaten
fall	fell	fallen
feel	felt	felt
find	found	found
forget	forgot	forgot, forgotten
forgive	forgave	forgiven
freeze	froze	frozen
get	got	got, gotten
give	gave	given
go	went	gone
grow	grew	grown
hang (suspend)	hung	hung
hang (execute)*	hanged	hanged
hide	hid	hidden
hit	hit	hit
hurt	hurt	hurt
keep	kept	kept
know	knew	known
lead	led	led
leave	left	left
let	let	let
lose	lost	lost
make	made	made
read	read	read
ride	rode	ridden
rise	rose	risen
run	ran	run
see	saw	seen

*Hang, to execute, is a regular verb.

Present Tense	Past Tense	Past Participle
shake	shook	shaken
shine	shone, shined	shone, shined
sink	sank, sunk	sunk
speak	spoke	spoken
stand	stood	stood
steal	stole	stolen
strike	struck	struck
swear	swore	sworn
swim	swam	swum
swing	swung	swung
take	took	taken
tear	tore	torn
tell	told	told
think	thought	thought
throw	threw	thrown
wear	wore	worn
win	won	won
wind	wound	wound
write	wrote	written

Number and Person   Verbs, like personal pronouns, must agree in number and person with their subject. Plural subjects require plural verbs and singular subjects, singular verbs:

We sing; he sings.

Verbs change form to indicate the speaker (first person), the person spoken to (second person) and the person spoken about (third person). These differences in form are shown below:

First Person   I am, we are; I was, we were; I go, we go.
Second Person   you are, you were, you go.
Third Person   he is, they are; she was, they were, he goes, they go.

Voice   The term *voice* refers to whether a subject of a sentence performs or receives an action. Verbs can be used either in the active or passive voice. If the subject performs the action the sentence is written in the active voice. The active voice should be used more often since it is more vigorous and emphatic:

The punter kicked the ball. (active)
The ball was kicked by the punter. (passive)

While the active voice is stronger and thus preferred, there are circumstances when the passive voice is more appropriate.

Use the passive voice when the doer of the action is unknown.

Our beautiful garden was destroyed by vandals.

When it is more important to emphasize the action than the doer, use the passive voice.

Robert Kennedy was assassinated by Sirhan Sirhan.

Mood   The mood of a verb indicates the circumstances under which a statement is made. The *indicative* mood is used for ordinary statements and questions:

I am leaving. Are you coming?

The *imperative* mood is used to make requests or give commands:

Please listen. Stop!

The *subjunctive* mood is used to express statements that are hypothetical or contrary to fact. In this mood the singular subject takes a plural verb. (In most cases this means changing *was* to *were*.)

If I *were* in charge, I'd do it differently.

Kinds of Verbs   Verbs can be classified as *transitive, intransitive, linking* or *helping* depending upon their use.

Transitive   A transitive verb transmits its action to a direct object. It requires the object to complete its meaning.

Henry *kissed* his *girlfriend*.   (*Girlfriend* is the direct object of the transitive verb *kissed*.)

Some transitive verbs may be followed by an indirect object as well as a direct object. This indirect object is usually a person and always precedes the direct object.

Henry *gave* his *girlfriend* a *kiss*.   (Here *kiss* is the direct object and *girlfriend* is the indirect object of the transitive verb *gave*.)

Intransitive   An intransitive verb can stand alone. Although it may have modifiers, an intransitive verb does not require an object to complete its meaning.

Grandfather *snored*.
Grandfather *snored loudly*. (Loudly is a modifying adverb.)

Linking   Linking verbs assert that a subject is, appears, or seems to be something. They connect a subject with a subject complement. This subject complement, an adjective, noun or pronoun, describes or renames the subject. The most frequently used linking verb is some form of the verb *to be* (is, am, are, was, were, etc.) Other verbs often used as linking verbs are: *become, grow, appear, remain, seem* and verbs denoting the senses: *feel, look, taste, smell* and *sound.*

Some verbs can be transitive, intransitive or linking depending on their use in a sentence. *Grew,* for example, is variously transitive, intransitive and linking in these three sentences:

1. Mrs. Jackson *grew tomatoes* in her garden.   (transitive verb and direct object)
2. While studying the Bible, Joan *grew in her faith*.   (intransitive verb and preposition)
3. As Gary approached the dentist's office, he *grew nervous*.   (linking verb and subject complement.)

Helping Verbs   Helping verbs are used in combination with main verbs. They change the meaning of the verbs they are coupled with. For example, they can change tense.

He *is attending* M.A.T.C.
He *will be attending* M.A.T.C.
He *has attended* M.A.T.C.

Helping verbs can also indicate obligation, permission or possibility.

He *must attend* M.A.T.C.
He *may attend* M.A.T.C.
He *might attend* M.A.T.C.

Helping verbs always come before the main verbs they modify although other words may be placed between them.

You *can pass* the course.
You *can* probably *pass* the course.

Will you *pass* the course?
Will the whole class *pass* the course?

Below is a list of commonly used helping verbs:

could   must   ought to
can   shall   will
may   should   would
might   have to

The verbs be (am, is, was, were), have (has, had) and do (did, does) can be used either as helping verbs or main verbs. They are helping verbs when they appear in combination with a main verb and main verbs when they appear alone.

As Main Verbs   **As Helping Verbs**
He *is* hungry.   He *is going* to eat.
She *has* the mumps.   She *has recovered*.
She *does* well.   He *does painting* and *wallpapering*.

Verbals   Verbals (gerunds, infinitives, and participles) are derived from verbs but actually function as nouns, adjectives or adverbs.

Gerunds   When a verb ending in –ing is used as a noun, it is called a *gerund*.

Playing the piano is fun.
Seeing is *believing*.

Infinitives   *Infinitives* can function as nouns, adjectives or adverbs.

He loves *to sing*. (noun)
It is her turn *to choose*. (adjective)
The children stopped *to look*. (adverb)

Participles   A verbal which modifies a noun is called a *participle*. The present participle ends in *–ing*.

The *rising* cost of food is appalling.

The past participle may end in *–d, –ed, –en, –n* or *–t.*

He went to look for a *used* car.
The *heated* stew was delicious.

John is a *broken* man.
She couldn't mend the *torn* pants.
The *lost* child cried loudly.

Problem Verbs   Some sets of verbs are frequently confused. Listed below are some problem verbs along with guidelines for their proper use:

1. Lie and lay. Lie, meaning to "recline", is an intransitive verb which does not require a direct object. Its principal parts are *lie, lay, lain.*

   LIE   I am going to *lie* down.
   LAY   The cat *lay* quietly in the shade.
   LAIN   You have *lain* in that bed all day.

Lay, meaning to "place" or "put", is a transitive verb that requires a direct object. Its principal parts are *lay, laid* and *laid.*

   LAY   *Lay* the book on the table.
   LAID   He *laid* the gun down.
   LAID   Having *laid* the gun down, he left.

2. Rise and Raise. Rise means "to ascend." Its main parts are *rise, rose* and *risen.*

   RISE   The sun *rises* in the east.
   ROSE   When the bell rang, the students *rose* and walked out.
   RISEN   Congress has *risen* to the occasion and passed the bill.

Raise means to "lift" or "elevate." Its main parts are *raise, raised* and *raised.*

   RAISE   I *raise* my eyes to heaven.
   RAISED   He *raised* the question of ethics.
   RAISED   The flag had been *raised* by six o'clock.

3. Sit and set. Sit means to "take a seat." Its main parts are *sit, sat* and *sat.*

   SIT   *Sit* down, please.
   SAT   He *sat* in the corner
   SAT   He felt like he had *sat* for hours.

Set means "to place" or "put." Its main parts are *set, set* and *set.*

SET   *Set* the alarm for midnight.
SET   She *set* the table for dinner.
SET   She knew she had *set* her hair carefully.

4. Let and leave. Let means "to permit" or "allow." Its main parts are *let, let* and *let.*

LET   *Let* me rephrase the question.
LET   Debbie *let* the water boil away.
LET   If they had *let* me, I would have joined.

Leave means "to depart" or "allow to stay." Its main parts are *leave, left* and *left.*

LEAVE   I wish you would *leave* soon.
         Leave some money for your rent.
LEFT   He *left* for home today.
LEFT   Theo *left* her purse in the car.

Nouns

Nouns name persons (Ellen, lady), places (Milwaukee, ballpark), things (trees, glasses), actions (riot, thunder), and ideas (love, honesty). The five basic classes of nouns are:

1. *Proper Nouns.* Proper nouns name specific persons, places or things and are capitalized: Marlene, Milwaukee, Easter, Friday, Declaration of Independence.

2. *Common Nouns.* Common nouns name more than one member of a class of things and are written in the lower case: girls, city, holiday, divorce, football.

3. *Concrete Nouns.* Concrete nouns name things that can be seen, heard, touched, tasted or smelled: jug, thunder, grass, coffee, smoke.

4. *Abstract Nouns.* Abstract nouns refer to qualities or ideas that cannot be detected by the senses: compassion, bravery, kindness, strategy, hate.

5. *Collective Nouns.* Collective nouns refer to a group of persons or things: team, congregation, committee, squad, fleet.

Function of Nouns   Nouns are used in sentences as subjects of verbs, as objects of verbs or prepositions, as complements, as appositives or as modifiers.

1. *Subject of Verbs.* In most cases, a noun along with its modifiers forms the subject of a sentence. It usually precedes the verb and answers the question who or what.

   Carl slipped. (Who slipped?)
   The big dog barked loudly. (What barked?)

2. *Direct Object.* A direct object is a noun that receives the action of a verb.

   Jane slapped *Ralph*. (Slapped whom?)
   Robin Yount hit the *ball*. (Hit what?)

3. *Indirect Object.* An indirect object occurs in conjunction with a direct object and indicates the thing or person upon whom the action is performed.

   Arnold gave his *teacher* a hug.
   Joan handed *him* the pan.

4. *Object of a Preposition.* The object of a preposition is often a noun.

   The girl behind *John* is beyond *belief*. (*John* and *belief* are objects of the prepositions behind and beyond.)

5. *Complements.*
   a. Subject complements—a subject complement (or predicate noun) follows a linking verb and describes or explains the subject.

   His *girlfriend is* a *scientist*. (noun, linking verb, noun)
   The *koala bear is* a *marsupial*. (noun, linking verb, noun)

   NOTE: Adjectives and pronouns may also be used as subject complements.
   b. Objective complements—the complement of a direct object of certain verbs (appoint, choose, consider, make, name) is often followed by an objective complement.

   He named his boat Exclusion II.
   She considers him a genius.

6. *Appositives.* An appositive is a noun whose function is to explain more fully the noun it follows. An appositive often has modifiers.

Edna's favorite pastime, *drinking,* led to her downfall.
Professor Blake, *our speech instructor,* was absent today.

7. *Modifiers.* Occasionally nouns function as modifying adjectives in sentences.

Nothing is as exhilarating as a *Wisconsin* winter.
Next week we are having a *garage* sale.

Forms of Nouns   Nouns can show number (singular or plural), gender and possession.

Singular and plural forms—Most nouns form plurals by adding *–s* to the singular; plurals of nouns ending in *–s, –ch, –x, –sh,* or *–z* add *–es:*

1. songs	**4.** taxes	
2. passes	**5.** ashes	
3. patches	**6.** buzzes	

Nouns ending in *–y* preceded by a consonant change the *–y* to *–i* and add *–es:*

universities,   companies,   agencies

Gender—A few nouns have one form for the masculine and one for the feminine

waiter–waitress,   host–hostess

Possessive form—Most nouns form the possessive indicating ownership by adding apostrophe *–s* (*–'s*):

Father's car,   Carl's horn,   women's rights

Plural nouns ending in *–s* form the possessive by adding only the apostrophe:

speakers' stand,   teachers' union,   readers' box

Singular nouns ending in *–s* form the possessive by adding either the apostrophe alone or apostrophe *–s* (*–'s*):

Amos' or Amos's brother
the waitress' or waitress's paycheck
the bus' or bus's capacity

With group or compound nouns, the −'s is added to the last term:

son-in-law's name
someone else's responsibility

An apostrophe and −s is added to each name to indicate individual ownership but only to the last name to show joint ownership:

Betty's and Art's cars
Betty and Art's house

Often when a plural noun is considered a modifier, the apostrophe is not added:

United States Senate
Veterans Administration
drivers education

Use of a and an with nouns. The article *a* is used before words beginning with a consonant sound: a woman, a year, a union. The article *an* is used before words beginning with a vowel sound: an hour, an uncle, an Indian.

Pronouns

Pronouns take the place of nouns as subjects or objects. If you had to write without pronouns, your sentences would read something like this:

"Carl washed Carl's face, combed Carl's hair and put on Carl's best clothes."

Pronouns free you from the necessity of awkwardly repeating nouns. The noun or nounlike element to which a pronoun refers is called its antecedent. The pronoun becomes a substitute for this antecedent. When a pronoun refers to an antecedent in a preceding sentence or sentences, it forms a connecting link between those sentences. These links provide continuity to your writing. Notice how the pronouns in the passage below provide continuity:

"*Those of us* who loved *him* and who take *him* to *his* rest today pray that what *he* was to *us,* and what *he* wishes for *others,* will some day come to pass for all the world.
As *he* said many times, in many parts of this nation, to *those he* touched and who sought to touch *him:* '*Some* men see things as *they* are and say why. *I* dream things that never were and say, why not.' "[1]

[1]*Vital Speeches* XXXIV:18 (July 1, 1968) p. 547

Reference of Pronouns. A pronoun must agree with and specifically refer to its antecedent. Unclear or ambiguous references will confuse your reader. For example, two or more references can be confusing:

Unclear: The *teacher* met her new *assistant* as soon as *she* arrived on campus.

Better: As soon as the *teacher* arrived on campus, *she* met her new *assistant*.

Unclear: The day after *Mrs. Jakes* got the *cat, she* was taken to the vet to be neutered.

Better: The day after *Mrs. Jakes* got *her,* the *cat* was taken to the vet to be neutered.

Pronouns should refer to definite rather than implied antecedents.

Unclear: I had a horrible toothache last week, so my dentist pulled it.

Better: I had a horrible toothache last week, so my dentist pulled my tooth.

Unclear: When I wrote my research paper, it made me realize the value of patience.

Better: Writing my research paper made me realize the value of patience.

It is sometimes wise to substitute a noun for an unclear pronoun.

Unclear: The robbery was pulled off too smoothly. They suspect it was an inside job.

Better: The robbery was pulled off too smoothly. The police suspect it was an inside job.

Unclear: Luke always wanted to drive a bus, but they have to sit too long.

Better: Luke always wanted to drive a bus, but bus drivers have to sit too long.

Personal Pronouns   Personal pronouns refer to the person speaking *(I, we, me, us, my, mine, our, ours);* the person spoken to *(you, your, yours);* or the person spoken of *(he, she, it, they, him, her, them, his, hers, its, their, theirs).*

Just between *you* and *me,* I don't believe *he* or *she* wants to come with *us.*

Relative Pronouns.   The relative pronouns (*who, whom, whose, which, that,* etc.) join a dependent clause to another part of a sentence, usually a noun.

Clarence, *whose* job was in jeopardy, was late for work.
The money *that* we found in the attic is counterfeit.

Note: Use the pronouns *who, whom, whose,* etc. when referring to people and the pronouns which and that when referring to places, things, and animals.

Interrogative Pronouns.   Interrogative pronouns *(who, whom, whose, which, what)* ask questions.

What are you doing?
Who is coming tomorrow?

Demonstrative Pronouns.   Demonstrative pronouns *(this, that, these, those)* point out the nouns to which they refer.

That is my girlfriend.
This is an old house.
These are my parents.

Indefinite Pronouns.   Indefinite pronouns refer to indefinite persons or things. *Some, all, most, none, anyone, everyone, everything* and *nothing* are typical examples.

Most of the volunteers showed up.
Everything went wrong today.

Intensive and Reflective Pronouns.   These are personal pronouns which end in *–self* or *–selves: myself, yourself, herself, himself, itself, ourselves, yourselves* and *themselves.* Intensive pronouns provide emphasis.

I *myself* am responsible.
He *himself* did it.

Reflexive Pronouns.   Reflexive pronouns indicate that the subject of the verb is also its object.

John hurt *himself*. (direct object)
I gave *myself* a haircut. (indirect object)
The students were proud of *themselves*. (object of preposition)

Note: *Myself* is mistakenly considered more polite than *I* or *me*. However, in standard English, the reflexive form is not used as a substitute for either.

Wrong: The committee and *myself* would like to thank you.
Right: The committee and *I* would like to thank you.

Wrong: The argument was between Lee and *myself*.
Right: The argument was between Lee and *me*.

Pronoun Case.   Pronouns change in form depending upon how they are used in a sentence. The grammatical term for this change is case. Personal pronouns and the pronoun "who" can take the subjective, objective and possessive case.

Subjective	Objective	Possessive
I	me	my, mine
we	us	our, ours
you	you	your, yours
he	him	his
she	her	her, hers
it	it	its
one	one	one's
they	them	their, theirs
who	whom	whose

Note: Only the personal pronoun *"one"* adds −'s to show possession.

Subjective Case.   Pronouns take the subjective case when they are used as subjects of verbs, as subject complements of linking verbs, and when they are in apposition to subjects.

She is a real genius. (subject)
It was *she* who called. (subject complement)
Those two, Jesse and *he,* are friends. (appositive)

Objective Case.   Pronouns take the objective case when they are used as the objects of verbs, verbals and prepositions and when they are in apposition to objects.

Alice kissed *him*. (direct object)
Jim gave *her* the book. (indirect object)
Seeing *him* was a thrill. (object of gerund)

This is between you and *me*. (object of preposition)
We asked the two of them, Larry and *her,* to play. (in apposition to them)

Possessive Case.   Personal pronouns have two forms for the possessive. One is used before the noun, the other after.

This is *my* jacket.
This jacket is *mine*.
She brought *her* friend.
She brought a friend of *hers*.

If you have trouble deciding which pronoun case to use, the following suggestions will help you decide which is correct:

To determine the case of a pronoun when it is paired with a noun or another pronoun, mentally omit the other noun or pronoun and see if what you chose sounds right in the sentence.

Wrong: The teacher wants you and *I* to help. (Wants *I* to help?)
Right: The teacher wants you and *me* to help.

Wrong: Sally and *him* are lovers.   (*him* is a lover?)
Right: Sally and *he* are lovers.

To determine the case of a pronoun that modifies a noun mentally drop the noun.

Wrong: *Us* Americans have to stick together.   (*us* have to stick?)
Right: *We* Americans have to stick together.

Wrong: The future belongs to *we* students.   (belongs to *we*?)
Right: The future belongs to *us* students.

To determine the case of a pronoun that follows *as* or *than,* mentally add the words that are omitted. The pronoun is subjective if it is the subject of the omitted verb.

He liked Jody more than *I*.   (liked Jody)
She needs it more than *I*.   (need it)

If it is the object of the omitted verb, the pronoun is in the objective case.

He liked Susan as much as   (he liked) me.
She needs him more than   (she needs) me.

Adjectives

Adjectives modify nouns, pronouns and other nounlike elements. They normally precede the words they modify except when they are used as subject complements, although other positions are possible.*

Joan was a *happy child*.   (adj. noun)
Her *beautiful singing* rang out.   (adj. gerund)
"Lucky me," I cried.   (adj. pronoun)
You *look wonderful*.   (linking verb adj.)

Types of Adjectives.   There are two types of adjectives: descriptive and limiting. Descriptive adjectives make the meaning of a noun or pronoun more exact by telling what kind: *fast* car, *strong* smell, *wonderful* you, *hot* day.

Limiting adjectives tell which one or how many. There are several important categories:

1. Possessive Adjectives: *my* life, *her* paper, *our* car.
2. Articles: *a* dog, *an* apple, *the* window.
3. Numeral Adjectives: *one* second, *third* Sunday.
4. Indefinite Adjectives: *any* subject, *all* students, *every* day.
5. Demonstrative Adjectives: *this* book, *those* flowers, *these* children.
6. Interogative Adjectives: *whose* name? *which* window? *what* message?

Nouns, pronouns and the present and past participles of verbs can be used adjectively.

The elevator stopped on the *ground* floor.   (noun)
This summer will be fun.   (pronoun)
He was captain of the *swimming* team.   (present participle)
The *dejected* student looked at her grade.   (past participle)

Adverbs

A distinguishing feature of adverbs is the *–ly* ending. However, because some adverbs do not end in *–ly* (*as, faster, down, well,* etc.) and some are identical in form to adjectives (*early, deep, fast, much,* etc.), you often have to distinguish an adverb solely by its function in a sentence. Adverbs modify verbs, adjectives and other adverbs. They answer the questions *when, how, how much* and *where*.

---

*The boy, *young* and *inexperienced,* fidgeted nervously. (Adjectives following the noun *boy* in apposition)

When? I *rarely* watch T.V. (modifying a verb)
How? Handle the kittens *gently*. (modifying a verb)
How much? Sally was *slightly* tipsy. (modifying an adjective)
Where? He wandered *far* away. (modifying another adverb)

Adverbs can be classified as adverbs of time, manner, degree and place.

Time (when?)	Manner (how?)	Degree (how much?)	Place (where?)
again	badly	better	away
always	carefully	considerably	down
immediately	cautiously	more	beyond
never	evenly	nearly	forward
seldom	quickly	once	here
soon	suddenly	slightly	there
then	tiredly	twice	up

Some adverbs such as *why, when, where* and *how* are used in questions.

When are we going?

Other adverbs called conjunctive adverbs (*also, however, nevertheless,* etc.) are connectives that join independent clauses. They are discussed in more detail on page 326 under conjunctions.

Comparison of Adjectives and Adverbs.   Adjectives and adverbs have three forms of comparison: positive, which suggests no comparison; comparative, used to compare two things; and superlative, used to compare three or more things. The three methods for indicating these comparisons are: (1) add *–er* for the comparative and *–est* for the superlative, (2) use *more* or *less* with the comparative and *most* and *least* with the superlative, and (3) use a different word with each degree.

Positive	Comparative	Superlative
attractive	more attractive	most attractive
bad	worse	worst
good	better	best
fancy	fancier	fanciest
fancy	more fancy	most fancy
some	more	most
big	bigger	biggest

Note: Adjectives and adverbs of three or more syllables always add *more* or *most* to form the comparative or superlative.

Problems with Adjectives and Adverbs.   Do not confuse the adjective *good* with the word *well*. *Well* can be either an adjective or an adverb.

Wrong: She did *good* on the test. (the adjective *good* cannot modify a verb)
Right: She did *well* on the test.
         She feels *good*. (in good spirits)
         She feels *well*. (in good health)

Use *bad* as an adjective and *badly* as an adverb.

Wrong: He plays chess *bad*.
Right: He plays chess *badly*.

Wrong: I felt *badly* about the accident.
Right: I felt *bad* about the accident.

Note: *Bad* is used as a subject complement (predicate adjective) following the linking verb. Although some people feel that the adverb *badly* can be used when the emphasis is on the verb, it is best to avoid such uses of *badly* when writing.

Use an adverb, not an adjective, to modify a verb, an adjective or another adverb. The following adjectives and adverbs are often confused:

Real/Really
Wrong: She is *real* smart.
Right: She is *really* smart.
Right: She is *very* smart.

Sure/Surely
Wrong: He *sure* is handsome.
Right: He *surely* is handsome.

Awful/Awfully
Wrong: I am *awful* tired.
Right: I am *awfully* tired.

Quiet/Quietly
Wrong: He talked as *quiet* as he could.
Right: He talked as *quietly* as he could.

Near/Nearly
Wrong: My dog was *near* killed.
Right: My dog was *nearly* killed.

Prepositions

A preposition is a connecting word that links a noun or pronoun (its object) to another sentence element. A preposition conveys a sense of time, direction or position.

Are you through *after* this? (time)
He rowed *across* the lake. (direction)
He crawled *under* the covers. (position)

Below is a list of the most commonly used prepositions:

about	behind	by	of
above	below	down	off
across	beneath	during	on
after	besides	for	since
at	between	from	upon
before	beyond	in	with

Since many prepositions can also function as adverbs, be sure to determine whether the word takes an object and functions as a connective. If it does, it is a preposition. If it has no object and functions as a modifier, it is an adverb.

He jumped *over the fence.* (prepositional phrase)
He jumped *over* and *over.* (adverb)

A phrase introduced by a preposition is called a prepositional phrase. A prepositional phrase includes the preposition, its object and all modifiers. When the object of a preposition is a pronoun, it is always stated in the objective case.

Wrong: The fight is *between she* and *I.*
Right: The fight is *between her* and *me.*

Wrong: The lecture was directed *at we students.*
Right: The lecture was directed *at us students.*

Wrong: He stood *behind he* and *Jeff.*
Right: He stood *behind him* and *Jeff.*

Prepositional phrases can function the same in sentences as adverbs, adjectives or nouns.

The lady *in blue* is mysterious. (adjective)
Peter crawled *under the house.* (adverb)
Before lunch is the time to exercise. (noun)

Common Errors with Prepositions

1. Do not use *of* in place of *have.*

    Wrong: He should *of* known better.
    Right: He should *have* known better.

2. Do not confuse *in* and *into.*

    Wrong: Go jump *in* the lake.
    Right: Go jump *into* the lake. (*In* refers to action taken *within* the location, *into* to action directed *toward* the location.)

3. Do not use *off of* for *off.*

    Wrong: He fell *off of* the stage.
    Right: He fell *off* the stage.

4. Do not confuse *between* and *among.* Use the word *between* to refer to two.

    The argument was *between* John and me.

    Use the word *among* to refer to three or more.

    A real friendship developed *among* the students in our class.

5. Do not confuse *beside* and *besides.*

    The bride stood *beside* the groom. (next to)
    Besides cake they also are serving cookies. (in addition to or except)
    Nobody *besides* me had any money. (except)

Conjunctions

Conjunctions connect words, phrases, or clauses. They may be coordinating, subordinating, correlative or conjunctive.

Coordinating Conjunctions.   The coordinating conjunctions *(and, but, for, or, nor, so, yet)* join parts of speech that are used the same way in the sentence.

Frank *and* Joan (two nouns)
win *or* lose (two verbs)
old *but* nice (two adjectives)

Remember: When a coordinating conjunction joins two independent clauses, it is preceded by a comma.

The phone rang incessantly, *yet* nobody answered it.

Beginning writers tend to overuse the conjunction *and*. A monotonous succession of *ands* makes for pretty dull reading. Check to see if another conjunction could do the job as well or better.

Subordinating Conjunctions.   Subordinating conjunctions are used to connect subordinate (dependent) clauses with main (independent) clauses. When used properly, they will add variety and precision to your sentences. A subordinate clause is not necessarily less important than a main clause. It is called subordinate because it cannot stand alone as a sentence. Below is a list of the most commonly used subordinating conjunctions:

after	if	until
although	since	when
as	than	where
because	though	wherever
before	unless	while

The relative pronouns *(who, whom, whose, which, that, what)* can also serve as subordinating conjunctions.

Subordinate clauses can begin sentences, end sentences or be included (embedded) in them.

Although John was late, we waited for him.
We ate the whole cake *because we were hungry.*
The paper *that Paul handed in* was without error.
Our cat, *which we love,* is Siamese.

Correlative Conjunctions.   Correlative conjunctions are coordinating words used in pairs. *Either . . . or, neither . . . nor, both . . . and,* and *not only . . . but also* are the most common correlative pairs.

He was *neither* young *nor* foolish.

The main purpose for using correlative conjunctions is to emphasize that two co-related ideas are involved. Therefore, you should be careful to keep your constructions parallel. If the first conjunction is followed by an infinitive, the second should also be followed by an infinitive, and so on.

Wrong: Max likes *either* fishing *or* to hunt.
Right: Max likes *either* fishing *or* hunting.

Conjunctive Adverbs.   Conjunctive adverbs join independent clauses either of which can stand by itself. Sometimes called transitional connectives, conjunctive adverbs establish a logical connection between a particular statement and a previous one. While the usual connection between them is a semicolon, a period is not uncommon.

Russell was sick; *nevertheless,* he had to go to work.
Edna came early. *However,* she had forgotten her present.

The most commonly used conjunctive adverbs are listed below:

also	indeed	similarly
besides	likewise	then
consequently	moreover	therefore
furthermore	nevertheless	thus
however	nonetheless	

Interjections

An interjection is an exclamatory word or phrase that expresses feeling: *well, ah, damn! oh, ouch! gosh, no, stop! help!* Interjections have little grammatical connection with other words in a sentence and are capable of standing alone. A mild interjection is punctuated with a comma.

Well, how are you?
Oh, all right I guess.

An emphatic interjection is punctuated with an exclamation point.

"Don't!" she gasped.
Come here!

Note: The interjection should be used infrequently. It is rarely appropriate in descriptive or expository writing and its overuse in narrative reduces its effectiveness.

Clauses and Phrases

Clauses.   Sentences are made up of single words and clusters of words called clauses and phrases. A main or independent clause expresses a complete thought and can stand alone as a sentence. It can also provide a framework to which modifiers, phrases or subordinate clauses can be attached.

The burglar surrendered.
(independent clause)

Caught in the act, the burglar surrendered.
(phrase)   (independent clause)

Caught in the act, the *cat* burglar surrendered *when the police arrived.*
(phrase)   (modifier)   (subordinate clause)

Subordinate Clause.   A subordinate clause (or dependent clause) is subordinate to or dependent upon a main clause. It cannot stand alone as a sentence. Subordinate clauses are preceded by subordinating conjunctions or relative pronouns.

because you are selfish
although she is blind
who missed the exam

Subordinate clauses are classified according to their function in a sentence as nouns, adjectives or adverb clauses.

Noun Clause.   Noun clauses perform as nouns in sentences. They may function as subjects, subject complements, or objects.

That we are all God's children is indisputable.
(subject)

The bad news was *that we lost the game.*
(subject complement)

Give credit *to whoever deserves it.*
(prepositional phrase)

I know *that we will win.*
(direct object)

Adjective Clause.   Adjective clauses modify nouns or pronouns.

I bought a new car *which I can't afford.* (modifies noun car)
Anyone *who knows baseball* knows Henry Aaron. (modifies pronoun anyone)

Adjective clauses are either *restrictive* or *nonrestrictive*. Restrictive clauses contain information so important to the subject that they can't be left out. Nonrestrictive clauses give information that is not vital to the sentence. Consider the two sentences below.

1. Students *who are caught cheating* will fail. (restrictive)
2. Students, *who are often short of money,* are not big spenders. (nonrestrictive)

In the first sentence, the clause is a necessary part of the subject and can't be left out without changing the meaning of the sentence. It limits the subject to a specific type of student: *those who are caught cheating.* When information is that important, it is *not* set off with commas.

In sentence two, the clause is not vital for the sentence to make sense and without it, the sentence would still make the same point. The fact that the information could be left out is emphasized by *framing it with commas.*

Adverb Clause. Used in a sentence as an adverb, an adverb clause can be introduced by a wide variety of subordinating conjunctions. Adverb clauses express relationships of time, manner, degree or place.

After the game was over, we all went out to celebrate. (time)
I baked the cake *as if you were here to help.* (manner)
As closely as we can determine, the test is completely accurate. (degree)
I will help *wherever I am needed.* (place)

Phrases. A phrase is another group of words that functions as a part of speech. However, unlike a clause, a phrase does not have both a subject and a predicate. A phrase may function as a verb, noun, adjective or adverb. Phrases can be classified according to their distinguishing words as prepositional, participial, infinitive, gerund, noun, verb and absolute.

Prepositional Phrases. A prepositional phrase consists of a preposition, an object and its modifiers. It can be used in a sentence as an adjective, adverb or noun.

The glass *on the counter* is clean. (adjective)
He spat *on the floor.* (adverb)
Behind that door is the answer. (noun)

Participial Phrase. The participial phrase is used as an adjective. It includes a participle with its object and modifiers.

Cheering loudly, the fans pulled at the goal posts. (present participle)
The letter, *marked "personal,"* looked interesting. (past participle)

Infinitive Phrase.   An infinitive phrase consists of an infinitive, its object and any modifiers. It can function as a noun, adjective and adverb.

To be rich would be wonderful. (noun-subject)
My goal is *to be rich.* (subject complement)
She wants *to be rich.* (direct object)
I have a paper *to write.* (adjective)
He is fascinating *to watch.* (adverb)

Gerund Phrase.   A gerund and its modifiers form a gerund phrase. It is used as a noun in sentences.

Having a cold is a bummer.

Noun Phrase.   A noun phrase includes a noun and its modifiers. It is used in a sentence in the same way a noun is used.

Bill Sanders, *the cartoonist,* is our guest speaker. (noun phrase as appositive)
Students with dedication and motivation are bound to succeed. (noun phrase as subject)

Verb Phrase.   A verb phrase consists of a main verb along with its helping verbs.

He says we *should have finished* long ago.

Note: A verb phrase is unlike other kinds of phrases since it contains a complete verb.

Absolute Phrase.   Although it is not grammatically related to it, the absolute phrase modifies the rest of a sentence. It includes a noun or pronoun and a participle. Absolute phrases are not joined to the rest of the sentence with connectors but are always set off with commas.

Considering that I stayed up all night, I feel pretty good.
To add insult to injury, he won the bet.

Punctuation

Punctuation shows the reader how a sentence is supposed to be read. Incorrect punctuation can result in confusion or misunderstanding.

This section deals with the fourteen kinds of punctuation you need to use in your writing: periods, question marks, exclamation points, semicolon, colon, commas, hyphens, apostrophes, quotation marks, parentheses, dashes, brackets, italics, and capitalization.

Periods. A period marks the end of most sentences. While the writer indicates with punctuation what the meaning of a sentence is to be, most sentences that are not exclamations or direct questions end with periods. Below are four types of sentences that are ended with periods:

Declarative Statement: Tuesday is election day.
Imperative Statement: Take a letter. (mild command)
Indirect Question: I wonder where Kai is.
Courtesy Question: Would you please be seated.

NOTE: These two questions are indirect in that they do not ask for an answer.
Periods are used for most abbreviations: Sgt., A.M., a.m., e.g., Dec., Ms. However, you do not need periods for abbreviations which are well known or commonly used.

NAACP, IBM, NBC, scuba

Periods are used after initials:

A. J. Foyt   J. P. Morgan

Periods are used as decimal points:

$.89, 98.6°, 3.11416, $39.95

Three spaced periods called ellipses (. . .) are used to show the omission of words in a quotation. When the omission occurs at the ending of the sentence, indicate this by adding the period as the fourth ellipse.

"The first American to die in the cause of freedom was Crispus Attucks . . . in 1770. The first doctor to perform open heart surgery was black. . . ."

Congressional Record. Speech given by Hon. Glenn M. Anderson of California in the House of Representatives, February 16, 1972.

Question Mark. A question mark is used to end a sentence that is a direct question.

Where are you going?

Use a question mark to end a sentence that begins with a declarative statement but ends with a question.

I might be mistaken, but isn't that the same shirt you wore yesterday?

A question mark occurs immediately after a question within a sentence. The question mark occurs inside the quotation marks if it refers to the statement quoted and outside the quotation marks if it refers to the entire sentence.

Claude asked, "Where did it go?"
Who was it who asked, "Where did it go"?

Use a question mark immediately after a parenthetical question within a sentence.

Someone once said (wasn't it a politician?) that bad publicity is better than no publicity at all.

Exclamation Point.   Exclamation points are used after emphatic interjections.

Stop!   Help!   Wait!   No, no, no!

They are used after sentences to indicate strong emotion.

My purse has been stolen!
What a fiend!

Do not overuse the exclamation point. It is seldom appropriate for expository or descriptive writing, and too frequent use in narrative weakens its effectiveness.
NOTE: Never use more than one exclamation point after any sentence.

Semicolon.   Use a semicolon between two sentences which are closely related. While either of the two sentences below could be made compound by using a coordinating conjunction, the use of the semicolon emphasizes the importance of each.

I guess they thought I was too young; I was only five.
The car is a good buy; it just needs a paint job.

Main clauses joined by conjunctive adverbs (*therefore, however, consequently, then,* etc.) are separated by a semicolon.

John didn't arrive on time; therefore, we left without him.
We forgot the food; however, there is plenty to drink.

Use a semicolon between main clauses connected by coordinating conjunctions if the sentences are long and contain commas.

Erik, who couldn't afford to, lost his shirt; but Allen, who had money to burn, won a bundle.

A semicolon may be used to separate elements in a series if the elements contain commas.

The members of the trio are Carl Harris, bass; Cal Jones, tenor; and Phil Morgan, baritone.

Colon.   A colon indicates that what follows will list, illustrate, restate, or amplify. Use a colon to introduce a list.

The note from school said to bring the following: a bag lunch, swim suit, bath towel, and spending money.

A colon is used to introduce a quotation.

As Robert Kennedy said many times, in many parts of this nation: "Some men see things as they are and say why. I dream things that never were and say, why not."

A colon can be used to emphasize an appositive.

He had only one thing on his mind: women.

Use a colon between two main clauses when the second clause restates or amplifies the first.

Betty couldn't decide which pastry to try next: she thought she had died and gone to heaven.

NOTE: Do not use a colon after a verb or a preposition.

Wrong: His favorite operas were: Tosca, Faust and Carmen.
Right: His favorite operas were Tosca, Faust and Carmen.
Right: His favorite operas were as follows: Tosca, Faust and Carmen.

Wrong: He wants to major in: English, Journalism or Communications.
Right: He wants to major in English, Journalism or Communications.
Right: He wants to major in one of the following areas: English, Journalism or Communications.

Conventional Uses of the Colon.   A colon is used in the following places:

1. After the salutation in a business letter: Dear Ms. Koenig:, Dear Doctor Backer:
2. Between hours and minutes when indicating time: 11:30 a.m., 1:15 p.m.
3. To link chapter and verse in Biblical references: Acts 11:16, Matthew 3:4–6.
4. In footnotes and bibliographies: William L. Rivers, *Writing: Craft and Art* (Englewood Cliffs, N.J.: Prentice Hall, 1975), p. 1.

The Comma.   Commas are used before coordinating conjunctions *(and, but, for, or, so, yet)* to connect coordinate clauses in compound sentences. Be aware that the comma is always placed before the conjunction.

Patrick really enjoys hunting, but his brother hates everything about it.
Sally hated her job, yet she was afraid to quit.

NOTE: The comma may be omitted if the clauses are short and closely related.

The picture fell and the frame broke.

Do not make the mistake of using a comma to join two independent clauses. This is called a comma splice. It is a serious error made by inexperienced writers who recognize that some division is necessary but are not sure which punctuation is correct.

Wrong: Answer the phone, it might be important.
Right: Answer the phone. It might be important.
Right: Answer the phone; it might be important.

Phrases and Clauses.   Use a comma after introductory parts of sentences. Subordinate phrases and clauses are often placed at the beginning of sentences for variety or emphasis. Unless they are short, they should be separated from the main clause with a comma.

As soon as I saw her, I knew I was in love.
Although he isn't good-looking, he is rich.
During the first half of the season, our team didn't win a game.
In spite of all his faults, my husband is a pretty nice guy.

NOTE: When a subordinate phrase or clause follows the main clause, no comma is required.

I knew I was in love as soon as I saw her.
My husband is a pretty nice guy in spite of his faults.

Transitionary Words. Words like *however, consequently,* and *therefore* often begin sentences to provide transition. They are set off with commas.

I got a "U" on the final exam. Consequently, I failed the course.

Transitional Expressions. Short transitional expressions like *in other words, for example, on the other hand, in spite of,* and *of course* should be set off with commas.

Of course, you knew it all the time.

Interjections. Mild introductory expressions like *no, oh, well,* and *yes* must be followed by a comma.

Well, how much will it cost?

Direct Address. Nouns used in direct address are followed by commas.

Mother, here is the money I owe you.
Nicky, give me a hand, please.

Coordinate Adjectives. Coordinate adjectives modify the same noun equally. They should be separated by commas.

a mean, selfish, contemptible liar
a loving, caring, sensitive person
two white picket fences.

In the first two examples, three adjectives modify the noun in a similar way. They could be rearranged or separated by *and* and make sense: selfish, contemptible, mean liar; loving and caring and sensitive person.
But in the following example rearranging the adjectives makes it glaringly awkward:

the two white picket fences
the picket, white, two fences; or two and white and picket fences.

Nonrestrictive Elements.   Commas are used to enclose nonrestrictive phrases or clauses: those which can be omitted without changing the meaning of the sentence.

My girlfriend, who is over eighteen, is eligible to vote in Wisconsin.
Anyone who is over eighteen is eligible to vote in Wisconsin.

In the first sentence, the clause *who is over eighteen* is merely adding information to the statement that your girlfriend is able to vote in Wisconsin. While the information is interesting, it isn't necessary to the meaning of the sentence. The clause is nonrestrictive, and it is set off with commas.

In the second sentence, however, the clause *who is over eighteen* is vital to the sentence because it identifies who is eligible to vote in Wisconsin: those who are over eighteen.

Nonrestrictive phrases and clauses require commas; restrictive phrases and clauses do not.

Restrictive clause—The school which we attended as kids burned down.
Nonrestrictive clause—Washington school, which we attended as kids, burned down.
Restrictive clause—From my vantage point on the roof I could see the parade clearly.
Nonrestrictive clause—The mailman, on time for once, brought the letter I had been waiting for.

Use two commas to set off nonrestrictive phrases or clauses unless they begin or end a sentence.

Maxine, convinced that she was doing the right thing, dropped out of school.
Maxine dropped out of school, convinced that she was doing the right thing.
Convinced that she was doing the right thing, Maxine dropped out of school.

Parenthetical Expressions.   Parenthetical expressions interrupt the flow of a sentence and are usually enclosed in commas.

Marta, of course, got all A's.
I opened the door and, wow, there he stood.
The speech, I told myself, would be easy to give.

Transitional Elements.   Transitional words and phrases that appear within a sentence are enclosed with commas.

The exam, however, has been postponed.
The steam room, for example, costs extra.

Appositives.   Appositives are nouns or noun phrases that explain or supplement a preceding noun. They are usually *nonrestrictive* modifiers set off by commas.

The boy, a newcomer to town, spent the entire morning trying to find a place to stay.
Ben just learned today that they published his letter in the Times, the school newspaper.

Restrictive appositives require no commas.

She preferred to be thought of as Sarah the woman rather than Sarah the actress.

Items in a Series.   A comma is the punctuation ordinarily used to separate words, phrases, or clauses in a series.

Kevin put lettuce, ham, bologna, cheese, tomatoes, pickles and mustard on his sandwich. (nouns)
Our parents told us how to eat, how to sleep, how to dress, but mostly how to work. (phrases)
We must know who is coming, what they are bringing and when they will be here. (dependent clauses)

Conventional Comma Use

1. *Letters*—Use a comma after the salutation of personal letters (Dear John, Dear Aunt Sally,) and after the complimentary close of all letters (Sincerely, Yours truly,).

2. *Numbers*—Commas separate numbers into thousands, millions, etc.

   3,150   38,794   6,483,000

NOTE: Telephone numbers, social security numbers and the like are separated by hyphens. 1 (414) 768-4324   399-52-0760

3. *Addresses*—When names and addresses appear on the same line, their elements are separated by commas. However, no comma is used before the zip code.

Fred Sutton, 6871 South Oak Street, Racine, Wisconsin 57301 is the applicant for this position.

4. *Dates*—Commas separate the day of the month from the year (March 9, 1928).

   On July 7, 1982, we moved to Milwaukee.

   If only the month and year are given, do *not* use a comma.

   It was during July 1982 that we moved.

5. *Titles*—Use commas to separate proper names from titles and degrees.

   Herman L. Thompson, Ph.D., F.A.S.M.
   Alice Rhodes, M.D.
   Elroy Hoffman, Jr.

6. *Quotations*—A comma is used to introduce direct quotations and to separate quoted from non-quoted material.

   George asked, "When are you coming?"
   "I'm coming," said Alice, "as soon as I can."
   "I'm coming as soon as I can," said Alice.

NOTE: When a quotation ends in a period, change the period to a comma if it is followed by non-quoted material.

Hyphens. Hyphens are used in two ways: to join compound words and to indicate that a word is continued from one line to the next.

There is no simple rule to follow when spelling compound words. Therefore, if you are in doubt, check your dictionary to determine whether or not to hyphenate a word.

1. Hyphenate two or more words when they serve as adjectives before a noun.

   well-known song, door-to-door salesman

2. All compound numbers from twenty-one through ninety-nine should be hyphenated.

   twenty-one, forty-four, sixty-seven

3. Fractions which are written out are hyphenated.

one-tenth, three-fourths, five-eighths

4. Hyphenate a word with a prefix and a capitalized noun.

pro-Nazi, anti-American, pre-Christian

5. Hyphenate between the prefixes *self-*, *all-* and *ex-* before all nouns and the suffix -elect after all nouns.

self-indulgent, president-elect, all-city, ex-officio

6. Use a hyphen to join words that are listed as compound words in your dictionary.

I borrowed money from my father-in-law.
Molly resigned as secretary-treasurer.

Use a hyphen to divide a word from one line to the next. If in doubt, consult your dictionary to determine how a word is divided.

The marching band began the fes-
tivities with a rousing rendition of "On Wisconsin."

NOTE: Always place the hyphen behind the division on the first line, never in front of the division on the second line.

Apostrophes. Use the apostrophe to indicate the possessive case of nouns and indefinite pronouns. Add an apostrophe and *s* to form the possession of words that do not end in *s*.

Gloria's hair	anyone's guess	a day's pay
the child's toy	a dollar's worth	the children's toy
yesterday's dream	the men's chorus	

Add either an apostrophe or an apostrophe and *s* to singular words ending in *s*.

Chris' coat—Chris's coat   the hostess' dress—the hostess's dress

Add only an apostrophe to plural nouns ending in *s*.

ladies' day	girls' gym
parents' blessing	three days' pay

In compounds, add the *s* to the last noun.

commander-in-chief's decision
son-in-law's occupation
someone else's responsibility

To show joint possession, make only the last noun possessive.

Dolores and Earl's boat
Ken and Lee's house.

To show individual possession, make both nouns possessive.

Dolores's and Earl's car
Ken's and Lee's children

Use an apostrophe and *s* to form the plurals of figures and letters of the alphabet.

three *A's* and two *B's*

The apostrophe is used to indicate the omission of one or more letters in a contraction.

it's = it is	o'clock = of the clock
isn't = is not	here's = here is
class of '72 = class of 1972	she's = she is
they're = they are	O'er = over (poetic)

Quotation Marks. Use quotation marks to indicate the exact words of a speaker or writer. Do not use quotation marks when you paraphrase (put into your own words) what was said.

Ginger said, "I love Mozart." (direct quotation)
Ginger said that she loves Mozart. (paraphrase/indirect quotation)

Use a direct quotation when something has been said so well that it shouldn't be reworded.

It was Shakespeare who said "There is no darkness by ignorance."

Quote directly when you want your reader to know *exactly* what someone (usually an expert) has said.

When a quotation is combined with explanatory words (she said, he asked) enclose only the quoted words in quotation marks.

"Help!" she screamed. "I'm being robbed."
"Did we win?" he asked.
"I am not unaware," he said, "of your talents."
"He is an excellent writer," she added.

Periods or commas should always be placed inside the closing quotation marks as in the examples above.

Unless they are part of the quotation, colons and semicolons are placed outside of quotation marks.

Most of us preferred "Sunrise, Sunset"; only two choir members voted for "Yesterday": Ruth and Harry.

Question marks or exclamation points go inside the quotation marks if they apply only to the quotation and outside the quotation marks if they apply to the whole sentence.

He asked, "Will you please pass the steak?"
Do you think I could get him to say "Thank you"? (the whole sentence is a question)
"No, no, no!" she screamed.
I did say "Please"! (the whole sentence is an exclamation.)

When a quotation occurs within a quotation, enclose it with single quotation marks.

The minister continued, "When Jesus said, 'Blessed are the peacemakers, for they shall be called the sons of God,' he was issuing a mandate for each of us to further the cause of peace."

When quoting several consecutive sentences, put quotation marks at the beginning of the first sentence and at the end of the last.

Sydney blurted, "I don't believe I can be of any help. The vandals had already left by the time I got there. Let me go home."

Quotations longer than three typewritten lines should be indented and single spaced. They do not have to be enclosed in quotation marks.

Use quotation marks to enclose the titles of songs, poems, short stories, and newspaper or magazine articles. Underline or use italics for longer works.

My favorite song is "If I Were a Rich Man" from *Fiddler on the Roof.*

Use quotation marks to identify words that you are defining or explaining.

The word "puppet" comes from Latin; the word "marionette" comes from French.

The threat of a nuclear war between Russia and the United States has resulted in a new word: "omnicide," the annihilation of all forms of life and vestiges of civilization.

Use quotation marks around nicknames, slang, or trite expressions. Avoid using these in formal writing.

"Madame Queen" isn't coming.
He was really a "weirdo."
"A stitch in time," they always say.

Parentheses.   Parentheses are used to enclose material that is supplemental to a sentence. This information might be explanation, example, detail, or reference. While such material may not be essential to the meaning of the sentence, it can often be useful to your reader. Parenthetical information should pertain to the material immediately preceding it.

The candidates are Anthony Earl (Democrat) and Terry Kohler (Republican).
Louis Pasteur (1822–95) was the founder of modern bacteriology.
For the first time in history, every living thing is confronted by an enemy more powerful than death—nuclear omnicide. (See Somerville's *The Philosophy of Peace.*)

Parenthetic material (including a main clause) which occurs within a sentence, requires neither a capital letter to begin it nor a period to end it. *NOTE:* Place the sentence period after the closing parenthesis.

A deposit of $100 per month for 25 years ($30,000 total), grows to $134,389 at retirement (based on 10.5% current interest rate).
I voted (my husband still can't believe it) for Ronald Reagan.

If the parenthetical material is a question or exclamation, use a question mark or exclamation mark within the parenthesis.

When he asked me, I agreed (what choice did I have?).
Cancer (I hate that disease!) killed my uncle.

When a statement is written as a separate, parenthetic sentence, the end punctuation comes before the closing parenthesis.

(The Pentagon has two rules for negotiating arms agreements: One is "Don't negotiate when you are behind." The other is "Why negotiate when you are ahead?")
Last semester I got A's in all my subjects. (I couldn't do better than that.)

Use parentheses to enclose numbers within sentences.

Your duties are to (1) chop kindling wood, (2) tend the fire, and (3) wash and dry the dishes.

The Dash   Dashes are used to emphasize material within a sentence or to show a break in thought. Dashes function somewhat like commas but the pause is longer and therefore more emphatic.

The boat—if you could call it that—bobbed up and down in the water.
The reason I failed—but why go into that?
He whispered, "Here's what we—"

A dash may be used to emphasize a short, final appositive.

When I heard her the first thing that came to mind was—magnificent.

Brackets   Brackets are used to include other parenthetic material within parentheses.

Only Mark came out to help his father. (His brother [Otto] was afraid.)

Use brackets to set off unquoted material within a quotation.

Jesuit peace activist Daniel Berrigan says, "If you're going to work for justice and peace, you better look good on wood [the cross]."

Use brackets to enclose the word *sic* which indicates that the mistake you are including appeared in the original.

My boss told me he'd like to congragulate [*sic*] me on my success.

Italics   Italics are used to call attention to a certain word or group of words. They are indicated in typing or writing by underlining.

Italicize the titles of all works published separately. (Short stories, poems, songs, and newspaper or magazine articles are set off with quotation marks.)

1. Books—*The Godfather, War and Peace*
2. Plays—*Hamlet, Death of a Salesman*
3. Movies—*Gone With The Wind, E.T., Jaws*
4. Musical Works—*Carmen, Fiddler on the Roof, Scheherazade*
5. Television and Radio Shows—*Mash, The Muppets, Amos and Andy*
6. Newspapers and Magazines—the *Milwaukee Journal*, the *New Yorker*, *Playboy*

Italicize the names of trains, planes, ships and spacecraft.

The first *Hiawatha* was a steam locomotive.
I was an ensign on the *USS Bristol* during the Korean War.
The space-shuttle *Columbia* completed a successful mission in November 1982.

Italicize words, numbers and letters used as examples.

Students often confuse the verbs *lay* and *lie.*
Many people are superstitious about the number *13.*
Bernard got all *A's* again this semester.

Italicize scientific names.

Robins belong to the *Turdidae* family of birds.

Italicize unfamiliar foreign words and phrases.

My mother makes Danish pancakes called *aebleskiver.*

Italicize for emphasis.

Do you know what it's like to be *really* needed?

Note: Italicizing for emphasis should be used sparingly or it loses its effectiveness.

Capitalization

Proper Nouns   Capitalize proper nouns, which name specific individuals, places, or things. Use the following list as a guide:

Capitalized Proper Nouns (specific)	Lower Case Common Nouns (general)
Bugs Bunny	a crazy rabbit
Mayor Jones	the mayor

Capitalized Proper Nouns (specific)	Lower Case Common Nouns (general)
Pastor Anderson	a minister
Uncle Cyrus	an uncle
Los Angeles	a city in California
Mud Lake	an inland lake
Venus	a distant planet
Yom Kippur	a religious holiday
Harvard University	a major university
Mona Lisa	a well-known painting
What Did You Say?	a text book
Lights Out	a radio program
Pepsi-Lite	a diet cola
Slavic	a language
History 211	a history course

Individuals (Proper Names)   The names of persons, animals or fictional characters should always be capitalized.

Elizabeth Taylor	Plato	Bugs Bunny
Lassie	Topol	Tom Sawyer

Groups   Capitalize the names of political, religious, national, or racial groups.

Democrat	Afro-American	Hispanic
Lutheran	Jew	Communist
Native American	Progressive	Norwegian

Note: When referring to people, the term *white* or *black* is usually not capitalized.

Organizations   Specific organizations and their abbreviations are capitalized.

YMCA	Girl Scouts	Knights of Columbus
Toast Masters	NAACP	Phi Beta Kappa

Titles   Capitalize titles that are used before a person's name.

Pastor Anderson	Dr. Disc	Rabbi Cohen
Queen Elizabeth	Mayor Jones	Captain Cook

Capitalize a title when it refers to the specific person holding it.

The Senator will return shortly.
The King is dead; long live the King.

Only titles of great importance are capitalized when they follow a name.

Hamlet, Prince of Denmark
George Washington, President of the United States.

but—

Dr. E. S. Johnson, professor emeritus, UWM.

Initials and Abbreviations   Capitalize a person's initials and all abbreviations used with his or her name.

Reverend P. Kuenning, D.D.
Ms. M. L. Beck, M.D.

Deity   Capitalize those words that stand for what is sacred or divine.

Father	Son	Holy Spirit
Shinto	Allah	Lord God

Family Members   Capitalize the names of family members when they are combined with a proper name.

Uncle Edgar	Cousin Claude
Aunt Millie	Mother White

Capitalize the names of family members when they are used instead of proper names.

Are you coming, Uncle?
We are having a party for Mother and Father.

Do not capitalize family names that are preceded by possessive pronouns or articles like *my, our, a, an,* or *the.*

An uncle of ours is visiting my mother and father.
All of your brothers and sisters are invited.

Places

Population Centers Capitalize the names of cities, states, countries, and continents.

Las Vegas	Africa	California
Ireland	Cairo	Greece

Travel Routes Capitalize the names of streets, boulevards, highways, and waterways.

Hollywood Boulevard	Erie Canal
Eden's Expressway	Alpine Highway
Front Street	

Points of Interest The names of specific parks, hills, mountains, and canyons are capitalized.

Yellowstone Park	Ural Mountains
Black Hills	Grand Canyon

Bodies of Water Capitalize the names of lakes, rivers, seas, and oceans.

North Sea	Nile River	Golden Pond
Indian Ocean	Mud Lake	Lake Michigan

Geographic Regions Capitalize the words *South, North, East,* and *West* when they identify geographical regions.

His parents come from the South.
Junko was born in the Far East.

Directions Do not capitalize *north, south, east,* and *west* when they refer to directions.

When the wind is west the fishing is best.
Milwaukee is north of Chicago.

Heavenly Bodies The names of planets, stars, and constellations are capitalized.

Mars	North Star	Aquarius

Do not capitalize the earth, moon, or sun.

Things

Dates Capitalize the days of the week and months of the year.

Saturday   Monday   July   April

Do not capitalize the names of the seasons.

Special Dates Capitalize the names of holidays and special occasions.

Yom Kippur   Easter   St. Valentine's Day   National Brotherhood Week   Christmas

Historical Data The names of historical events and documents should be capitalized.

Dark Ages   Sermon on the Mount
Crusades   The Great Depression
Civil War   Declaration of Independence

Languages Capitalize the names of different languages.

English   Mung   Slavic   Chinese

Trademarks Capitalize brand names but not product names.

Cheerios   Pepsi-Lite
Ivory soap   Ajax cleanser

Institutions The names of public and private institutions should be capitalized.

University of Texas   The Pentagon
Central High School   Racine Public Library

Tourist Attractions Capitalize the names of specific monuments, statues, and buildings.

Washington Monument   Lincoln Memorial
Grant's Tomb   Empire State Building
Statue of Liberty   The Little Mermaid

Educational Classes Specific academic or language courses must be capitalized.

Afro-American History   Russian
Speech 201   English Literature

Note: Do not capitalize all the important general subjects like chemistry, speech, or psychology.

Titles   Capitalize all the important words in the titles of the following:

Textbooks and Novels—*What Did You Say?*   *Watch on the Rhine*
Magazines and Periodicals—*Ebony   Science Digest*
Newspapers and Speeches—*Milwaukee Journal   Martin Luther King's "I Have a Dream"*
Songs and Poems—*"Yesterday"   "Slow Down"*
Plays and Movies—*Death of a Salesman   Jaws*
Radio and TV—*Lights Out   Mash*

First Words   Capitalize the first word in every sentence.

Time is money.

Capitalize the first word in direct quotations.

Alice explained, "Time is money."

Capitalize the first word in each new line of poetry.

And here the buzz of eager nations ran,
In murmur'd pity and loud roar'd applause,
As man was slaughter'd by his fellow man.
                    —Byron, "Childe Harold's Pilgrimage"

Capitalize the first word of a salutation and all the important words that follow it.

Dear Ted and Alice,
Dear Mr. Walker:

Only the first word in a complimentary close is capitalized.

Sincerely yours,   Very truly yours,

Always capitalize the personal pronoun *I*.

INDEX